D0499962

ROUGHHOUSE FRIDAY

ROUGHHOUSE FRIDAY

A MEMOIR

JAED COFFIN

FARRAR, STRAUS AND GIROUX   NEW YORK

Farrar, Straus and Giroux
120 Broadway, New York 10271

Printed in the United States of America
First edition, 2019

Library of Congress Cataloging-in-Publication Data
Names: Coffin, Jaed.
Title: Roughhouse Friday : a memoir / Jaed Coffin.
Description: First edition. | New York : Farrar, Straus and Giroux, 2019.
Identifiers: LCCN 2018045292 | ISBN 9780374251956 (hardcover)
Subjects: LCSH: Coffin, Jaed. | Boxing—Alaska. | Fathers and sons. | Masculinity. |
    Boxers (Sports)—Alaska—Biography. | Thai Americans—Biography. | Alaska
    (Biography)
Classification: LCC GV1132.C5255 A3 2019 | DDC 796.83092 [B]—dc23
LC record available at https://lccn.loc.gov/2018045292

Designed by Jonathan D. Lippincott

Our books may be purchased in bulk for promotional, educational, or business
use. Please contact your local bookseller or the Macmillan Corporate and
Premium Sales Department at 1-800-221-7945, extension 5442, or by e-mail
at MacmillanSpecialMarkets@macmillan.com.

www.fsgbooks.com
www.twitter.com/fsgbooks • www.facebook.com/fsgbooks

10 9 8 7 6 5 4 3 2 1

This is a work of nonfiction. However, the names and identifying characteristics of
certain individuals have been changed to protect their privacy, and dialogue has
been reconstructed to the best of the author's recollection.

To my father and Victor

CONTENTS

PART III

ROUGHHOUSE FRIDAY

PROLOGUE: GALAHAD

When I was a boy, my father, during our weekly phone conversations, used to tell me stories about the mythical kingdom of Camelot. I am not certain how closely his versions adhered to the canonical legends, but I think he got the basics right: there was King Arthur, an orphaned peasant boy who pulled the magic sword, Excalibur, from a stone; there was the wizard Merlin, Arthur's adviser, and Guinevere, his beautiful queen. And then there were the Knights of the Round Table—a gang of impressive but indistinguishable men who, unhindered by domestic life, upheld the moral order of Camelot and protected it from evil. The most valiant of Arthur's knights, my father told me, was a mysterious figure called Lancelot. He came from nowhere, lived alone, and spent his days wandering the forest looking for someone to fight.

At the time, I was living with my mother and older sister in an unfinished apartment building in downtown Brunswick, Maine; my father lived five hours away, in an old farmhouse called the Birches, in the Champlain Islands of northern Vermont, with a white woman named Martha and her five children. I knew the Birches well: the property stood a few miles down the road from the house where I was born, the same house, just months ago, my mother had left behind to start a new life in Maine.

My mother had come to America from a small village in rural Thailand—she'd met my father, a soldier, on a military base during the Vietnam War—and every year, for about three weeks, she took us back to visit. I knew much less about where my father had come from; the Camelot stories were his way of acquainting me with his cultural origins, origins that, he said, came from a place called Great Britain.

To connect himself with this lost heritage of men, my father had begun taking riding lessons at a local stable. I liked the image of my father atop a horse. Though I knew that he was not a real knight, I understood that he'd been a soldier of some kind, and the combination of horsemanship and war made me believe that my father belonged to a special class of men. During one of our phone conversations, my father told me he'd recently been thrown by his horse—an accident that, he said, could very well have killed him. As I pictured my father soaring through the air, I reminded myself that, despite his recent absence from my life, the sound of his voice was proof that he was alive. So the image of my father falling was replaced by a vision of him rising to his feet, adorned in a suit of armor.

When I told my mother about my father's fall—thinking that she would want to know that a man we both loved had survived a near-death experience—she paused before responding. I was, by then, used to my mother's delayed comprehension. But the nature of my concern, that my father—a man who had left our family to live in the house of another woman and her five children—had been injured while galloping around a stable on a horse, would likely not have made sense to her even in Thai.

My mother dismissed my concerns with the same pragmatic indifference she employed in her work as a psychiatric nurse at the local hospital. Every night at ten o'clock, she would leave our apartment for an eight-hour shift, only to return the next morning to relieve a babysitter and deliver my sister and me to school. She slept only two or three hours a day. My sister and I had invented a game called "I need to sleep!" in which one of us would lie in bed while the other person would tiptoe around it. Any noise and the sleeping mother would explode upright and scream, *"I need to sleep!"* and the game would be over.

Somehow I still believed that my mother's fatigue had something to do with a failure to adapt to our American life. Every time she took my sister and me back to Thailand, the twelve hours of time difference cast her past and present worlds in stark opposition. All night, my sister and I lay awake beneath the white drape of a mosquito net, telling each other jokes or listening to the sound of my grandfather snoring, waiting for the first call of a rooster, or the opening bars of the Thai national anthem erupting from public speakers, to signal the arrival of first light. During the day, we wandered around our family's village—a dusty collection of stilt houses gathered along a muddy canal—paying respects to slow-moving old people whose mouths dripped red with betel-nut juice. That these people were introduced to me as blood relations, and that they seemed to know me, expected something from my mother, and always asked after my father, only made the dream of my mother's past more impossible. Whenever we returned to Maine, I always felt less certain about my relationship to that place than when I'd left.

■

By the time I was in second grade, my sister and I began to spend our summers at the Birches. I do not know what emotions my mother put aside before allowing her two children to be cared for by her former best friend; perhaps, finally able to get some sleep, she was glad to see us go. On the days my father arrived, my mother would take extra time to comb my hair—"Like a prince!" she said—and dress me in a button-down flannel shirt with a clip-on necktie. But she often packed my bags full of soiled socks and underwear (a phrase that my sister and I always mimicked as "sock and underwears"), perhaps to remind my father and his new lover that our dirty laundry was theirs to clean.

■

During drives to Vermont my father would continue his stories. In his version of the Arthurian legends, few of the knights had children, but he did reveal that Lancelot had a son, whose name, he said, was Galahad. How Lancelot had raised a son while serving his king was a mystery to me, but my father assured me that Galahad was the purest and most righteous of any knight at the Round Table. It was Galahad, after all, who, before ascending to heaven, had been the only knight virtuous enough to behold the Holy Grail.

"What's a Holy Grail?" I asked my father.

He nodded solemnly, then held his hands before him as if supporting an invisible ball. "It's a big cup. A cup of God."

A cup of God. "What color is the cup?"

My father paused. "Gold."

Yes, I thought. Of course. I looked out my window, at the rolling contours of the Green Mountains scrolling along the highway, until I saw him: a young white knight with a sword at his hip, rising through the clouds in a beam of light, bearing the golden Grail skyward like a sports trophy.

Later, toward nightfall, as we followed Route 2 past hazy glimpses of Lake Champlain, past the swamps and apple orchards and cedar forests of my former life, I felt the silent spell of destiny moving through me. As we turned onto the long gravel driveway, the windows of the old farmhouse glowed with soft candlelight, and the tilting barns rose above fields of cow corn like the walls of a fortress. To be free from the sleepy shadow of my dark-haired mother filled me with a magical sense of power; to be on my own, under the care of my father, told me that manhood was not far off. I knew nothing of what deeper emotions were at work inside me; nothing of the past that would curse my father's love; nothing of how complicated love could become when woven through a loom of race, culture, and war. Then, I believed only in the truth of what lay before me: that the willow trees bowing to my arrival were the sentinels of my father's kingdom.

■

During the day, while my father worked in Burlington as a drug and alcohol counselor, my sister and I stayed home with Martha, whose five children, the youngest of whom was six years my senior, paid me little attention. While my sister spent entire days in her bedroom, reading thousand-page novels without breaking to eat, I spent my mornings guiding a small LEGO knight on a plastic horse across the mountainous topography of my bedspread, to the hummed soundtrack of "Stairway to Heaven," which I heard on my stepbrother's boom box every night. Then I would wander outside, snooping in old pig sheds and chicken coops, examining the gravestones in a cemetery across the street, exploring the barn where a farmer named Burt kept his cows in exchange for winter plowing and fresh milk. In the back of the barn stood a rickety wooden ladder that led up to a hayloft, where, among litters of feral kittens and handfuls of hairless baby mice, I discovered a small pile of boxes that my father had not unpacked since his recent move. In one box: several boring photo albums from his boyhood in Needham, Massachusetts; in another: a yearbook from Middlebury College, dated two years before he met my mother. At 220 pounds, six foot two, my father had the build of my He-Man action figures, but his profile—angular and chiseled, stern and serious—looked nothing like my chubby, round face.

Hidden behind the boxes was a long wooden cylinder, painted

black, with red tassels hanging off the handle. I paused before picking up the object. Right away, I knew that the object was a sword; right away, I knew that the sword—curved slightly, like the ceremonial elephant tusks in my mother's closet—was of a different species from the Excalibur of my father's stories. Then I removed the sheath. The blade was rusted and dull, but I could feel its danger running through my hands like electricity. I spit on my finger and ran it over an inch or two of text engraved just above the hilt. It was the same flourishing but unreadable script that I had seen on letters from my aunts that occasionally arrived at our apartment in Maine. I studied the writing, half expecting that I might be able to decipher its meaning, half imagining that it might bear the name of a soldier whom my father had killed during the war. I took one last look, then hid the weapon precisely where I had found it.

When my father came home from work that night, I did not mention the sword. By that time of day, my sister and I were usually droned out on television—*Star Trek* reruns, or double features of *DuckTales*—but out of the corner of my eye, I always watched the way my father kissed Martha each evening, the way she rejected his affection with embarrassed repulsion. But I saw the hidden hypocrisy in their love: often, early in the morning, I heard Martha crying in the bedroom—a whimper that I at first mistook for sadness, only to later see my father's powerful white body striding down the hallway.

With the last hours of daylight, my father liked to mow the lawn—one of the few jobs that did not require the kind of manual skills he lacked. Or else, I'd play in the yard while my father practiced a form of Korean martial arts that he'd been studying for several years under a young master in Burlington. Some nights he'd throw me batting practice with tennis balls, using the barn as a backstop. Or else, if arguing with Martha—which was often— he'd take me to the stable where he rode horses. His horse looked nothing like the horse I'd imagined: it was tall and dark and violent looking, an adversarial beast who resisted my father's every command. My father rode stiffly, unsure of himself, clenching the reins in tight fists. As I sat on a bench watching him ride, I chewed on white strips of paint that I'd peeled off the corral fence, diffusely choosing between what angered me more: that my father had created in my imagination a vision that did not exist, or that I had been so eager to believe a lie. When the lesson was over, his teacher led me around the corral on a deferential little pony named Duke.

Afterward, I often asked my father to take me on drives along the shore of Lake Champlain—a choppy dark pasture of wind-beaten water that stood beneath the heavy granite shadow of the Adirondack Mountains—until we drove up the dusty dirt road that led to our old house. It belonged to someone else now—strange cars were in the driveway—but my parents, yet to be legally divorced, owned several acres of the adjacent field. He pulled off the road, and together we walked into the field, to the top of a hill where, in the pale dusk, you could see across the field to our old home. As waist-high grass moved along the tree line like liquid, I sat in my father's lap and asked him what he planned to do with the land. But even after he explained that a farmer wanted to buy it, and mow it, and put it to good use, the sense that the land would forever be mine did not leave me. Then the sky began to shift and change shape, and a column of golden light poured through the clouds and touched the earth, and I was sure that I was seeing the exact image of God, and when I told that to my father, he seemed impressed and nodded in agreement, then wrapped his arms around me a bit more tightly.

■

Each night, Martha would cook a large meal for the whole lot of us: my father, five stepsiblings, my sister, and me. Before eating, my father liked to offer a long meditation about how happy he was to have us with him, a moment of confession that made my cheeks burn and that drove my stepsiblings wild with hungry irritation. Dinners—casseroles and potatoes, pasta and homemade bread or biscuits, sometimes fried bass that my stepbrothers caught from the lake—were so different from the hastily assembled cabbage-broth, egg-drop noodle soups that I ate under my mother's care, and I remember feeling confused by my total absence of guilt when it occurred to me that I preferred meals at the Birches over quiet dinners in our apartment in Brunswick.

Then we'd spend evenings in the living room, watching eighties movies on a recently purchased VCR. My father had little discretion about what sex or violence passed before my eyes. To this day, I can still picture the topless woman standing in a lit doorway in Clint Eastwood's *Tightrope*, can still transport myself to the subway scene at the end of Tom Cruise's *Risky Business* as if I were standing right there on the platform. As for the violence, it came primarily in movies about the Vietnam War—*Platoon*, *Full Metal Jacket*, *Hamburger Hill*—but it did not once occur to me that the war in the movies was the same war that had brought my parents together. In many ways, the violence was more perplexing than the sex: while the sex always took place among similar-looking people, the violence was always inflicted upon disillusioned white men who wandered through steaming jungles, hunted by endless hordes of nameless soldiers in black pajamas who, in the rare instances when I saw their faces, reminded me a bit of my uncles.

One night, my father brought home a movie that he was particularly eager to share: the film was called *Excalibur* and was, he said, based entirely on the legends of Camelot. I felt great excitement as the video loaded—to see Camelot in full color would prove to me that my father's stories were true. But *Excalibur* was not the movie I'd expected: I could not tell one knight from another. I could not tell who was good and who was bad. There were wars, at night, upon flaming battlefields, between anonymous men in dented armor who killed one another for reasons I didn't understand. And there was a great deal of sex in *Excalibur*, too: In one scene, a knight in full armor made love to a naked woman while a small child stood watching. In another, Lancelot and Guinevere—there was no mistaking it—had a secret encounter in the forest until, in the middle of the night, Arthur came upon his best friend and his wife and drove Excalibur between their naked bodies, nearly killing them both.

I looked around the living room for some validation that I was not alone in my confusion, but by then, my stepsiblings and sister had all retreated upstairs, while my father remained in his chair, legs spread wide, casually eating ice cream from a coffee cup. Martha sat at the end of the couch, as far from my father as possible, carefully stitching an elaborate quilt that I had seen her working on long before my parents' separation. As *Excalibur* continued, I knew that the only hope for Camelot now would be the redeeming arrival of Galahad, as promised by my father, but even after the credits rolled, the virtuous young knight from my father's stories never showed up. The only boy in the movie was the cherub-faced young Mordred, bastard son of Arthur, who, in the final scene, rides into battle in golden armor only to drive a spear through his father's chest.

"Wow," my father said. "What a story. What a story." He rose from his chair, asked me if I wanted some ice cream. Later that evening, I lay with my father in bed singing our nightly songs. "Peace I Ask of Thee O River" was always followed by a Korean Buddhist prayer that my father had learned from his martial arts teacher. As I chanted the empty syllables (*kwan say am bo true saw*), it occurred to me that neither my father nor I understood their meaning.

■

Toward the end of June, my father presented me with a gift: a pair of matching yellow T-shirts—one for him, one for me—that read

CHEERIOS across the chest and, on the back, in tall capital letters, our nicknames: LANCELOT and GALAHAD. My father had ordered the shirts off a cereal box with the hope that we could wear them together to the annual Fourth of July celebration downtown—the seminal event of the Champlain Islands summer, which began in the morning with a 5K footrace and ended with an old-fashioned country parade.

My father's shirt fit beautifully across his muscular frame and shoulders. While many of my friends' fathers had grown doughy and round in middle age, my father, at forty-five, still had the biggest biceps of any man I knew, still carried himself with the focused self-seriousness of an athlete in training. I was the shortest and smallest boy in my second-grade class, and my shirt hung off my wiry frame like a bright yellow curtain. But I was eager to wear something that testified that my father and I shared the same blood. With my straight black hair, and skin that was almost as dark as my mother's, I was becoming aware that I looked less like my father's natural son than any of my three stepbrothers.

"What a couple of dorks," one of my stepbrothers said the morning of the race, as my father and I stood in the kitchen dressed in our matching uniforms.

"You don't have to wear that," Martha said. Occasionally, she mediated my father's grand gestures of love with maternal reasonability—an effort that made me feel that, together, we shared the unspoken secret of his weaknesses.

I looked at my father, saw in him an image of the man I might become. "I don't mind."

Later, I stood with my father in a crowd of runners. A pistol fired and we were off: trotting through a jiggling sea of legs and butts until the crowd thinned and we ran alone. The road we ran down was the same road that led to my old house, the same road that, two years earlier, I had watched my mother run down as she completed her first marathon. Back then, Martha had been her training partner, and later in my life I would see pictures of those days: my mother in denim cutoffs, a bandanna around her neck, a long black braid swinging at her waist. Behind her: Martha, holding on to my mother's braid for support.

Along the road, familiar faces—friends from my playgroup, mothers who had known my mother—cheered us on. "Go, Jeddy!" they yelled. "Go, Jeddy!"—Jeddy a baby name that I had shed since moving to Maine. But as we approached the finish line, I saw their overly cheerful faces as masks of pity. These were the faces who had invited my mother into their community upon her arrival in America; these were the faces who had whispered about my father's infidelity behind my mother's back; these were the faces who had stopped talking to her after she left the Champlain Islands; these were the faces of people who, now, accepted me as the youngest member of my father's new family. Perhaps the joy on these faces was in celebration of what they'd secretly wanted to believe all along: that my parents' union, like the horrible war that had brought them together, was doomed to fail.

In the last hundred yards, as my father and I sprinted through a gauntlet of noise, my breath became short, and the vision I held of myself—a young champion running alongside his impressive father—began to fade. My legs wobbled, and my chest began to hurt, and my head filled with white fog. What I did next felt even more natural than running: just steps from the finish line, I let myself tumble to the ground, in a gesture so dramatic and obscenely false that I cannot imagine anyone believing its sincerity.

I was not in pain. I was not out of breath. I was not even tired. But as I lay facedown on the street, my face hidden beneath my arms, I listened for what I needed to hear: gasps of concern, worried footsteps rushing to my side, any evidence at all that the people who had cheered me on understood what invisible thing I carried with me. Though I was not exactly sure why I had fallen, whatever condition I was pretending to suffer from—hyperventilation, a twisted ankle—felt as real to me as any pain. I remained on the pavement for several seconds, performing various forms of injury that I'd likely seen acted out in *Platoon*, until I heard my father's voice above me:

"He'll be all right."

Then I felt his hands on my shoulders, lifting me to my feet. I shook my head, pretended to fight off the pain. Flinching, I limped a few steps forward. Then, to an explosion of applause— "Go, Jeddy! Go, Jeddy!"—my father and I, Lancelot and Galahad, sprinted across the finish line.

■

Back at the Birches, my father did not ask me to explain why I had fallen. But inside, I held a quiet shame, coupled with the unsteady conviction that what I had done was necessary. As for my CHEERIOS T-shirt, I felt a strange discomfort wearing it, as if its bright yellow color drew attention to a part of me that I wished to remain secret.

One afternoon, I slid through the doors of the old barn and climbed up into the loft. There, beneath a beam of dusted, slanted window light, I found the sword. When I was sure that I was alone, I unsheathed the blade and set my feet just as my father had taught me to when swinging a baseball bat. Then I lifted it high above my head and drove it into the thick body of a wooden post.

Whack!

The impact ignited all the little muscles of my forearms with a clean rush of power, similar to the way it felt when I hit one of my father's pitches clear over the barn. I wanted to feel that power again. But when I tried to pull the blade free, the weapon did not budge. I worked the handle up and down, pulling with all my strength, until I felt the smooth glide of release, followed by a metallic pang. When I opened my eyes, only the red-tasseled handle remained in my hands. The blade—curved and rusty, like an old farm tool—lay at my feet. I knelt, tried to force the two pieces back together as best I could. Then I buried the broken weapon beneath the boxes of my father's past and, for the rest of that summer, and for the rest of my life, never went back to find it. Instead, in some foggy chamber of my imagination, I convinced myself that the beautiful weapon, forged in my mother's country, brought home from my father's war, still remained—in some other kingdom, in some other time—unbroken.

PART I

I. WHACK!

I was lifting weights in the Sheldon Jackson College Gymnasium on a Friday night in early October when I heard the sound coming down the hall.

Whack! Whack! Whack!

The weight room was on the second floor of the SJ gym, in an upstairs loft overlooking a basketball court. Long ago, the college had served as a boarding school and was named after an American missionary who'd come north to reform Native children after the Alaska Purchase. Now SJ had about a hundred students—some hippies, some Christians, some Native kids from the Interior—but few of them did much working out, so I usually had the place to myself.

Whack! Whack! Whack!

After a few more bench presses, I let the bar fall into the yoke. I did not particularly like lifting weights, but ever since I'd showed up in Sitka at the end of the summer—alone, by sea kayak, at the end of a cross-country road trip and a one-thousand-mile paddle north up the Inside Passage—working out was the only thing that filled my days with any kind of ritual. I was one year out of college, wandering through that shapeless in-between period of my early twenties when I wanted to become a man but didn't know how to start. For the past month, I had been living in a basement apartment, working as an academic tutor for a tribal organization, having a first crack at life on my own. Lifting weights brought definition to my physical self when every other fact about who I was pulsed inside of me with furious uncertainty.

Whack! Whack! Whack!

I got up from the bench and followed the sound to a small room where several men were working out like boxers. In one corner, two Native boys followed each other under a bob-and-weave rope. In the opposite corner, two white men took turns hitting a heavy bag. In the middle of the room, a short man in a baseball cap and hooded sweatshirt held a pair of mitts for a shirtless redheaded boy whom I recognized from the high school. His name was Richie, and I often saw him wandering the halls as if lost in a foreign city.

"Six!" the man called out, and Richie attacked the mitts— Whack! Whack! Whack!—with three rights and three lefts. "Ten!" the man said, and Richie dove forward with more punches. They continued for thirty seconds or so, the man calling out combinations—"Right hand–hook–right hand!"—as Richie, shoulders and chest glistening with sweat, kept punching. Then the man said, "To the bell!" and Richie hit the mitts until a beeper sounded in the corner. "Push-ups! Twenty!" the man said, and everyone fell to the floor.

I remained in the doorway until the session was over, when all the fighters unwrapped their hands, dressed for the weather, and filed past me out the door.

The man who'd been holding the mitts stood in the middle of the room, stuffing helmets and gloves into a duffel bag. "You need something?"

I paused. "You ever take new guys on?"

The man shook his head. "Got two guys fighting Roughhouse

in November and the high school boys training for amateurs this spring." He looked over his shoulder. "We just don't have a whole lot of room in here."

I thanked the man, turned to leave.

"You ever do any fighting?" he called out behind me.

"Yes," I lied. My senior year at Middlebury College, me and some guys from my dorm had read a few chapters of Nietzsche and watched *Fight Club* too many times and come to the bold conclusion that our luxurious liberal arts existence was turning us into overeducated, technology-obsessed boy-bots. In a small room above the tennis courts, we started working out like boxers, trying to imitate the men in the movie. We did lots of push-ups and sit-ups, hit an old heavy bag with our bare hands until our knuckles bled, always with our shirts off so that the girls who used the room for yoga class could witness our rapid Becoming. After a few weeks, we bought some boxing gloves, named ourselves the John Keats Club, and started fighting for real. This was in the late fall of 2001, and it is hard to say what larger forces compelled us to perform such theater of violence. By late winter, the John Keats Club had mostly run its course: my training partners, perhaps aware that their imminent delivery into the upper-middle classes of America would likely protect them from most kinds of physical danger, all quit. I continued training on my own. Some nights, I looked at the young man scowling back at me in the long mirrors on the wall, wondering what he wanted to know.

"You want to give it a shot?" the man said. He was on his toes now, flicking half punches. He'd pulled off his sweatshirt and removed his hat, so that he wore only a tank top and shorts. The man stood around five foot eight, with hair and skin about the same shade as mine. He looked like he might be Native or part white or Filipino—in a town like Sitka, where many people had mixed blood, it was hard to tell. Standing across from him, I was sure I held an advantage. At five eleven and a lean 190, I had inherited my father's build. The rest of me—flat nose, full lips, small hands—came from my mother.

"Sure," I said.

The man offered me a pair of gloves and a helmet. Then he traced a square of duct tape on the carpet. "That's the ring," he said, through his mouth guard. "But you don't have to stay inside it." Then he tapped a small plastic box in the corner. "Beeper's set for three minutes."

For several seconds, the man swayed in place, chin tucked into his chest, feet set, hands low, squinting at me beneath the padding of his helmet. I had no plan for how I was going to attack him, but I believed that somewhere inside me I possessed the power to beat him.

Whack! Whack! Whack!

A series of jabs—bouncing off my forehead in such quick succession that I could not tell the first punch from the third. Then a volley of harder punches—straight left hands that smashed into my nose, clubbed the side of my head, and drove me into the wall. I had never been hit like that before, but I did not experience the impact as pain. Instead, I felt as though the man's punches were trying to tell me something, tapping out their message in code. As he slid away, I stalked after him, and swung for his head with a swooping left hand. But the punch found only air. Then I felt a dull ball of pain settle into a soft pocket of flesh beneath my ribs. The ball grew, traveled into my stomach, trickled down my legs, and pulled me to the floor. I tried to stay on my feet, but my knees buckled and I fell to all fours. Drops of blood from my nose dripped onto the carpet.

Above me, the man stood with one glove extended, the white knuckles stamped with small rose shapes. "You got any more?"

"Yeah," I said. I took the man's hand and came to my feet.

For the next two rounds, the beating continued: jabs off my nose and forehead, followed by thudding left hands. By then, my chin and chest were covered with blood and I was out of air and I had all but given up. Even when I could see his punches coming, I was too winded to move my head out of their way. But nothing in my brain told me to avoid the impact. Toward the end of the third round, I put up my gloves and charged the man, thinking I might be able to tackle him. But as I came forward, his fist split my elbows, clicking my jaw shut and snapping my head back. I stumbled to the wall, dropped my hands, waited for more. But the punches never came.

Across the room, the man stood in the opposite corner, hunched into a ball, his head buried in his shoulders, his hands up. "Your turn." He waved me forward.

I didn't move.

"Come on. Hit me."

I shuffled across the room and tapped my fist off his forehead.

"Fuckin' hit me!"

I hit him again, in the same place.

"Hard!"

I set my feet like I was about to swing a baseball bat, reached back with my left hand, and drove my fist into the side of his helmet.

"*Unnhh.*" The man rocked to his left, then righted himself. "Again."

I hit him a second time. Then I kept punching: powerless slaps that glanced off his shoulders.

When I couldn't lift my arms, the man lifted them for me. "To the bell!"

I punched until the beeper sounded. Then I sat on the floor.

He took off his gloves and unbuckled his helmet, reached into the duffel bag, and handed me a towel. "Sorry about that. I don't usually do that on the first night. I just get so many guys coming in here that I got to have some way to figure out who's serious.

Most guys think they're pretty tough till they get beat up. Then I never see 'em again."

I stood, took off my gloves and helmet, and put them in the duffel bag.

"You new in town?" the man said.

"Yeah. Summer."

"Fishing?"

I shook my head. "I work at the high school. Native Education Program."

The man paused. He was looking at me in that confused way that people sometimes looked at me when they were trying to figure out where I came from. I didn't mind the scrutiny: such hesitations gave me time to prepare an explanation. A phone rang in the man's pocket. "Home in five minutes!" he said into it, then stuffed the phone back into his pocket. "I got to go. Got a wife and son back home."

I followed him downstairs to the entrance of the SJ gym. We stood outside under an awning. It was raining again, for the fifth or seventh or tenth day straight. The gravel parking lot was full of deep puddles that reflected the orange light of the streetlamps like giant orange moons. I pulled my bicycle off the rack—a girl's model, once teal, that a Tlingit man named George had given me when I'd first arrived in town. I'd stripped the frame down to bare metal and spray-painted it black.

"You got a truck?" the man said.

"No."

"How'd you say you ended up here?"

I told the man about my trip.

"A fucking kayak?" He laughed. "What the hell did you eat?"

"Mostly rockfish. A couple sculpin."

"Sculpin? You know they eat shit off the bottom?"

I laughed. "It had green meat. It wasn't very good."

The man shook his head, looked at me more closely. "You Native or something?"

The only thing I knew about what it meant to be Native was that sometimes people mistook me for one. "No. I'm from Maine."

"Maine. Well, I hate to break it to you, but winter isn't the best time of year to be up here. If you don't fish or hunt . . . or box"—the man shrugged—"I don't know what the hell you do. Summer, that's the time to visit. All sorts of things to do. This time of year, people go kind of crazy." His phone rang again. This time he didn't answer. He held out his hand. "Victor Littlefield."

I shook it. "Jade Coffin."

Back East, everyone had pronounced my name Jed for as long as I could remember. But for some reason, as soon as I landed in Sitka, people had started pronouncing my name as Jade, and I'd never bothered to correct them. The only person I knew who said my name right was my mother, so—Jade, Jed, what was the difference?

"Well, Jade," Victor said, "we're in here Monday, Wednesday, Friday, six o'clock. I can't promise you work, but if you come back around, I'll see what I can do." He crossed the parking lot to a black electrician's van and drove away.

2. SOLITARY MAN

I rode home that night as I often did—along the dark streets of downtown in a light rain, through the quiet neighborhoods above Lincoln Street, where a heavy mist hung over the channel and buried the booms of the fishing trawlers in Crescent Harbor. I rode on—past the teardrop steeple of the old Russian cathedral, the vacant windows and storefronts of cruise-ship tourist shops, before turning right onto Katlian Street, past the steamy windows of the Pioneer Bar and Kenny's Wok, beneath the sidewalk shadows of the clan houses and the Alaska Native Brotherhood Hall in Indian Village, through the whirring neon glow of the seafood cannery and Old Thomsen's Harbor. From there, it was a short ride uphill onto my street, Halibut Point Road.

HPR was one of two main roads in Sitka. It ran about nine miles north to the end of town, out past the ferry terminal and Mosquito Cove. The other major road in town was Sawmill Creek Road, or SMC, which ran about ten miles south, under a wall of steep mountains, to the narrow inlet of Silver Bay. Though Sitka had about nine thousand full-time residents—a relatively big population for a community in Southeast Alaska—the town occupied less than 1 percent of Baranof Island, most of which was covered in thick rain forest and a sharply carved labyrinth of rugged mountain ranges. When I had first arrived in Sitka, I had spent my weekends hiking up streambeds along Indian River, following vague hunting trails into the woods, trying to familiarize myself with the topography of the wilderness. But something about its vastness—you could almost hear it breathing in the air—made me feel at odds with the forest in a way I never had before.

My apartment was about two miles down HPR, across the street from a McDonald's, beneath the house of a white fisherman and his Native wife who went south for the winter. They'd furnished my apartment with a couch, a bed, a small TV/VCR, a breakfast table and two chairs, some pots, pans, and silverware, and a freezer full of leftover fish. The fish was nothing good— mostly oily cuts of black bass and lingcod—but I'd been eating it for dinner for the past several weeks, with a pot of brown rice and chili sauce, and it was still only half gone.

The other thing my landlords had left me: a stack of nine envelopes, stamped and addressed to the First National Bank downtown, where I was to send my rent check—$475 utilities included—on the first of each month. The nine envelopes were enough to get me through to June, when the fisherman's helper, a white kid from San Diego, would take my place.

The only items that belonged to me were a banjo I'd bought off a teacher at the high school but didn't know how to play, and a small stereo that I'd bought at a thrift store downtown called the White Elephant. I had one audiocassette that I listened to every night: Johnny Cash's *American Recordings*. Since his death that fall, I'd been mimicking his model of macho nihilism, trying to see how it held up against the backdrop of the Last Frontier. I'd even gone so far as to dye my favorite jean jacket black, but the dye job hadn't come out right and my jacket had turned a faded shade of purple and I probably looked more like a half-Asian Prince than the Man in Black.

I hadn't done much decorating since moving in. The cinder-block walls were bare save for two items I'd brought with me all the way from Maine. The first was a certificate I'd been given from the temple in my mother's village, after I'd spent a summer as a monk two years earlier. I had entered the temple with the hope that locating myself within the deep traditions of her culture, and stripping myself down to a more basic form, might soothe the strange restlessness that I often felt boiling inside of me. And yet, ever since returning to Maine, those feelings had only grown stronger and more violent, and every time I tried to meditate something seemed to bark back at me from across the still waters of my breath. Anyhow, I had no idea what the certificate on my wall even said—I could barely speak Thai, never mind read it. Already the corners were curling, the paper fading to a pale yellow.

The second item on my wall was a Hallmark card my mother had given me the morning I'd left Maine. I had been living at home, working on a lobster boat, trying to figure out what to do with my time now that I was supposed to be an adult. I had no desire to follow in the footsteps of my college peers, who seemed so willing—hungry, even—to begin purposeful lives in the alpha cities of the Northeast. A part of me wished that I could join them, but a swirl of feelings—a mix of betrayal and fraudulence, disgust and disdain—held me back. My resulting condition was a kind of numb and cynical paralysis, for which staring across the Gulf of Maine from the stern of a fishing boat from dawn to dusk seemed the only salve. And yet I knew that my mother had not spent the past thirty years of her American life working the night shift just so that her only son could stuff bait bags for twelve hours a day.

Just after the New Year, when my mother and I could barely look at each other without the gravity of her sacrifices haunting our house like a hungry ghost, I loaded my car with a backpack of clothing, a crate of books, and some camping gear and told my mother that I was driving west, to look for a job as a teacher. It was an odd declaration—I had no ambition to teach, only a desire to do what I considered to be masculine, physical work—and it was probably naive to assume that my mother would buy my story. In an unspoken way that transcended our common half language, my mother often understood what motivated me better than I did. The morning I left town, she'd placed an envelope on my steering wheel, containing four one-hundred-dollar bills and a note: *I am proud of you*, she'd written in her very precise penmanship. *No matter what you do.*

No matter what I do.

For the next six months, I drove south and west in a trance. It was a strange time to bear witness to my country: we were at war, again, against an invisible enemy that had no name, and all around me the spirit of the nation offered itself in blurry visions of duplicity and simulation. In Washington, DC, I killed an afternoon marching with protesters against the war in Iraq; an evening getting shit-faced with several young soldiers on their way overseas. In Pigeon Forge, Tennessee, I spent a night in an eleven-dollar casino hotel room, beneath the glowing, cascading billboard of Dolly Parton's beaming face and chest. On a snowy night in Humansville, Missouri, I wandered into an empty public library to find nothing but a single computer humming and dinging with the hollow song of the bodiless, digital future. While wandering around central Mexico, I found two donkeys—one dead, one living—on a barren plateau in the mountains. From the Hollywood Hills, the blinking red lights of a distant radio tower projected a holograph of itself against the glowing grid of a smog-filled night. Occasionally, I made gestures toward putting down roots—an inquiry about an apartment or a job, a promise to be in touch—but I was mostly just trying on the lives of generous friends who, by some miracle, did not feel a similar need to keep chasing down whatever was next.

By June, I had made my way into the San Juan Islands of Washington State, where I stayed at the house of a college friend and found work tending to the property of an elderly woman who sometimes mistook me for one of the Mexican men who over-mowed her lawn. One weekend, while I was hitchhiking around the Olympic Peninsula, a young Makah man named Daniel picked me up on the side of the road, assuming that I, as one of his own, was heading back to Neah Bay. As we drove, Daniel told me that he'd recently returned from an Indian college in Kansas, where he'd been recruited to play quarterback on the football team, but that he'd come home because he missed his family and girlfriend too much. "People don't know much about us. They just know that Greenpeace bullshit about us killing whales. They don't know that in our language *I love you*"—and here he said the Makah phrase—"means 'My heart aches for you.'" That evening, after introducing me to his family, Daniel dropped me off at a sea-cliff campsite overlooking the northwesternmost point in the Lower 48. I gazed into the fading light of the Pacific, comparing my centerless, rootless life to Daniel's, contemplating my compass of worn-out options: to go back East would be total failure; to go south was to retrace my steps; to go west, in the direction of Asia, accomplished nothing. Then I looked north—into a parting mist hanging over the Pacific. For the next several hours, I remained on that cliff, watching the mist, waiting for it to tell me what to do.

Just after the Fourth of July, I blew the last of my fishing money on a seventeen-foot sea kayak made of bright yellow bulletproof plastic and stuffed the hull with several canisters of oatmeal, sacks of potatoes, and bags of rice, and enough camping and fishing gear to last me through the summer. The only rule I imposed upon my journey was that I would swear off all modern technology: no cell phone, no EPIRB or VHF radio, and no navigational devices beyond a simple compass and a nautical chart displaying the nine hundred miles of coastal wilderness between the Strait of Juan de

Fuca and Glacier Bay. I was not without my models then: I imagined myself the newest member of a lineage of American men—Jack London, John Muir, Chris McCandless—who set off into the Last Frontier to cut their teeth on the raw truth of the wilderness. But I sensed, too, that my imitation of the past would never be exact. I did not possess London's viciousness. I lacked Muir's longing for sublime communion with nature. I felt closest to the angry mysticism of Chris McCandless—grunge martyr of my generation—but was too uncertain about the motivations behind my journey to claim for myself an Alexander Supertramp avatar.

The night before I left town, I called my mother, left her a message that I was heading out on the water but would be in touch in a few weeks. By then, she'd grown used to me taking off into the mountains of New England for long periods of time, but likely didn't understand the difference between that quaint wilderness and the one I was about to enter. The next morning, I dragged my boat down an empty beach and, under a cottony weave of clouds, against a rippling breeze from the north, began paddling. The world that hung before me—a lush, rain-forested mosaic of islands divided by emerald veins of water—appeared like an amplified, inverted dream of the world I had left behind: a foggier, rockier coast of Maine, blended with the drearier, darker lake valleys of northern Vermont.

I spent the next twelve days making my way up the inside coast of Vancouver Island, sleeping in city parks, foraging for dinners from gas-station hot cases. I was still getting comfortable spending long days in my boat, still acclimating to the incessant silence of my own head. Just north of the narrows of Johnstone Strait, I stopped in a small island village called Alert Bay, hoping to find someone to talk to, until I came upon a phone booth in a grocery store parking lot. The only person in my life whom I could reliably count on to chat was my father. For most of my life, our conversations had taken place over the phone, and in some ways, I was more comfortable talking to his disembodied voice than spending time with him in person. Over the past nine months, I'd been calling him at home, offering dispatches from the open road like an explorer reporting back to his colonial king. He listened to my stories with voyeuristic pleasure. When my father was my age, he'd shipped off to Thailand, only to come home a year later, married. Since then, he'd been tied to a property that he had inherited from another man, devoted to a family to which he held no blood relation. His was not exactly a wandering life.

While I was waiting for my father to answer, a white sedan with a cracked windshield pulled over. A woman got out and began knocking on the glass. "Jeremy?"

I looked at the woman. "I'm not Jeremy," I said.

The woman squinted. She looked as much like my mother as anyone I had ever seen: dark hair, copper skin, round face. She continued to stare. "You sure look like Jeremy." I hung up the phone and stepped outside. The woman explained that Jeremy was her nephew, who had left Alert Bay several years ago and never come back.

"Not me."

The woman nodded. "You're cute like Jeremy!" Then she drove away.

That night, I paddled into the middle of Queen Charlotte Sound, across a dangerous stretch of open channel, and made camp on an island about the size of a tennis court. Off the rocks, the entire Pacific Ocean seemed to yawn and groan with its massiveness, and yet I slept soundly, on a slab of rock, under a crisp, star-filled sky. But in the morning, a storm had rolled in, and I woke to a fog so thick, so heavy and white, that I could barely see where I'd tied off my boat. The right thing to do would have been to wait for the fog to burn off, rather than risk being steamrolled by one of the giant container ships from China or Mexico that moved through the channel like enormous spaceships. The currents in

Queen Charlotte Sound were strong enough to wash me a hundred miles out to sea. But as the mist swirled in front of me, that shapeless white world withheld an irresistible secret. I broke camp, duct-taped my compass to my deck, set the arrow in the general direction of the mainland, and started paddling.

For the next several hours, time obeyed different laws. Every time I took a paddle stroke, the dark water flowed by my boat, leaving me unable to decipher if it was moving forward or backward. I looked down at my compass, half expecting it to start spinning. I squinted into a receding distance, listening through the silence for any hint that I was moving in the right direction. In a panic, I began paddling faster and faster. By my map, the crossing to the mainland was all of five miles—but I knew only what I saw: that this was the fog at the end of the world. Then a faint shadow rose out of the mist like a ghost ship, and the bow of my boat rammed into a rocky ledge with a hollow, definitive thump.

In a shallow inlet, I came upon a rusted old barge. Two men came out from below. Dressed in logging boots and union suits, they looked like a pair of steampunk Rip Van Winkles. I asked them what they were doing way out here. Collecting cedar chunks for shingles, they said. Then the two men started laughing. "We were about to ask you the same thing!" I told the men I was headed to Alaska. "Jesus," one man said. "You got a long way to go."

From then on, I left the living world behind, as the remote coast of British Columbia—a scroll of empty beaches and haunted forests—turned more wild. I rarely saw boats. All day, I watched killer whales and porpoises rolling across the horizon, silver salmon slapping the surface, humpbacks exploding out of the water, then disappearing in a boiling ring of foam. At night, I sat naked at driftwood bonfires, carving little animal statues out of wood, improvising lyrics to songs I didn't remember. I had stopped shaving by then, and had gone three weeks without seeing my reflection, and one night, after watching a pack of sea otters swimming through a kelp bed, I decided to smear Vaseline all over my body, through my hair, with the hope of turning myself into an otter. Then I dove underwater with a knife, thinking that I might spear a fish. It was weird. I knew it was weird. As I sat by my fire cleaning myself, I could only laugh at my strangeness.

When I did come across people, they took me in with a lonely generosity that I'd never experienced before. A gang of charter fishermen who'd been flown into a remote camp stuffed me with so much chili and leftover fruit that I shit it all out in the middle of a crossing and had to spend several hours cleaning out my cockpit. Some wealthy yachters from Friday Harbor got me drunk on gin and tonics and fed me massive steaks, before telling me racist stories about an aggressive Native man who'd yelled at them for steaming past a burial ground. "Me Big Chief Tom-Tom!" the captain shouted, recalling the encounter. "You get off my land!" A German woman in a fishing camp called Big Bay took me into her bunkhouse for a night, shared her bed, sent me out the next morning with bags of cookies. A drunk man in a cabin called me in, poured me a glass of white wine, then asked if we could take pictures together.

In a village called Bella Bella, a man named Barry took me in for three days. We stayed up until four in the morning, eating fried salmon with soy sauce and mayonnaise, smoking cigarettes, as he told me his life story. After being abused by missionaries in his village, he'd left his community behind to be an "urban Indian." Only now, after all the people he once knew were dead, had he come back to relearn his culture. The morning I left Barry, I woke to the sound of chants blasting from a boom box in his front yard. The songs sounded so much like the chants from the temple in my mother's village, which I used to hear as a boy and had later learned as a monk. "Don't know what they mean," Barry said, as he cut back the overgrown shrubs on his property with a machete. "But when I listen to them, I can work all day. Don't even need to eat." As a present, he gave me the machete and a hatchet that he'd had since he was a boy.

As I paddled into the channel, a man on a missionary boat with a crucifix on its stack asked me where my heart was with God. I'd gotten word that the boats showed up in villages like Bella Bella, lured local kids aboard with free pizza and video games, then told them stories about heaven and hell. "I don't know," I told the man. He nodded sadly, handed me a film case, inside of which was a small cross on a necklace. I threw the cross overboard, but kept the film case as a waterproof container for matches.

Three to four weeks into my trip, when I could no longer stand the feeling of being treated like a stranger, I took two days off the water in Prince Rupert, hoping to shake my isolation by checking into a hotel room. I sat up all night, staring at myself in the mirror, marveling at what I'd become: overgrown, haggard, sinewy with muscle. I couldn't sleep, and I kept thinking that the walls were caving in, that the ceiling was collapsing. Around two in the morning, I packed up my things to sleep under a wharf where I'd tied off my boat. At sunrise, I wandered the streets, staring into windows of buildings with FOR RENT signs, imagining lives I would never live. Then I went into a Tim Hortons and was nearly brought to tears by the sparkling vision of ordinary people doing ordinary things.

That evening I crossed the open water of the Dixon Entrance as if gliding over a swimming pool. I made camp on a small island across the channel from Ketchikan. As night fell, several bonfires burned on the far shore, igniting the darkness like orange lotus flowers. I paddled toward one of the fires, until several teenage boys, drunk and amazed by my emergence, helped me carry my boat to the fire, where they toasted my arrival back to American soil with cans of beer. Then it began to rain. As the high school kids retreated to their trucks, a young girl came up to me. "No one here does anything," she said. I could see her eyes glowing in the firelight. "Not me, though. I'm going to do something." I watched her leave, then wrapped myself in a tarp and lay down in the wet sand. Several hours later, I woke to a smoldering fire. Without my glasses, I saw something so strange, so surreal, that I was sure I was dreaming: a vision of massive pastel-colored seagulls floating in the channel. When I put my glasses on, I saw them for what they were: cruise ships bobbing in the swell, little orange boats shuttling their passengers to the southernmost city in Alaska.

I walked into town, through crowds of tourists. I ate a massive breakfast at a diner called the Pioneer: biscuits and gravy, served with a full thermos of coffee. I wandered into the street, buzzing with a jittery sensation of being lost. When I saw a barber pole spinning on the corner, I went inside and sat in the chair.

"What are we doing?" the barber said.

I looked at myself in the mirror. "Shave it off," I said.

By the time I'd arrived in Sitka, I'd grown tired of being a nameless, vanishing person, tired of eating rockfish, of sleeping in the sand, of being wet. The only contact I had in this part of the world was a friend of my godfather's named George, who worked as a park ranger at the Cultural Center. I didn't know much about George other than the fact that he was Tlingit, and that he and my godfather had become friends over their common service in Vietnam. "Heard you had quite a trip up here," George said, laughing to himself. We were standing on the beach. "Those are some pretty big waters. I used to fish those waters." He paused. "You must have had some help." By help, I figured George meant something mystically Indian; later, I learned he was a Russian Orthodox Christian. When George asked me where I was headed next, I told him that I intended to paddle on to Glacier Bay, in the footsteps of John Muir. George didn't seem all that impressed. "That's where I'm from. Hoonah people. But we don't go in there unless we got a reason." He looked at my boat. He looked at me.

"I got an old fifth wheel in my yard," George said. "Full of junk, but a place to stay until you figure out what's next."

It was late August. In the past few days the air had gotten colder, the water in the channel a bit rougher. Off the beach, in the shoal waters, a pack of deformed pink salmon swam in dizzy circles, headed back home to spawn before they died.

"I'd like that," I said.

That night, George made me dinner. There was muktuk from his Yupik wife's village, seal oil, seaweed, herring eggs, and canned salmon. While we ate, we watched a Chuck Norris movie about Vietnam. Norris was running around blowing up thatched bunkers, throwing knives into the chests of little men in black pajamas. "That guy's quite a warrior," George said. Then he showed me a picture of himself on the wall, shirt off, standing with several other American soldiers. "Those white boys, they thought it was pretty funny when I used to let those kids from the village sit by my fire, cook 'em the little crawfish I caught in the river. But they didn't know I was Alaskan Native; I was taught to respect people's cultures. Pay attention to my surroundings. Old people in the villages, they used to come up to me, say, 'You me same same,' and that's when I knew I was going to be okay." He looked at me over the bridge of his glasses. "Your people, they understand my people."

The next morning, George called me in for breakfast. He showed me a brochure he'd been working on for his bentwood boxes—steam-bent ceremonial boxes with formline designs painted on them. He was trying to sell the work, wanted to explain where he was from, but he needed someone to read over his writing. "My people, we've got a language so good we never had to write anything down." I read through his narrative—right down to the name of his clan and his house, he could pin down his origins. I cleaned up the grammar a bit while George read the *Sitka Sentinel*. When I was done, I gave him the paper, and he slid me the classifieds section. "You know," George said, "I saw some jobs in there you might like. You young guys, you don't like to stick around, but I think you ought to stay up here, see if you can learn something from my people, just like I learned something from yours."

I showed up to my interview with the Sitka Native Education Program wearing a polyester suit jacket and a pair of too-short slacks that I'd bought the day before at the White Elephant. The SNEP office was in the back of the Alaska Native Brotherhood Hall, in an old building on Katlian Street. I met with four people—a white man who was the principal of Sitka High, and three members of the Native community: a representative from the ANB named Wilbur, a school board member called Hank, and a woman called Laura, who was the director of SNEP. The demands of the position sounded basic enough: about one-third of Sitka's student population was Native; my job was to help them keep their grades up. Pay was thirteen dollars an hour, thirty-two hours a week. No one seemed to mind that I had no experience in education; their primary concern was whether I'd be able to work with students with a complex cultural history.

I did not know then that the very building I was sitting in was the meeting place for the first chapter of the Alaska Native Brotherhood, founded in 1912 by a group of Natives—Tlingit, Haida, and Tsimshian—who led the fight for Native rights to land and citizenship. The early members of the ANB had banned the use of Native language at all meetings, in an attempt to keep pace with the white-speak of their opponents. They'd also adopted as their anthem "Onward, Christian Soldiers." Following passage of the Alaska Anti-Discrimination Act of 1945, championed by Natives, and the Alaska Native Claims Settlement Act of 1971, SNEP was created by the Alaska Native Sisterhood to celebrate the very culture that the federal government had spent the past century trying to erase.

On George's advice—that my people understood his people—

I answered the interviewers' question with a story about my mother: where she came from, and what it was like to grow up in Maine in the house of a woman from rural Thailand.

"Ha!" Hank said, rubbing his chin. "This whole time, I thought you were a Tsimshian!" He looked at Wilbur. "Doesn't he look like one of those Tsimshians?"

Wilbur looked at me sideways. "Little bit."

Then Laura asked me if I had any questions. I asked what I thought was the most obvious one: What was so bad about the local high school that the Native students needed their own special tutor? The room fell silent. The principal of Sitka High shifted in his chair. Hank looked at his hands. Wilbur studied the floor. Finally Laura said, in a clear but careful voice, "When you learn something about the history of our people, maybe you'll understand."

Later that afternoon, I sat in George's fifth wheel, mulling over the logic of Laura's final words. If my people understood George's people, and if the only way to understand Laura's students was by learning about the history of her people, then . . .

"Hey, Jade!" George's wife was calling for me through the window. "Got someone on the phone for you."

It was Laura. She was calling to offer me the job. I took it on the spot.

■

No matter what I do.

I lay in bed, staring at the ceiling, singing along to Cash's cover of "Solitary Man" while spinning a ring on my finger that my parents had given me as a graduation present. The ring was made of two halves of their wedding rings—flower designs for my mother, vague shields for my father—that had been cut apart, then soldered together. The gift meant as much to me as anything I owned: it reminded me that, despite my parents' separation, their past was bound by something more powerful than war and circumstance. The only time I'd taken the ring off was while I was paddling north, when the ring had left a welt on my hand, so I'd worn it around my neck on a piece of rope.

If this—living alone in a basement like some melancholy Gollum—was the best I could do with my mother's sacrifices, there seemed little sign that it would get any better. In the past weeks, all the cruise ships and summer workers had gone home, and the light had begun to fade by several minutes a day, and even the salmon, which had been vigorously spawning for most of September, now lay on the banks of Indian River in ribbons of putrid, rotting white flesh. Most mornings, I woke to pale rainy light streaming through my windows, feeling as though everything inside me, too, were turning dark, rainy, and rotten. But that night when I closed my eyes, none of that blurry mist was hanging behind my lids. Instead, I saw only the bright flashes of impact—Whack! Whack! Whack!—of Victor's gloves snapping in front of my face. Then, as if no time had passed, I bolted awake to the beep-beep-beep of my alarm clock, to a tardy dawn light pouring through the narrow windows above my bed, painting the cinderblock walls with the bland promise of another gray day.

3. THE SAVAGE

My classroom was in the back wing of Sitka High School, next to the shop and special-education rooms, in a practice studio for the SHS drill team. It wasn't a very uplifting place to learn: there were no windows, and little furniture beyond a few tables and chairs. Three of the walls were covered in shiny whiteboards, while the fourth wall was hidden behind an ominous black curtain, behind which stood a floor-to-ceiling mirror. A series of stage lights hung from the ceiling, which you could control from a small panel in the closet. The bell didn't ring until 8:00 a.m., but I liked to get to school a few minutes early, even though I didn't have much to prepare for.

On my first day, a guidance counselor told me that I might not have much to do for the first couple weeks because it took a while for kids to start falling far enough behind to justify a period with me. But now, six weeks into the school year, my periods were starting to fill up. In the morning, I worked with two Native boys, Danny and Nathan. Danny showed up most days with a can of Pimp Juice energy drink and his fingertips covered in Doritos powder. He looked white, but according to his paperwork, his mother had roots in Klawock, and his father lived Down South. Danny was supposed to have ADD, which made him an odd best friend for Nathan, who moved slowly and spoke little. The two boys loved basketball and always raced through their algebra homework so they could spend the last fifteen minutes playing one-on-one. I'd tried to enforce a rule that the boys couldn't bring a basketball into my classroom. Now, though, I let them keep a ball under my desk.

Recently, Danny had gotten all fired up about his upcoming ferry trip to Juneau, where he planned to blow his dividend check—an annual bump from oil industry profits, distributed evenly at about a thousand bucks per full-time resident—on a pair of basketball shoes and a new game console and as much candy as he wanted. The capital city, located on the mainland about ninety miles northeast, had four times the population of Sitka, and a lot more stores. Nathan, on the other hand, didn't seem to care about the "free money." We balanced a few equations, I made sure the boys' homework was in decent shape, and then we spent the rest of class working on a spinning Allen Iverson move they'd seen on TV. When the bell rang, Danny shouted, "See ya later, Jade!" while giving me a sideways peace sign. Nathan just nodded and waved.

Then I worked with two young women, Carrie and Donna. Carrie also looked white but her paperwork said she had ties to Prince of Wales Island. She didn't say much in class, just stared off into the distance, silently chewing on candy. She weighed perhaps eighty pounds, always wore bright blue contact lenses over her brown eyes, and rarely showed any effort in school. Sometimes I'd quietly ask her to start her homework, and she'd snap out of her trance and apologize and shuffle some books around on her desk. One morning Carrie came to class in a Sitka Wolves JV cheer-leading outfit, with red-and-blue pom-poms dangling from her backpack, and matching sneakers. She'd just gotten moved up from the freshman squad and was excited to show me pictures of herself standing atop a human tower, arms raised in a V. She was smiling, gazing proudly at an invisible crowd with a self-possession that I was yet to see in the hallways of Sitka High. But when I asked her to focus on her math, her fake blue eyes glazed over, and she became silent and still again.

Donna was more outspoken than Carrie, but it took her a twenty-ounce Pepsi before she could get going in the morning. She struggled in math, and I even spent a few periods in her classroom trying to figure out what her teacher was doing that Donna didn't understand. Donna came from a local Tlingit family, and her grandparents were well-known members of the Native community. When I learned how deeply involved Donna's family was in the history of Sitka, and how they'd spent the past seven decades fighting to keep their language alive, I didn't blame her for being so uninterested in algebra and Spanish. Some days I let her skip homework to draw formline designs in her workbook, to practice her Tlingit phonetics and vocabulary. But her favorite thing was to make me and Carrie laugh. She loved to do impressions of her elders. "Oh! Chee whiz! Choover the chaweekend I go to Choonah to cheat some chalibut!" was one routine. Or: "Holy chumping mukluks, Donna!" But her best impression was of her white father: "If it wasn't for your mother," she said in a gruff man-voice, "you'd be nothing but a dribble of goo sliding down my leg!"

In the afternoon, I worked with a kid named J.B. He showed zero interest in receiving any help or even recognizing my existence. I think this was largely because his buddies on the basketball team always poked their heads in the door, heckling and shooting spitballs at him, teasing him for having a special babysitter. J.B. could also pass for white, so rather than be the one to blow his cover, I always kept my distance and sat a few tables away.

That afternoon, with about fifteen minutes left in the period, the guidance counselor showed up in the library with a young man in a hooded black sweatshirt, black pants, black sneakers, and giant headphones blasting speed metal over his ears. "Jade! This is Peter!"

Peter nodded but didn't speak. I offered him a chair. He sat down.

"Peter is having some trouble in math this semester. I thought he could use a period with you, see if we can get those grades up?"

"Sure." I liked the guidance counselor; she was compassionate and cheerful, but sometimes I felt like she was living in a different world.

"Great!" As she walked out, she gave me double thumbs-up behind Peter's back.

Peter took out his math book, plopped it on his desk.

"You understand any of this stuff?"

Peter stared at the clock on the wall.

"What about this?" I turned several pages to that week's unit.

Peter remained silent. So I just sat with him for the rest of the period, shoulder to shoulder, eyes on the clock, waiting for the bell to ring.

■

For the next two weeks, I went back to the SJ gym to work out with Victor every Monday, Wednesday, and Friday night. There wasn't much space in the small room, so I remained in the corner, teaching myself to jump rope while the high school boys worked the heavy bag and bob-and-weave ropes. Meanwhile, Victor gave most of his attention to the two white men who had fights in November. I knew nothing about Victor beyond what I'd gathered from our first meeting: he was older than me, maybe in his midthirties, married, with a one-year-old son. He'd grown up in Sitka and worked full-time as an electrician at the town hospital. But every time I heard him talk about the "Roughhouse show" with the other men, his voice grew more serious, even solemn, in a way that made me want to know more about it. I didn't have any idea what

Roughhouse Friday was, or why Victor called it a "show," but being the new guy, I didn't think it was my place to ask.

The first Roughhouse fighter was named Todd Thompson. Todd was from Newark, New Jersey, and had been living in Sitka and working as a fisherman and at the cannery for about a decade. He had a shaved head, sunken eyes, and sinewy forearms covered in tattoos of wolves and fish. His skin was so white that it was almost translucent, and whenever he threw a punch, little waves of muscle rippled across his cheeks. Todd lived on a houseboat with his dogs, in a slip down at Old Thomsen's Harbor, and every night after practice he showered and changed in the locker room downstairs. One night when I asked Todd how long he'd been training with Victor, he told me that they'd been working out together for over a decade. The only reason Todd hadn't had a Roughhouse fight yet was because he'd "never stayed clean long enough." "If it wasn't for Victor," Todd told me, "I'd probably go right back to being a crackhead again."

The other Roughhouse fighter was an Australian lightweight named Scott Robinson, who, in the Roughhouse ring, was known as Kid Roo. Roo was only about five foot seven and barely 150 pounds, but his torso was stacked with tight bundles of muscle. Roo had ended up in Sitka after a yearlong walkabout when he'd met his wife, Nicole, on the interisland ferry and decided then and there that he would marry her. Back in Australia, Roo had fought under any number of names—Scott Robinson, Robert Scott, Scott Robbins—racking up, as Victor would later tell me, somewhere between eight, eighteen, or twenty-eight fights. Scott showed up at Victor's gym one day, challenged Victor himself, and dropped him with a body shot in the first minute. "Balls of steel," Victor sometimes said, when recalling that night several years ago. "To show up from nowhere, walk into another man's gym, and drop him in front of all his fighters . . . you gotta have balls of solid fucking steel." As the reigning lightweight champion of Southeast Alaska,

Roo held the record for the fastest knockout in Roughhouse history (eleven seconds, round one). When he hit the mitts with Victor, it was easy to see why: his power rose out of his legs until it exploded through his fists with a deep, hollow thud.

After Victor worked with the two men, he gave his time to the high school boys. In addition to Richie, there were two Native brothers, Wyatt and Ethan Ojala. Wyatt, the older of the two, was pink cheeked and built like a bulldozer. He had heavy, methodical hands and, with one leg shorter than the other, moved with a natural puncher's rocking motion. Ethan was leaner and darker than his brother, but didn't yet have the muscle to give his punches any pop. Victor had been working with the boys for over three years. When he called out punch combinations—"Double jab–hook–right hand!"—they attacked his mitts with dutiful precision. The boys had only had one fight each, at a small tournament in Ketchikan. It was expensive to fly off Baranof Island and difficult to find kids their age with any experience.

The last half hour of training was dedicated to sparring. Roo was by far the most technically sound fighter in the gym. Against Todd, he stalked forward, closing the distance between them by dropping his forehead onto Todd's chest, then driving him back into the walls with short hooks and uppercuts. In between rounds, while Roo chatted with Victor, Todd punched himself in the helmet, shaking his head and swearing. When the high school boys fought, Richie's wild style lined up nicely with Wyatt's patient, steady attack, but Ethan was just too little to hurt the older boys and sometimes left the gym crying. Then Victor would step in with Wyatt and Richie to even the score. Once Victor was warm, he would fight with Roo. The two men circled each other, gradually punching with more and more force, until they were all but swinging for each other's heads. I knew little about each man's history, little about their pasts and what made them fight, but the stiff silence in the room told me that something bigger was taking place, less a confrontation than a conversation, as if in fighting each other they were defining some larger truth about where they came from and who they were. And yet, when the beeper sounded, Victor and Roo would bump gloves and act as though nothing had happened.

After practice, while stretching, Victor sometimes played old videos of his Roughhouse fights, on a TV/VCR that he kept on a cart inside the closet. They were vicious, violent affairs with lots of screaming fans, a gravel-throated man in a bow tie and derby barking over a microphone from the center of the ring. Victor's fighting style—plowing forward through a tangle of blind, wild punches, dropping club-like left hands until the other man crumpled into the corner—looked nothing like what he taught in the gym, but after three rounds, he was always the one lifting his hands in victory. While watching his fights, Victor would sometimes narrate the footage with stories about growing up in Sitka, and how he'd become the number-one-ranked Roughhouse fighter in all of Southeast Alaska.

Victor was born in 1973, two years after the Alaska Native Claims Settlement, during a period of cultural resurgence. His father and mother spoke Tlingit at home and raised their three sons at a fish camp on ancestral land that his father had won back in a fifty-year legal battle with the Bureau of Land Management. "It was all about subsistence," Victor once told me. "Hunt, fish, learn the woods." But Victor still felt alienated at school. He didn't play sports, and his teachers always made him feel like he was too dumb to be good at anything. Though he was quiet in class, he got suspended for fighting every year. Once, when I asked Victor what he'd been fighting about, he laughed. "About? About fucking whatever," he said. "I have no idea. I was just a mad little guy. I guess I didn't want to be just another Native kid who slipped through the cracks." Some nights, Victor would sneak out of his house and ride his bike to the bars downtown to wait for last call, when local men—drunk, looking for action—would stumble into the parking lot and fight each other inside a circle of spectators. "It was so fucked-up," Victor said. "I couldn't fuckin' wait until it was my turn to get in the circle and prove to everyone how much of a man I was."

Through high school and into his early twenties, as he pursued a career as an electrician, Victor held on to a singular goal of becoming "a better bar fighter." He ordered boxing and karate magazines from Down South and started working out. Then, one night, while walking home shit-faced from a buddy's house, Victor got stomp-kicked and stick-beat by two white kids who jumped him behind the old movie theater on Sawmill Creek Road. It was an unlucky encounter—the only witness had reported to police that the victim was white, the assailants Native—but Victor's girlfriend and future wife, Miranda, wasn't surprised that Victor had gotten his due. That year, for his eighteenth birthday, she bought him two sets of sparring equipment, presenting the gift under one condition: that Victor fight only with his buddies, on the concrete floor of his father's machine shop, instead of against drunk strangers in a parking lot.

In footage of those early fights, Victor is always the smaller, chubbier fighter. But as soon as the two young men exchange first blows, it's clear that Victor possesses some strange power. "I used to line my friends up, five, six in a row, and knock them all out," Victor recalled. In one exchange, his opponent hits the deck and begins seizing on the floor. "I thought I had the sleep button back then. Thought I had the magic touch. If I ever got into trouble, I could always just drop a guy with a left to the body. I guess I was just a little bit tougher than everybody else."

In Sitka, Victor quickly ran out of guys to fight, so he went looking for opportunities beyond Baranof Island. One year, he flew himself up to Anchorage with leftover money from his oil dividend check to fight downtown, in front of a thousand people, at the

Thursday Night Fights at the Egan Center. Undertrained and over-matched, against a bigger, more experienced fighter—"Native guy, Oliver something?"—Victor took a beating and felt lucky to get a draw. But something about the sound of the crowd heckling Victor's small-town roots, their jeers when he was getting beaten down in the corner, broke his spirit. As he flew back to Sitka the next morning, he figured he'd never amount to anything but a local bar fighter.

For the next several years, Victor committed himself to a life with Miranda: they got married, bought a house. Victor got his journeyman's license and was getting good hours in the union. Then one afternoon, while wiring a building downtown, Victor heard a radio announcement on KINY, the only station to air in all the towns and villages up the Inside Passage. A man from Anchorage named Bob Haag was holding a boxing tournament in Juneau called the Southeast Showdown, with thousand-dollar prizes in three weight classes, given out to "the toughest guy in Southeast Alaska." Victor had heard of Haag: Haag's mother, Frankie, owned a bar in town called the Kiksadi Club—named after the Sitka clan—that had once held fights in a jury-rigged thirteen-foot ring over the dance floor. Victor wrote down Haag's number and, on his lunch break, signed himself up. The next morning, Victor started a training regimen—push-ups, sit-ups, roadwork—and told his father and commercial-fishing buddies to book their flights to Juneau. On a Friday morning in April, thirty pounds leaner, in the best shape of his life, Victor landed in the capital city, ready to fight. "The moment I stepped off the plane," he said, "I knew I was going to win."

John "the Irish Indian" Smith, a father of six from Hoonah; Dan "the Animal" Fink, a stand-up comedian from Juneau; Gabe "the Steel" Duckworth, the oldest son of a fighting family from Ketchikan. One after another, the Tlingit electrician from Sitka dropped his opponents with the same quiet violence that had lived inside him since he was a boy. His picture appeared in local papers; in the airport, people often recognized him as the Champ. Even the principal of Sitka High—the same man who had once suspended Victor for fighting—called him personally to congratulate him on his success, and for being a role model and mentor to young people in the community. For the next three years, Victor, racking up a record of seventeen wins and two losses, was widely regarded as the number one middleweight at Roughhouse Friday. After he won two Southeast Showdowns, Miranda, ready to have a child, told Victor that if he didn't quit fighting, she'd leave him. As a consolation prize, she helped him give Sitka the one thing he'd never had: a boxing club.

As Victor watched his fights, he nodded at the vision of his younger, fighting self. "No one could fuckin' touch me. Back then, my motto used to be 'Crush skulls, steal souls.'" Then he paused the tape to show the expression he wore in the ring: the muscles of his face were contorted into something like a joyful snarl. "Miranda used to call that my angry Native face." And with the screen frozen, you could see his ring name stitched into the band of his red-and-black trunks: THE SAVAGE.

◼

I sat on a stool at the Pioneer Bar on Katlian Street, watching Game 7 of the American League Championship Series between my beloved Red Sox and their archrival, the New York Yankees. Had I been in Maine, every dive from Madawaska to Eliot would have been packed to the walls, but the P Bar was mostly empty that night. As the bartender wiped down the counter, as a drunk man a few stools down ripped off another round of pull-tab tickets, the Sox blew a three-run lead, after the Yankees tied it at five in the bottom of the eighth, and sent the game into extra innings. I ordered another beer, trying to pretend like I was just another lonely guy blowing a night at the bar. But inside me, I felt as if the rivets of my soul were starting to shake loose. Though it had been years since I'd followed the game with any dedication, few things made me feel as madly connected to my New England heritage as watching the Red Sox blow it to the Yankees. Part of it was the cruel predictability of the Curse—the knowledge that even the best, most hopeful circumstances in life could suddenly unravel into despair and tragic defeat. Part of it was that my father had instilled in me an affection for the Red Sox since I was barely old enough to tie my own shoes.

The first year that my mother and sister and I lived in Maine, my father took a trip to the Red Sox spring training, in Winter Haven, Florida, to track down his boyhood hero, Ted Williams. I was too young to understand the motivation for his trip: that spending a few weeks watching baseball in Florida was my father's way of taking time to decide whether he should leave my mother to live with Martha. When he returned north, he came to visit me in Maine. By all accounts, his trip had been a great success—he had the souvenirs to prove it. He showed me a picture of himself and the Splendid Splinter riding around in a golf cart, a meeting he'd engineered after several days of scouting Williams from the stands. He even got Williams to autograph a charcoal drawing of himself that had hung on my father's wall in his boyhood bedroom. *To the Coffins*, Williams had written, in looping cursive. *Best Wishes, Ted Williams.*

The other things my father had brought back: a red, white, and blue baseball jacket, matching ball cap, and a beautiful wooden bat with my name engraved in the barrel. In the side yard of my apartment building, my father showed me how to stand over home plate, feet evenly spaced, bat cocked over my shoulder, hands choked an inch above the knob, elbows down. It took me a while to get the stance right—a natural lefty, I kept mixing up my hands, standing with the wrong foot forward, dropping the bat too low—but my father was patient. "Good," he'd say, showing me his own stance before hitching his arms to take a practice swing.

The mechanics of hitting—so concrete and specific—were a welcome change from the ambiguity of my father's situation. I still didn't fully understand where he lived. On some occasions, he spoke about Martha, and his life in Vermont, with a familiarity that made it sound like he'd been there for years. As he took me through several more instructions—eyes on the ball, chin down, knees bent—I became bored with the tedious details. But I also knew that as soon as the lesson was over, my father would get in his car and drive back to Vermont. After we'd gotten the basics down, my father took a few steps back. He'd forgotten a baseball, but using acorns as a substitute, he threw me my first pitches. I swung, gently at first, then with more force. My father laughed at my seriousness, was impressed by the intensity of my concentration. "Good," he said each time I connected bat to acorn. "Good." When the lesson was over, my father gathered himself for the drive home. My sister often began crying as my father's car disappeared. But I never felt that sad: I had a swing to practice, and I knew that the next time I saw my father—a week from now, maybe two—I'd be even better.

One afternoon, while I was taking cuts in the backyard, my mother came outside. I can imagine that no matter how tired she was, the image of her son dressed in a baseball uniform, pretending to swing at imaginary pitches, made sleep difficult. By then, my father had left me with a baseball, and my mother, despite having zero knowledge of the game, asked if I wanted her to pitch. I didn't like the idea: baseball was something I shared with my father, a game played by lean, stern men like Ted Williams. The sight of my mother entering that vision violated the masculine beauty of the game.

"Let me try," my mother said.

I gave her the ball, walked back several feet, then positioned myself just as my father had taught me. My mother's throwing motion was even worse than I'd imagined it would be: less a throw than a jerky, inelegant whip. Her pitch—way high, way outside, an arcing, wobbly lob—was slow enough for me to reach out and tag with the fat barrel of my bat. As the ball shot back toward my mother, she ducked, flinching as the ball disappeared into the bushes near the street. As she gamely jogged after the ball, the sight of her searching embarrassed me. I dropped my bat and went inside.

The Red Sox blew it in the bottom of the eleventh, just as I knew they would. By then it was nearly midnight back East, and I'd gotten a bit drunker than I'd meant to. I stumbled into my apartment, then into the bathroom to brush my teeth, and I looked at my reflection in the mirror. My face was flushed bright red as usual—the bad luck of my mother's genetic inheritance—but behind that redness I saw another face. I stood there for several seconds, trying on different expressions, trying to coax that hidden face into the light. I stuck my tongue out, squinted my eyes, rearranged my cheeks. But no matter how much I tried to imitate the expression I'd seen Victor wear into the Roughhouse ring, I just couldn't call it up.

■

I showed up to school the next morning nursing a mournful hangover. It was just a dumb baseball game—but being so far away from New England, with no one to share my losses with, made the usual despair all the more lonesome. Luckily, it was a short day—just three periods long—and I was glad to have my final period with Peter, who didn't require much beyond my presence. Though his grades were slipping, my new policy with Peter was total, relentless patience. I decided that Peter had enough people trying to get him to talk, and that he didn't need me to be one more. In recent meetings with my SNEP colleagues, Laura had cited several studies that showed that culturally

Native students, unlike their white classmates, weren't encouraged to speak up with the kind of bold authority that was rewarded in American classrooms. Rather, the virtue of listening, often for long periods and without interruption, was a way that information could be passed down from one generation to the next. Stories, songs, knowledge about fishing grounds were transmitted between the old and the young not through answering questions correctly but by the humble act of memorization. To raise one's hand, to assert one's superior knowledge, showed disrespect and a lack of humility—traits that, Laura said, weren't valued in traditional Tlingit culture. In mainstream classrooms, such reserve was often mistaken for stupidity. Laura's analysis was supposed to help me work with my students at Sitka High, but it also made me think about what Victor had told me: how his teachers had always made him feel like he was too dumb to be good at anything, that fighting was his way of proving them wrong.

I sat for the better part of an hour, waiting for Peter to say something. He didn't—just sat next to me with his head down. For now, I was content to sit with him until he was ready to speak. It was a comfortable place: to say nothing, do nothing, exist in the cocoon of your own head, provided security and protection from the world.

Finally, Peter reached into his backpack, carefully pulled out a small metal box—about the size of a Rubik's Cube, welded roughly along the edges—and placed it on the table.

"What is it?"

Peter paused. "It's a box."

I asked him where he'd made it.

He shrugged. "Shop."

I held the small box in my hands, examining it from different angles. The corners were a bit uneven, but it was a rugged little box, heavy and sturdy. I handed the box back to Peter. "Cool."

Peter nodded, put the box in his backpack, and put his head back down.

■

The Friday night before Alaska Day—Alaska Day was like Alaska's Fourth of July, and every year the biggest celebration in the state took place in the historic capital of Sitka—Victor was particularly rough on the high school boys. In a sparring session, he gave them a beating like the one he'd given me the first night I met him: lips split, noses bled, and by the time practice was over, the boys stumbled out of the room like they'd been drinking. Victor explained that he'd gotten a call from the boys' mothers the night before. They were concerned that with all the Alaska Day festivities going on that weekend, the boys would get into trouble. "So they asked me to beat 'em up extra bad so they'd be too tired to go out drinking." It wasn't exactly how I'd been brought up— while my mother worked the night shift, I was usually free to come and go as I pleased—but there was something admirable about the way that Victor held the boys accountable to the best versions of themselves, that fighting was the medium for their agreement.

Then Victor got a call from Haag, the Roughhouse promoter in Juneau. Even though the first fights were still a month out, Haag wanted Victor to give Todd and Roo extra rounds on the mitts. The November Roughhouse Friday was the first of eight fight nights in the season, and a good show with well-trained fighters would give Haag's fans something to come back for. After he hung up with Haag, Victor gave Todd extra rounds of mitt work, but when it came to Roo, he wasn't interested. "I'm all set, Veek," Roo said, waving him off. "Most of them fakahs in Juneau I reckon I could beat one-handed."

Victor shrugged, stood in the middle of the room. "You want some, Jade?"

I put down my jump rope, pulled on a pair of gloves, and met Victor inside the square of duct tape.

First he showed me how to stand: feet shoulder-width apart, hands up, shoulders bladed, in a position that Victor called "fight stance." When he learned that I was a lefty, Victor said he'd waited his whole life to train another southpaw like himself. He showed me a jab and a cross, then a basic punch combination, thrown in a simple, pat-pat one-two rhythm. In Roughhouse boxing, Victor said, where most fighters came into the ring without any experience, "straight punches" were all I needed to know. We repeated the sequence several times, slowly increasing my speed and power. To increase the pop in my punches, Victor slammed his mitts into my fists, grunting in time with the impact. We worked like that for several rounds, Victor moving in a wide circle, shepherding me around the room. When my stance became too square, he'd smack my shoulder, turn his feet sideways, and show me an image of how I should position myself. When the beeper sounded and Victor dropped his mitts, I felt like I was coming out of hypnosis.

"Good stuff, Jade." Victor paused. "You know, the promoter in Juneau, he told me he's still looking for guys to fill up his November card. I told him about you. Said you paddled a kayak up here. Said I beat the crap out of you the first night but that you kept coming back around. I said you didn't know much about fighting, but that you were tough, and in shape." Victor explained that the promoter paid for the plane tickets and hotel rooms, and if I won, he'd write me a check for $150.

I looked at Victor. The experience of hitting his mitts had awoken something inside of me. But now I felt an equal force willing that thing back to sleep. "Who would I fight?"

He shrugged. "Probably some guy like you. Maybe a fight or two under his belt, but nothing like what you seen in here. I mean, it's no ballroom, Jade. Basically, you go into a bar, take your shirt off, and show everyone how much of a man you are."

4. MISS MARY AND THE GOAT

Alaska Day morning, I had a date with a local woman named Miss Mary. I'd met Miss Mary not long after I'd arrived in Sitka, while I'd been walking around downtown. She had just finished giving a walking tour to a group of cruise ship passengers. Our initial exchange was brief: when she asked me what I was doing in town, I told about my paddling trip, and my plans to continue on to Glacier Bay. Miss Mary was impressed with my ambition, but the way she looked at me told me that she wasn't buying my story. "Well," she said, with a note of condescension, "I think you'll find that Sitka is a magical place." A few weeks later, while I was walking downtown, Miss Mary came riding past me on a bicycle, her hair blowing in the wind, smiling so hard her eyes were nearly closed. I had spent the hours since the end of the school day trying to invent errands to run just so I'd have an excuse to talk to someone. The sight of her filled me with hope.

"Well!" Miss Mary said. "It's not often that I see such a strapping young lad walking through my town!" When she learned that I'd settled in Sitka, she nodded as if confirming her premonitions. We didn't exchange numbers, but as we parted, Miss Mary looked at me longer than I expected her to. "Until we meet again." A few days later, I ran into Miss Mary a third time, in an aisle of the Sea Mart grocery store. By then I had begun to wonder if Miss Mary possessed a secret power of staring into the future. She looked inside my basket. I had gathered my usual bachelor fare—a bag of rice, eggs, bacon, and some kind of Mexipino egg rolls called taquitos that you could buy in the hot case for half off after six o'clock. Miss Mary's basket was full of little bags of seeds and grains, and lots of vegetables. She was wearing logging boots and a wool sweater and laughed when she saw the way I looked at her. "Aren't you cute?" she said, smoothing down the collar of my flannel shirt. Based on appearances, it was clear that Miss Mary was significantly older than me. In my limited experience with women my own age, they seemed to know what they wanted better than I did, which often left me feeling even more lost and wandering than when I was on my own. I'd dated a few girls while traveling west—kind young women doing productive things with their postgraduate years—but I was too consumed by my own unfolding story to offer them much beyond a stoic cowboy persona that had no correlation whatsoever to the person I was.

Before we parted this time, Miss Mary asked me to be her date to the Alaska Day Parade. I'd never been asked out on a date by a woman. I'd never asked a woman out on a date. I paused, pretending to consider my other plans. I'd been spending my weekends wandering the mossy forests and mountains, losing myself up streambeds and ravines, following vague deer trails along unnamed ridges, passing eight hours a day in total silence. "Sure," I said.

The morning of the parade, I rode my bike downtown and joined the crowds on the sidewalk along Lincoln Street. It was local tradition for men and women in Sitka to celebrate the holiday by dressing in the costume of Americans at the time of the 1867 Alaska Purchase. Several white men wore peacoats and had grown beards; white women wore hoop skirts and bonnets. The parade offered the usual floats that I'd grown used to back East—the fire department, Shriners in little cars, the Elks Lodge, the high school marching band—but then there were several floats you'd see only in Sitka.

First came a replica of a Russian frigate called the *Neva*, which had cannonballed the Kiks.adi fortress in a decisive battle in 1804. The battle took place at the end of Lincoln Street, on a rocky beach near the mouth of Indian River, and, by most historical accounts, was considered the last major uprising of Native Alaskans against foreign powers. Depending on whom you asked, the Kiks.adi flight from their fortress to a more secret stronghold across Baranof Island could be remembered as either a final surrender or a highly strategic survival march. By then, the future was in the cards: in a matter of years, disease would ravage many of Southeast Alaska's indigenous communities, the explosive fur trade would dry up, and the lords of Russia would withdraw from operations in Alaska, forking over their frozen territories to the United States. As for the *Neva*, it sank off the coast of Kruzof Island during a horrible storm.

Then came a regiment of stern-faced men with rifles on their shoulders: a reenactment of the American military brigades that came after the United States bought the Alaska territories—for about eight million bucks—as a diplomatic favor to Russia. To Washington, the prospect of inheriting several thousand depleted Native people held no advantage for an emerging nation like the United States—America had seen how this had played out Down South, seen the uprisings and the reservation disasters, and it was just an expensive, violent, and logistically tedious hassle (of course, back then, no one knew about oil deposits in the North Slope). When Sheldon Jackson was appointed the minister of education, he went about organizing indigenous youth into centralized schools, thereby destroying millennia-old clan affiliations intimately bound to the geography of the land and sea. In 1912, the federal government allowed a final potlatch ceremony before outlawing cultural traditions altogether.

Then came a group of dancers—young and old—from the SNEP program. Dressed in full regalia, they marched past me, singing and dancing to songs that had belonged to their people for thousands of years. I would learn that there was a name for such possessions: *at.oow*, or "owned things." At.oow were songs, clan crests, names passed down from one generation to the next. Fishing grounds could be at.oow. Constellations, hunting knowledge. At.oow could be shared, traded, inherited. In time, I would consider that perhaps the faint pang in my chest that morning had something to do with a lack of owned things in my own life. But as I stood along Lincoln Street observing the parade, my only conclusion about history was that maybe the Tlingit people had the deepest understanding of how to keep the past alive. The rest of us— Americans posing as Russian soldiers, white men posing as white men from a long time ago, me wordlessly observing it all—were just pretending.

Then I saw Miss Mary coming down the street, surrounded by a pack of women dressed in gowns, waving from under a bonnet like a pageant model. I did not have a good feeling as I waved back at her, but when she smiled at me and threw me a handful of candy, I picked it right up off the street.

Later, I met Miss Mary at the corner of Lincoln and Katlian, where that year's floats were being judged. (The *Neva* won.) Afterward, Miss Mary took my arm and together we walked up to the old Castle Hill monument—a turret-like cylinder overlooking downtown—to witness the reenactment of the land-transfer ceremony between Russia and the United States. In the original ceremony, the Kiks.adi had come to Castle Hill to honor the departure of their Russian rivals. But the Americans, worried there might be an uprising, had not allowed the Kiks.adi to witness the exchange up close, instead forcing them to watch from behind a garrison wall or from their canoes. Where the Russian presence in Southeast Alaska had been marked by relatively peaceful trade agreements—the Russians relied on Tlingit knowledge to supply otter fur, the Tlingit enjoyed the use of metal to amplify their artistic traditions—the American agreement would offer the Tlingit little in return. There was also a legend that during the transfer ceremony, the Russian flag as it came down the flagpole got snagged on an American bayonet. But none of those things were part of the reenactment ceremony that day.

■

Miss Mary's apartment was up the hill from mine, also in a basement of another person's house. But her apartment felt like a home: her living room was decorated with lots of fluffy pillows and blankets, her kitchen was full of spices and little jars of grains, and she even had a bedroom separated from the main living quarters by a red velvet curtain hanging in the doorway. For dinner that night, Miss Mary cooked me a stew-like dish served on toast, made with the meat of a mountain goat that, she told me, she'd shot on top of Bear Mountain. I hadn't had a home-cooked meal in months, and I devoured several plates while Miss Mary told me about how she'd ended up in Sitka. Like me, she'd come to Southeast Alaska—from a former life in Minnesota—to live more simply. She came from a complicated family—she no longer spoke to her father—and putting space between herself and that past gave her a fresh start. She smiled. "Everyone I've met up here is running away from something Down South." She paused for a moment, as if silently posing the question of my motive to me, but I just nodded and kept eating.

When I was done, Miss Mary stood up and asked me if I would allow her to teach me a few things. I agreed. Four thousand miles away from the judgmental gaze of people I knew back East, it struck me how inapprehensive I was about trying new things.

First, Miss Mary tried to show me how to tango. We stomped around the kitchen for several minutes, until it was clear that she didn't know how to tango much better than I did. Then she asked me to sit on her couch so she could teach me how to comb her hair. "A man should know how to care for a woman's hair," she told me. I brushed a few strokes—her hair was long and smooth. Then Miss Mary went into her bathroom and came out with a tub of warm water and a bag of nail polishes. She told me to soak my feet, then asked me to pick a color from the bag. I searched through several bottles before settling on a dark shade of blue. As Miss Mary washed my feet, she looked up at me and said, "I believe that washing a lover's feet is a very sensual act. When Mary Magdalene washed Jesus's feet, I believe that was very erotic." While I sat there, I tried to make sense of who I was supposed to be: Was Miss Mary telling me that I was Jesus?

As she painted my toenails, Miss Mary asked me about my life back East. I told her I'd graduated a year ago, left home after a season of commercial fishing, then wandered my way north without any plan. When she asked me about my childhood, I told her my history: I'd grown up in Maine with my mother, spent summers at my father's house in Vermont. I explained that my parents had met during the Vietnam War, when my father had been stationed on the military base where my mother ran an officers' club. They'd married, then come to America to start a life. What had happened next? Miss Mary wanted to know. I paused. A blank cloud filled my head. I had no memories of my parents together. My mother had once told me that by my second birthday, my father was already gone. "They got divorced," I said.

Miss Mary stopped painting my toes for a moment. "I'm so sorry, Jade." She appeared more baffled by my past than I was.

"I was pretty young. I don't remember much." What memories I did possess of that life in Vermont existed as little more than a string of vague impressions like postcards from another world: a blue Dodge truck in the front yard, parked under a maple tree. A red fox disappearing into the cornfield across the dirt road. A rotted log that I'd lifted out of a swamp in the backyard, only to find a city of grimy insects squirming over one another's bodies. A dream in which a massive blue bear tried to pull me out of my bed in the middle of the night, but I escaped out the back of a sleeping bag before he disappeared into the darkness. My father, on a motorcycle, driving away down a long dirt road, his face obscured by a helmet, a green army backpack on his shoulders, upon which was sewn a tattered American flag.

Miss Mary blinked. "Your mother didn't take you back to her country?"

"No." By now, my mother had been living in Maine nearly as long as she'd lived in Thailand. Then I showed Miss Mary the ring on my finger and explained to her what it meant. But as I held up my finger, I was less interested in the two sides of the ring than in the smudged, poorly soldered area that held the two broken pieces together.

Miss Mary was quiet, thoughtful. "Jade, I've had a dishonest lover myself. It is very painful." She looked at me—that same knowing stare that she'd regarded me with when I'd first shown up in town. "And I, too, was abandoned by my father." She paused, swallowed. "I am still trying to forgive him."

I had an impulse to correct her use of the word *abandoned*—I had never thought of my father's departure from our family that way—but I couldn't think of another word.

"Jade"—she sighed—"would you mind if I shared an observation about you?"

"Sure."

Miss Mary lowered her head. "You seem to be a person who does not allow himself much comfort in life. As for me, I believe that comfort is essential." Most days, Miss Mary said, she was up early, doing productive things: cooking, exercising. But some days, she forced herself to spend the entire day in bed. She looked at the entrance of her bedroom. "My bedroom is the most comfortable place I know. But I only let another person inside if I trust them."

I glanced at the red velvet curtain hanging over the door to her bedroom.

Miss Mary put her hand on mine. "I trust you, Jade."

For the next several nights, I stayed over at Miss Mary's place. She was conscious of my youth and inexperience and aware that I was new to town, so she didn't put too much pressure on me to act like her boyfriend. She called me every day, but usually waited for me to invite myself over. One night, she told me that after living in Sitka for several years, she'd developed rules about dating local men. The first: "You don't have a boyfriend. You have a turn." The second, for women like Miss Mary: "The odds are good, but the goods are very, very odd."

Later that week, when I came down with a bad cold, Miss Mary brought a big pot of chicken soup to my apartment. While I was asleep on my couch, she cleaned my kitchen and bathroom— an amazing feat. My toilet had some kind of green growth in the bowl; I'd been using my sink less as a washing basin and more as storage for dirty dishes. I thought it was sexist for a woman to clean up a man's messes, but Miss Mary insisted that she enjoyed it, that it made her feel good to take care of someone else. Then, one night, I woke up to find her reading at the end of my couch. When she realized that I was awake, she said that she wanted to ask me something. "Jade, what do you do with your time when you're not with me?"

I told her that I spent most of my evenings at the boxing gym.

Miss Mary flinched, then collected herself before continuing in a stern but trembling voice. "Jade, I need to know something . . ."

She paused, took a deep breath. "And I need you to tell me the truth."

"Sure."

"Jade, I need to know . . . if you are a player."

"A player?" I could have come up with a list of fifty other questions that I would have been more ready to answer. A player? I didn't have a car; I rode a spray-painted bike. I had a job at a high school, lived in a basement, had just recently gotten my phone hooked up. I had about a hundred dollars in savings. Not exactly the portrait of a player.

"Please tell me the truth. I'd prefer a difficult truth to an easy lie."

"I'm not a player."

Miss Mary shook her head, as if to recalibrate her thoughts. "I'm sorry. That was unfair." She paused. "I think you're an honest man." She ran her hand over my head. "And kind." Then she looked me in the eyes. "And very exotic."

I had never had anyone call me exotic before. I knew I was supposed to be offended by the word, but I kind of liked the sound of it.

Miss Mary stood up to leave. "Sleep, Jade. Sleep."

I nodded, closed my eyes, and went back to bed.

■

Ever since Victor had offered me the chance to fight, I had been uneasy about going back to the gym. Something about the idea of—as Victor put it—taking off my shirt, getting into a ring, and showing everyone how much of a man I was made me want to run back East, pretend I'd never come to Southeast Alaska, and go network my way into a straight job in a city where I could blow my weekends getting drunk with my fellow postgrads.

While Todd and Roo and Victor doubled down on workouts, I trained off to the side. But I still paid careful attention to the way the men prepared for their fights. Roo remained calm about facing his upcoming and still unknown opponent. He jumped rope only until he broke a good sweat, then hit the heavy bag gingerly, now and then loading up on power punches as if to test his strength, but never taking himself to a limit of desperation or exhaustion. I admired the self-possession of a man like Roo: he had shown up in a strange place with a trade, carpentry, and a skill, fighting, and from those things had invented a life for himself out of nothing.

Todd, because of weight-class restrictions, was trying to shed almost fifteen pounds off his already-lean frame. In Roughhouse boxing, unlike in amateur and professional classes, there were just three weight divisions—light, middle, and heavy—since most fighters didn't stay in shape and couldn't be relied on to make weight before a bout. Roo had no trouble coming in under the 165-pound lightweight limit, but Todd, who hovered right around 175, had begun the painful process of starving himself. In the last days, his eyes and cheeks had hollowed out, and every few minutes he ran into the locker room to step on a scale, only to come back shouting the new number—"One seventy-two!" "One seventy!"—out loud. This mad obsession made Todd's unsteady demeanor even more precarious. But I admired the discipline of depriving oneself in the name of accessing something more pure. Even my brief encounter with a semi-ascetic life in the temple had revealed to me that beneath all the layers of who I'd become at the molten age of twenty-one, there existed a still, clear pool of being, which, with practice, I could access, one breath at a time, whenever I wanted to. My Buddha nature, my empty, flickering soul—whatever it was, knowing that such a self existed inside me soothed the lonely, wild confusion I sometimes felt about the rest of my life. In that steady state of unsureness would always be something solid and strong. And yet, in the past couple years, without the temple or my faith or my mother's heritage to contain it, that pure, steady thing no longer felt stable.

One night after practice, as I was changing out of my sneakers and into rubber boots for the ride home, I listened in on a conversation between Victor and Roo and Todd about their potential Roughhouse opponents. Neither man wanted an easy opponent, but rather a game and straightforward fighter who would give them a fair test. Roo had beaten just about every fighter in his weight class from Ketchikan to Yakutat, and Victor said it was likely that Haag would find him an opponent who outweighed him by twenty pounds. For Todd, there were plenty of guys in the 165 range who had never fought before. But few of them trained like Todd did. Then, on a dime, Victor stopped talking. "What the fuck?" He was looking at my toes.

It had been a couple of days since Miss Mary had painted them blue, but the paint was still visible. "A woman did it."

"A woman?" Victor said.

I shrugged. "Her name's Mary."

Victor paused. "Calls herself Miss Mary?"

"Yeah. Miss Mary."

"Mate," Roo said. "Mate."

"Mary's the Goat's girl," Victor said.

I asked him who the Goat was.

"The Goat is the fuckin' champ." Victor went into the closet, wheeled out the TV and VCR, and popped in a tape of a well-built white man with a nearly shaved blond head, traps like giant bat wings, puffy pectorals and biceps, demolishing his opponent. After the fight, the man scowled at the crowd, nodded like a pro wrestler, and held up a single fist.

After Victor had retired as the middleweight champion of Roughhouse Friday, the Goat had come on as his understudy. In two years, the Goat had won sixteen fights straight, back-to-back Southeast Showdowns, and was half the reason why the middleweight title belt had remained in Sitka for four years running. He was also the reason why the Roughhouse Friday boxing show, once located in the center of downtown Juneau at the Alaska Native Brotherhood Hall, had been moved nine miles out the Glacier Highway, to a second-story barroom above a diner. In the world of Roughhouse Friday, the legend was sometimes referred to as the Microphone Debacle.

To win the 2003 Southeast Showdown, the Goat had to fight through a family of Ketchikan men known as the Duckworths. The patriarch of the family, Jack, had drawn the Goat in the semi-final. Jack knew he had no chance—he was almost fifty, not half the fighter that the Goat was—but hoped to at least do enough damage to soften the Goat up for his son, Gabe "the Steel" Duckworth, whom the Goat would likely face in the final. As predicted, the Goat gave Jack a beating, retiring him in the second round. Before his title bout with the Steel, the Goat asked Haag for the microphone. As a rule, Haag never let fighters on the mic—more than anything else in life, Haag liked to be the center of attention, and letting a fighter do the talking compromised this power—but this was the Goat, a man who had, Haag knew, become as synonymous with the Roughhouse Friday brand as the Big H boxing glove logo.

"Well, I grew up on a farm in Pennsylvania," the Goat began, addressing the seven hundred drunk and rowdy fans in the ANB Hall. "And I ain't never seen a duck kick a goat's ass." The crowd erupted. They liked the pun. They liked the Goat. Then the Goat turned to the Steel. "Now"—the Goat lowered his eyes—"I'm going to beat your ass, just like I beat your old man!" This insult to the Steel's father, Jack, tipped the scale. Gabe and his little brother Tyson—a young lightweight who expected to face Roo in the final—rushed the ring. Several security guards held them back, but the commotion ignited a grand brawl in the ANB Hall. Beers flew through the air. Strangers shoved one another into other strangers. As the Duckworth boys were escorted outside, the Steel, in a fit of rage, punched through a window and had to be carted away to the hospital in an ambulance, where he received treatment for an eviscerated forearm. The Goat, observing the chaos from inside the ropes of the elevated ring, was later crowned the default champion of the middleweight division. Roo, who'd expected to face the now-disqualified Tyson Duckworth in the lightweight final, got his belt, too.

But the real fallout of the evening was that the abiding members of the Juneau ANB decided that Haag—who already had a questionable reputation with tribal organizations in town—needed to find a new venue for his show. Ever the promoter, Haag chose Marlintini's Lounge. Though the upstairs barroom could hold only half the fans as the ANB Hall—four hundred max—there were advantages to running boxing shows in a bar. Haag could use their liquor permit and their staff, and as a man who'd spent his adult life pulling off boxing shows in Last Frontier watering holes, Haag knew that "most dance floors in Alaska, they just happen to be the exact same size as a boxing ring."

I'd become so enchanted by the vision of a young man following in Victor's footsteps, rising through the ranks of a world of fighting men, then becoming champion by desecrating the paternal lineage of his opponent that I almost forgot to ask the most obvious question: "Why do they call him the Goat?"

Victor laughed. "He was hunting up on Bear Mountain one day and shot one, but then the weather came in too fast, and he had to spend the night under its dead body to survive."

"Oh." I guessed Miss Mary hadn't shot the goat herself.

Now, Victor said, after winning a few fights up in Anchorage, the Goat had run through most of the competition in Alaska and had moved to Philadelphia, to train with pros in a real gym. He was jogging nine miles a day, working out in double sessions, with plans to fight in the Golden Gloves amateur ranks before going pro himself. "I don't know where he's at with Mary," Victor said. "He wasn't very loyal to her when we went to Juneau. But last I talked to him, he was all fucked-up about her still." Victor shrugged. "But I'll let you guys figure it out. I mean, you're the one who paddled a damn kayak up here."

■

When I got back to my apartment, I found a box on my doorstep, with a small note attached: *Can't wait for this weekend! XOXO, Miss Mary*. A few days earlier, Miss Mary had invited me to a Halloween costume party called the Stardust Ball. It was a very public event, and I sensed that this was her way of calling my bluff, to see how serious I was about being a couple. I had no interest in dressing up in a costume and pretending to be someone else, but since I didn't have the courage to tell Miss Mary how I felt, I had just shrugged and said, "Sure." Inside the box was a piece of chocolate cake. I entered my apartment, took a piece of fish out of the freezer, then put it back in. I sat at my kitchen table and ate the chocolate cake for dinner.

■

I showed up to Miss Mary's house without a costume on. When Miss Mary answered the door, she frowned in disapproval. She was wearing a black flapper dress with little tassels hanging off it, a mask over her eyes, and her hair in a swirl on top of her head. Several of her friends—middle-aged women dressed like forest queens and fortune-tellers—stood behind her, waiting for me to explain myself. They, too, seemed disappointed in my appearance.

"This will not do!" Miss Mary said, and led me into her bedroom, where she began digging through her closet until she produced a plastic package off a shelf. It was a medieval court jester costume: black tights, black shirt with red, blue, and green ruffle sleeves, and a hat with puffy horns, little bells hanging off the tips. On the package was a picture of a guy wearing the costume, a blank expression on his face. It just happened to be my size exactly.

"Perfect!" she said. Then we drove downtown in one of her friends' minivans.

The Stardust Ball was a big event in town: crowds of people milled about outside the door of the Centennial Building, dressed like zombies, ghouls, witches, cats. I followed Miss Mary and her friends through the crowd, noting that, despite some goofy out-fits, there weren't a lot of other guys wearing a silly hat and pointy shoes with bells on the ends. If I'd been drunk, I might have been more willing to act the part, but instead I felt like a child on dis-play. In the ballroom, a live band was playing dance music, and Miss Mary jumped into the crowd, where she started noodle danc-ing, shaking the tassels on her dress. I just stood still, bobbing my head, waving now and then to teachers I recognized from the high school, who looked at my outfit, looked at Miss Mary, and gave me a limp thumbs-up.

"Loosen up, Jade!" Miss Mary yelled, several times, and even took my hands in hers and tried to get me to move. I kept pretend-ing that I had to use the bathroom and wandering out into the lobby. From a distance, I saw a tall refrigerator box making its way through the crowd, a fist-size hole in the middle of the box for the man to look out of. As he came closer, I could see the little people on strings hanging from the top of the box, flames running up the sides, a plane sticking out the middle. Inside the hole, the man was grinning, getting a real kick out of the way he was offending everyone, getting under their skin. I watched him pass, a white column wandering through the crowd, making his way onto the dance floor.

After an hour of putting up with my pouting, Miss Mary finally gave in, and her friend gave us a ride back to her apartment. Inside, Miss Mary asked me what was wrong. I knew she would take my remoteness personally. So I took a deep breath, let my shoulders fall, and pretended to be hurt. "You know, I know about the Goat."

Miss Mary blinked several times, searching for words. "When you told me you were boxing, I . . . I just didn't know what to do."

I didn't speak right away. If I could just maintain my silence, I knew that Miss Mary would start to feel like this was her fault.

"I used to go to his fights in Juneau. I didn't like it. It was very violent. The women at the show, they did not respect themselves." Miss Mary looked down. "He was not honest with me about what he did in Juneau. There was a great deal he did not tell me."

I watched Miss Mary from a distance. She was still in love with the Goat—I could see that truth surrounding her like the low light of her apartment. I went into the bathroom, changed into my clothes. As I made my way out the door, I handed Miss Mary the jester costume.

"Jade!" Miss Mary called out behind me. She was standing in her doorway, framed like a silhouette from a noir movie. "If you ever fight him . . ." In her voice I heard an emotion that made me wince: honest concern for my well-being. "Please. Just watch out for his uppercut." She nodded to herself. "It's his best punch."

5. THE STONE

Another rainy Sunday. I lay in bed, reading a piece of mail I'd received from my father a few days earlier. I'd been receiving mail from my father for most of my life. At first, in elementary school and junior high, the mail was newspaper clippings—columns from *The Boston Globe* about the Red Sox rookie prospects or the Celtics' playoff runs. By high school, the clippings were replaced by long photocopied feature stories from *Sports Illustrated* and *Esquire*. The stories didn't interest me so much as the messages that my father would sometimes write in the margins of the pages: short reflections on life, updates on his recent doings at the Birches. A few times a year, my father would write me full letters, on notebook paper, in all-capitals penmanship, in which he would take stock of my development as a man. When I was thirteen years old, after I'd somehow netted thirteen goals in a weekend soccer tournament, my father wrote, *I've always looked at you as my lovely son who always fills my heart just to be with you and see you. Today, however, you were a man . . . You were a lion. You were indomitable . . . as Robert Bly would say*—Robert Bly, the author of *Iron John: A Book About Men*, was my father's favorite thinker—*You showed your sword*. It was heavy stuff—but as much as I had learned to value my father's expressions of love and support, I had also learned to distance myself from the intensity of his confessions. No matter how many times he expressed his love, no matter how many times he penned missives about the man I was becoming, there seemed to exist some basic gap between his words and the emotions I felt at the other end of them, as if the grandiosity of his language were spackling over the more obvious truth standing between us. I could count on a single hand the number of times my mother had expressed her love with such effusiveness, but in a way I had spent most of my teenage years rejecting, I had always felt her blood pumping more powerfully through my veins.

But his most recent piece of mail was of a different tone than I'd been used to. It was a dispatch from Ernest Hemingway, published by the *Toronto Star* in 1923, when the young writer had been sent to Pamplona to cover the San Fermín festival, which became the material for *The Sun Also Rises*. I had read the book several years ago, but had missed entirely that Jake's injury was a fundamental feature of his character. Without this detail, I found the book to be little more than a tale of drunk expats wandering around Europe without enough to do.

What brought my father to Hemingway was more complicated. After September 11, my father—now a full colonel with some thirty years in the military—had been serving as the staff psychologist for the Vermont National Guard. For the past year, he'd been flying to military bases across the country to debrief soldiers as they arrived home from tours in Iraq and Afghanistan. In many ways, it was the perfect job for him: he loved nothing more than to talk to other men about their most complex feelings, to plumb the depths of the human (male) soul, to give air to the rage and anger, self-hatred and pain that the experience of war had created within them. Reading the nihilism of Hemingway's heroes perhaps made him feel that he wasn't so lost—that, when everything was meaningless, he could rely on the singular truth of himself.

And yet this simple and solitary vision of masculinity didn't totally find justification in the details of my father's life and character. He was physically fit, and strong, but he was no warrior. In his thirty years of military service, he had never seen combat, and yet, with his shaved head and broad frame, adorned in his fatigues, he'd earned himself the nickname Monk Rambo. When I was a boy, during sports events, my father would sometimes run laps around the playing fields, dropping for a set of push-ups or pausing to run through a series of martial arts forms. Such performances led my friends to ask me if I knew how many people my dad had killed in battle, as if in his other life in Vermont he spent his days fighting alongside the action heroes of our imagination. Sometimes, I witnessed his exchanges with the kinds of capable men—mountaineers, builders, hunters and fishermen, even some local boxers—whom he liked to surround himself with, but who I often caught rolling their eyes at my father's mechanical ineptitude, his preference for talk rather than action, feelings rather than thought. I did not think of my father as a phony—he'd be the first to fess up to his weaknesses and limitations and would certainly be willing to spend multiple hours dissecting their origins. But I did recognize the contradiction between the man he presented himself as—a warrior, a soldier, a knight—and the man he was: a highly emotional, deeply sensitive, physically delicate person who often lost himself within his own needs and feelings.

But there were consequences to talking to soldiers about death and darkness; the work was heavy and brought up old feelings about his own war. Recently, my father had told me that his commitment to such work had made him feel distant from my stepmother, who didn't understand or care why the experience of war was so important to him. "The other day I asked her what she remembered about Vietnam," my father said, "and she barely knew it happened." This had made him feel isolated from his wife, he told me, and yet I remember thinking that if having a wife who understood Vietnam was so important, he could have stayed with his first one.

The allure of the Hemingway passage he'd sent me caught me off guard. "Pamplona in July," it was called, and the descriptions of that world—*a white-walled, sun-baked town high up in the hills of Navarre . . . the cafés under the wide arcades . . . Really beautiful girls, gorgeous, bright shawls over their shoulders, dark, dark-eyed, black lace mantillas over their hair . . . the streets were solid with people dancing*—made the dreariness of the rainy morning disappear. I closed my eyes, imagined myself in Spain, sitting in the dry heat of an afternoon, sweating in a bullring while sipping on a beer . . . and it was like inhabiting a luscious and vivid dream. *Some beautiful stuff in here . . .* my father wrote in the margins of the letter, and expressed his interest in one day traveling to Spain with me. But the way my father signed off his note broke the pleasant vision of 1920s Spain. *This fighting game you have been involved in of late is extremely interesting to me. And vexing. Anyway, my fight for the weekend was planting 50 lily and tulip bulbs. I scrabble for noble opportunities, Dad.*

Fighting. Noble opportunities. Vexing.

I suppose my father had a point. Unlike Victor, I did not have a history of fighting. There was a period in elementary school when, after exhortations from my friends, I was convinced that I had an innate knowledge of karate. My favorite movie was *The Last Electric Knight*, a one-off Disney production starring a prepubescent Filipino boy from the fake Asian country of Patusan, who could drop a gang of hooligans—led by a young Don Cheadle—by summoning waves of glowing blue light. But my sense of power quickly disappeared during a scuffle over a kickball dispute, against the middle brother of the only African American family in my school. He was a grade older than me, and he was stronger than me, and I knew going into the confrontation that I would surely lose. And yet—as a crowd of boys chanted, "Safe! Out! Safe! Out!"—what I remembered most about the encounter was not a feeling of pain, but a quieter emotion that rose up inside me as the boy dropped me to the ground with a knee to the groin. I wasn't hurt—his knee had only glanced my thigh—but I knew I had a reason to be, and so rather than stand up swinging, I writhed on the pavement in tears until a teacher separated us. Maybe I was gaming the system and knew, somehow, that my opponent, who'd already been targeted as a troublemaker, would get the bulk of the blame. Or maybe I just didn't have the kind of fury inside me to fight back. Either way, I spent the afternoon at home, in my bed, staring out the window while my mother slept, trying to convince myself that the pain I felt in my stomach was real.

In junior high, I sometimes dabbled with fighting, usually only on occasions when the violence was brought my way. One afternoon, I was cornered by the youngest brother from a family of four boys, who'd wrongly assumed that I'd stolen his baseball hat. We wrestled in front of a small crowd until, by luck, I accidently flipped the kid onto the pedal of my bike, which left him in a howling mess in the dirt, me as the default victor. But rather than celebrate my win, I spent the next two days apologizing to the kid, worried that his older brothers would come for me.

Small for my age, and late to puberty, I'd had a couple of encounters with man-child bullies. One of them, Dean, liked to put me in headlocks during gym class and make me dance around like a puppet, until I, copying a move I'd learned from a Steven Seagal movie I'd watched with my father, whipped his arm around his back and pushed him into a locker. Dean hadn't expected me to fight, and when he turned on me, I begged his forgiveness. On another occasion, a boy named Jason, who used to pick on me at a summer day camp, told me, "Go back to China and eat your rice!" in front of about forty other boys. I had no comeback—

physical or verbal. Then another boy—not much bigger than me, but somehow braver and more witty—came to my defense: "He's not from China, shit for brains! Get it right!" As I watched the two boys stare each other down, I made no vows of revenge or loyalty. Instead, I just felt numb, confused, and empty—as if spectating on a world in which I had no part.

At the beginning of high school, I began to feel urges to fight, but never was able to cross the line into violence. Once, during a soccer game, an opposing player, after a hard tackle, had called me a "fucking refugee." Something exploded in my brain, but even after leaving my position to run across the field in the kid's direction, I pulled up short just inches from his face. He looked at me, more surprised than fearful, and yet all I could bring myself to do was look back at the boy, fists clenched, mind screaming, paralyzed by a feeling with no name.

A few years later, the night before I left my hometown for college, I was hanging out at a buddy's house, late, when a giant football player who'd been rumored to use steroids pulled up to the stoop in his SUV. There'd been some incident with his girlfriend and one of my friends, and the football player wanted to know which one of us needed an ass-kicking.

I stood up off the stoop. "Go fuck yourself."

The football player looked at me, turned his head sideways. "What'd you say?"

"I said go fuck yourself." My friends—none of them the fighting type—turned to me, confused. But I was not afraid. I was in the best shape of my life: I'd been working on a framing crew all summer, lifting weights, and running at night in preparation for playing soccer in college. My body was ready.

The football player opened his door. He had a broken leg, in a large white cast. He pointed to the cast. "I got a busted leg. But if you say one more word, I'm gonna come over and kick your ass."

I looked at him. I looked at his cast. I could feel the air

tightening all around me, the cosmos contracting around the single point of pause.

"One fucking word," he said.

I can still hear the triumphant laugh of the football player as he got back in his SUV, the sound of my silence as he left me behind.

Fighting. Noble opportunities. Vexing.

I let the letter fall to the floor. A current of feeling spread through my body with the same unfurling sensation as when Victor had dropped me with a shot to the lower kidneys.

I got out of bed, dressed, put on a raincoat and rubber boots, then walked around the side of my apartment, lifted my kayak onto my shoulder, and carried it across the street and a few hundred yards to the McDonald's parking lot. I stepped down a rock retaining wall into a mudflat, then slid my boat, which I had not touched since arriving in Sitka, into the still water of the harbor and began paddling into a heavy mist that hung over the channel and buried the bowl of the volcano on Kruzof Island in clouds. When I was about halfway across the channel, I stopped paddling, stared into the green-gray world on the horizon, studied the clouds as they moved above me. Then I just stayed there, floating.

■

Every week, I had to fill out a form for SNEP detailing the number of Native students I'd been working with. This wasn't a straightforward task: since a lot of my students were part white and part Native, or part Filipino, it was often hard to put a finger on who was who. Sometimes these facts revealed themselves on individualized education program paperwork, but not always. Usually, I just filled out the form—which read BUREAU OF INDIAN AFFAIRS across the top—and rounded up, figuring that a lot of my students were underreporting their identity.

On my way to the gym, I stopped off at the ANB Hall to put the form in a folder on the SNEP office door. It was late in the evening. Outside, a bus driver named Karen Williams was dropping kids off for afternoon classes, one of the services SNEP offered to local families. In the ANB auditorium, the walls were covered with pictures of the old days: people standing in front of house poles, dressed in full regalia. At a pair of long tables, a woman named Vida Davis was teaching young people Tlingit. I loved the sound of spoken Tlingit: it sounded so different from English, and as a tonal language with forty-one consonants, interspersed with catches in breath, sometimes resembled a harder, more definitive version of Thai. A lot of the kids were pretending to not pay attention, but I knew from experience that even familiarity with the sound of a language could, without warning, call up a bolt of memory and longing.

I dropped my form into the box. On my way out, I ran into one of my coworkers, a master bead worker named Paul. Paul was a few years older than me—midtwenties, maybe—and he was short, compact, and quiet. He liked to wear bright Hawaiian shirts, with flames and dragons on the back, his hair in a hard part down the middle. Paul and I liked each other—we were the only two male employees of SNEP—but rarely took the time to talk.

"How's it going up there?" I said.

"Good." Paul's workshop was in a small loft over the office. He had been spending the afternoon working on regalia for men's dance shirts. He invited me upstairs to have a look. There were several bins of beads of various colors, which were being woven into black-and-red felt vests, adorned with the imagery of Tlingit crests and clans.

"Looks like my people's regalia," I said.

This was not exactly true. It reminded me of the hill tribe clothing I had seen on a trip up north with my mother. I had no relation to hill tribe people. My cousins were modern Thais: they had cell phones before I did; they dressed in cheap American clothing and bleached their skin.

"Oh yeah?" Paul said.

"Yeah. Same."

"That's cool. I'm all about respecting other people's cultures." Paul told me that I ought to come to the next dance class. "Not only for Natives."

On my way out, the kids were still finishing up. As I walked by their tables, I passed the photographs of the old days of Sitka, studying the house and clan poles adorned with different animal crests, the people sitting beneath them. As I stared at the photos, the people in them stared back.

■

I rode my bike down Lincoln Street in a light rain, pumping my pedals as fast as I could. When I got to the gym, I climbed the stairs and found Victor.

He was unpacking his duffel of boxing gear, waiting for the rest of the club to show up. "Hey, man, I just talked to the Goat. He's fuckin' pissed. He called me from Philadelphia and was like, 'Vic, man, you know some guy named Jed?' And I said, 'Guy named Jade started coming to the gym?' And the Goat said, 'Well, apparently he's going out with Mary now!' Then he starts going on and on about how you're trying to take his place. He was like, 'I'm so fuckin' pissed off, I'm gonna name my dog after him just so I don't forget to kick his ass!'" Victor shook his head. "I don't know, man. I never seen the Goat mad like that before. Haag was supposed to fly him back to town to fight in a show this spring. I hope he can cool down before that."

I tried to explain to Victor that I'd stop hanging around with Miss Mary if it meant that I was causing problems in his gym. But I knew there was only one way to fix things. "I want to fight," I said.

Victor dropped the duffel bag. "Fuck yeah, Jade."

■

For the next three weeks, my life took on a new clarity of purpose. I went to bed early every night, slept well, and woke up at the same time—seven—every morning. My days at school were efficient and orderly, and when I got home, I took a brief nap before jogging to and from the gym—a distance of about four miles there and back. During training, Victor devoted as many rounds on the mitts to me as he did to Roo and Todd. In addition to working on "straight punches," he also showed me a basic slip maneuver, tailored especially to southpaws, wherein you countered with a lead off a righty jab, driving your fist into the pocket right beneath your opponent's chin. We did it over and over until I didn't have to pause before throwing it; then at night, I stood in the mirror with my shirt off, imagining the punch coming at me from different angles, throwing my left into the face of an invisible opponent.

As we approached the fight date, the pace of our workouts increased, too: One night we did two hundred jumping jacks in a row. Another night, we did a hundred burpees. We doubled up on sets of push-ups and sit-ups and often worked with partners, punching each other in the back of the head and whaling each other in the stomach. I started sparring with Roo and Todd and the high school boys. I rarely landed more than a single punch. I had limited hand speed and still hadn't figured out how to circle and punch at the same time, but that didn't matter. The basic routine of taking off my ring, wrapping my hands, adorning myself in sparring equipment, all felt like the basic rites of a sacred ritual.

On weekends, I got out of bed early, put on my boots, and rode my bike to the end of HPR, to the gates of the Starrigavan Wilderness. I bushwhacked through groves of devil's club, crossing muskegs, following neon tags of old hunting trails, and scrambling up loose ledges until I broke through the tree line and onto the open ridges. There, you could jog for miles and miles with full views of the coastal mountains and the waterways surrounding town. I climbed until I stood above the clouds, looking down into the labyrinth of valleys and ravines, the clouds threading between the clefts, filling in the empty spaces. The swirling script of ridges and shoulders appeared like a topography of broken lines. But when I traced those lines, they all led to the same mass of land: an island, surrounded by dark water, floating on the edge of the world.

■

The last night before my fight, Victor led us through a light workout. We did some mitt work, shadowboxing but mostly just breaking a sweat. After we were done, while we were stretching, Victor asked me if I'd picked out a name yet.

"A name?"

"Yeah. A ring name. If you don't pick one out, someone else will." Victor shrugged. "Roo hates his name, but the Goat made it up for him and Haag loves it, so it stuck. Some asshole tried to call me Big Chief until I came up with the Savage."

I asked Todd what name he'd chosen.

He put his hands over his head, jogged in place. "From the slums of Newark, New Jersey, Todd 'the Dirty Dog' Thompson!" Then he dropped his hands and shrugged. "I live with my dogs in a little boat, so I figured it made sense."

As we put gear away for the night, I thought of all the names I'd been given in the past. My father had once told me that before I was born, he'd wanted to name me Jethro, to honor my Nantucket heritage. Jethro Coffin was a direct descendant of the founder of Nantucket—an honor that my father seemed to claim for his own blood, despite that the only times I'd ever heard of Nantucket were among the kids I disliked the most in college. For a period during my boyhood, my father had tried to call me Galahad, but the name—honorific, complicated, loaded with irony he didn't seem to recognize—hadn't stuck. Then, when I'd spent summers at his house, playing on his town Little League team, he called me the Hammer, perhaps because I, the catcher, the power hitter, captain of the all-star team, could do the most damage. One summer, my father had sent me to a boys' camp where you had to dress up like a Native American, in handmade clothes, and pretend to live in a tepee as part of a tribe. You also had to make up an Indian name. Most boys chose names like Owl Moon and White Fox, but I, in bold recognition of my mixed blood, had chosen Many Rivers. After the camp was sued by the American Indian Movement for exploitation of cultural rituals in the name of profit, I'd felt so stupid to have been part of such a thing that I'd sworn to never speak the name again. In college, my freshman-year roommate—a prep school kid from a Boston suburb who was a star on the lacrosse team—had called me Mohammed the Asian Buddhist Prince in front of a one-hundred-person psychology class. The name stuck, was shortened to Mohams and then Mo before cycling out of existence. When I got drunk, my friends called me the Red Baron because of my bloodshot eyeballs and blotchy skin. The only name that seemed to honor my origins without any irony or denigration was when I'd been given the Pali name Jaed Da Wat Tat No Namat—an auspicious moniker whose meaning had never been revealed to me—by the head monk of my mother's temple. But outside Thailand, the name sounded silly.

On our way downstairs, Victor said, "You know, Jade, I was wondering—where you from?"

"Maine." Just like I'd told him the first night we met.

"Where's your blood from?"

I told Victor the story I'd grown comfortable with: my mother was from Thailand, my father was American, they'd met in the Vietnam War. There, always, was where the story ended.

"What about the Half-Asian Sensation?" Todd said.

I thought about that. Why not the Half-White Knight?

Victor was still thinking. "Jade . . . Jade Coffin . . ." He paused. "What about the Stone?"

"The Stone?" I said.

"Jade 'the Stone' Coffin," Victor said.

I repeated the name a few times to myself. "The Stone." It did not occur to me that Victor had likely associated *the Stone* with jade stone and coffin—perhaps in his mind's eye he'd seen a glowing green tomb where my opponents would all be laid to rest.

"The Stone," I said. "Sounds good."

Victor and I squared up plans for our departure on Friday morning, then parted ways. But later, as I ran down Halibut Point Road, I imagined a blank, featureless tablet, waiting to be engraved with a story. I threw punches into the rain, hissing my new name— "The Stone! The Stone!"—into the mist.

PART II

6. ROUGHHOUSE

All night, I'd been having visions of my opponent standing across a dirty canvas, in the corner of a dimly lit ring, his face hidden in shadows. He did not move much: just the rising and falling of his chest as he breathed in the dark. Even with my eyes open I felt as though the man remained in my apartment, hidden in my closet, buried inside the walls. I lay in my bed, fists clenched, heart pounding, staring at the ceiling, waiting for daylight. Then, around five in the morning, two beams of lunar light passed through my windows, projecting themselves onto my walls like a pair of giant moons. I jumped out of bed, swung my backpack over my shoulder, and went outside.

"How you holding up?" Victor said. He was sitting in his truck, his hat pulled low over his eyes.

"I'm all right. Didn't sleep much."

"I used to get so worked up the week before a fight I'd get sick. It's just nerves. They'll go away."

We drove down Halibut Point Road, the pavement shiny with ice, the lights of the harbor bridge blinking through the clouds like low-hanging stars. In the airport terminal, two men in line for the 6:00 a.m. Juneau service asked Victor if he was going over to fight.

Victor shook his head. "Retired. Got a wife and kid." Then he looked at me. "Now I just train badasses like this guy."

One of the men held out his hand. "Those guys in Juneau are fuckers. Go over there and kick some ass. Win one for Sitka."

I shook the man's hand, made a face that I hoped would project seriousness and malice, and promised him I would.

■

The flight to Juneau took about twenty minutes. Off the wing, as the sun rose, the black water of Chatham Strait moved between the masses of Chichagof and Admiralty Islands, the ridges and peaks of the dark coastal mountains made bright by white handprints of snow. While Victor slept, I studied the Rorschach shapes as if trying to decode their secret meaning, but one shape blended into another, and the mountains went on forever, thousands of miles north into ice fields and more mountains and more wilderness that likely didn't stop until the Arctic Ocean.

When we landed in Juneau, Todd was waiting for us at the terminal. Losing all that weight had hollowed out his cheeks and pulled his face forward into a beak-like shape. With his hungry eyes staring out from beneath the hood of his sweatshirt, he looked like a scared and emaciated little bird. Though Roo wouldn't be coming until the evening flight, Todd had flown over the night before, so that he could weigh in early and still have a full day to get some food down. But when Victor asked Todd if he'd eaten yet, he grew quiet. "Spent my last ten bucks on a bacon double cheeseburger, but I was so nervous I puked it right back up."

"You gotta eat something, Todd," Victor said.

Todd nodded. "I know. I know."

We walked down the airport road with our packs over our heads. The rain turned to ice. In the distance, the drab mountains of the Mendenhall Valley rose up around the city. A long chain of clouds passed over the mountains like a gossamer curtain.

When we got to the intersection with the Glacier Highway, Victor pointed to a two-story building on the corner. On the first floor was a diner called Donna's, but above the diner hung a large white wooden sign, burned at one corner, with a picture of a marlin jumping out of a martini glass. Along the bottom of the sign it read MARLINTINI'S LOUNGE. (Years ago, the bar had been called the Landing Strip because of its proximity to the airport. Then it was renamed Hoochies, after the salmon tackle, before closing down. The owner of the bar, Ethan Billings—"Like Montana!"—once told me that he and his late partner, Jim Cashem, had bought the bar and "stomped butt" because they were the kind of guys who always "put our necks—well, our ball sacks—on the line.")

We stopped in the parking lot, looked up into several dark windows decorated with neon beer signs.

"It looks small up there," I said.

"Biggest barroom in Southeast Alaska," Victor said.

■

The Travelodge where Haag was putting us up for the night was a short walk across the Glacier Highway. The parking lot was almost empty, and the stucco walls were faded and stained. Several posters for Roughhouse Friday hung in the lobby windows: a cartoon of two bloated lumberjack-looking men dressed in jeans and work boots, thumping each other with red gloves. Beneath the men, the poster read CASH PRIZES! FIGHTERS IN ALL WEIGHT CLASSES! RING GIRLS FROM AROUND THE WORLD! with a picture of a little blue boxing glove with BIG H PROMOTIONS written across the knuckles. The *H* stood for "Haag."

Our room had only two beds, so Victor gave one to Todd and one to me, then lay down on the floor on top of his jacket, using a boxing glove for a pillow. I tried to sleep, but after about ten minutes Todd got up and stood in front of the mirror and started hissing and throwing punches. Then Victor got up next to him and did the same. His mouth guard was hanging off his lip. "This morning on my way out the door," Victor said, "I saw my mouth guard sitting on my dresser. It was all 'Take me with you, Vic! Take me with you!' And I was like, 'Shut the fuck up, mouth guard!' but I couldn't help it." He looked at me in the mirror. "Don't let me fight. Miranda'll leave me if I ever get back in the ring."

We spent the afternoon driving around Juneau in a car that Victor had rented for the day. First we went shopping at the Fred Meyer department store, where Victor bought the new 50 Cent album and some bulk groceries for Miranda. I bought a hooded sweatshirt that I hoped would make me look more like a boxer. Todd walked the aisles nodding at things he planned to buy with his fight money. Then we drove the Glacier Highway twenty miles to the end of town, blasting the 50 with the windows down. Thick spruce forests ran along both sides of the road, the tree line opening occasionally to reveal the dark mountains across Douglas Channel. If Sitka had reminded me of Maine—the rocky coastline, the thick pine forests—then the geography of Juneau looked a bit like northern Vermont. The mountains were more rolling, the valleys more open, but the water in the channel was shallow and spreading like Lake Champlain.

At the end of the road, Victor pulled over at a beach overlooking the channel where, on the horizon, a chain of small islands, arched with tough little trees, melted into the fog. Todd and I shadowboxed in the mudflat, as Victor tried to give us last-minute pointers. When it started raining again, we drove back to our hotel past a neighborhood where Todd said he used to live with a now ex-girlfriend. "Until I walked in on her fuckin' my best buddy." I studied Todd's face, trying to understand what he must have felt. "Whatever," Todd said, waving his hand. "We were all just a bunch of crackheads."

By three thirty, the daylight began to disappear. By five, it was night, and a hard flurry of snow had all but covered the Glacier

Highway with white. While Todd and Victor watched a hunting show on television, I sat at a small table, staring out the window at a line of cars turning into the Marlintini's parking lot, their lights glowing in the snowfall like a parade of ghost lanterns. I studied the snow as it fell through the orange halo of a streetlamp, tracing the hypnotic path of each flake before it fell to the earth and melted in the street.

"Yo, Jade!" Victor said.

I looked up.

He was standing next to the door, his duffel bag over his shoulder, his jacket on. "Come on, man. It's time to fight."

■

At the entrance to Marlintini's, a pair of bouncers in yellow T-shirts checked IDs with a flashlight. When one of the bouncers saw Victor, he waved us to the front of the line, through a set of large metal doors. We climbed up a stairwell filled with music and smoke. At a second door, another bouncer checked our names off a list and let us inside.

The fight ring stood in the middle of the barroom, over the dance floor, glowing beneath neon tubes of light. A large American flag hung behind the ring. Victor walked across the barroom, put his foot on the bottom rope, and told Todd and me to step inside. The canvas was speckled with dark bloodstains. I shuffled around a bit, trying to get a feel for its size. The ring was much bigger than I'd thought it would be. When two men in BIG H T-shirts came into the ring to tighten the turnbuckles with giant wrenches, Todd and I got out.

In a corner of the barroom, in an elevated area with several pool tables covered in boxing gloves and hand wraps, a dozen or so men stood in line waiting to see a doctor for a prefight physical exam. Most of the men looked older than me but were dressed in similar clothing: winter hats, hooded sweatshirts, mismatched track pants, dirty sneakers. The men smacked their fists, rolled their necks, took deep breaths, then exhaled swiftly. I tried to predict which one would be my opponent, but everyone looked the same.

When it was my turn to see the fight doc, I stepped behind the sheet, then sat in a metal chair across from a white man about my age, with several earrings and lip rings, dressed in a cutoff T-shirt with a stethoscope around his neck. "You been drinking tonight? Any drugs?"

"No."

He squeezed my fists. "Broken bones?"

I shook my head.

He shined a small flashlight in my eyes. "All right, buddy." He slid a piece of paper across the table.

I started reading it but then just signed my name.

"It's so you don't sue us if you get hurt."

■

I sat with Victor and Todd on a tattered couch, watching the barroom fill with fight fans: men in overalls and jeans and hoodies and frayed baseball hats, dressed like they'd just stepped off the slime line at a cannery; women in slinky tops and tight pants, dressed like they were going out for a big night in Vegas. White men, Filipinos, Samoans and Tongans, and Tlingit and Haida. Tickets were forty-five bucks for ringside seats, thirty-five for general admission. The Marlintini's waitresses wove through the crowd, platters of shots and pint glasses over their heads. Meanwhile, more fighters continued to arrive—sometimes alone, sometimes flanked by wives or girlfriends.

A stout man in a black derby and red NASCAR jacket appeared next to Victor, a tumbler of whiskey in his hand. "Vic 'the Savage' Littlefield!"

Victor shook the man's hand. "Haag, this is Jade Coffin."

Haag took a drink, wiped his mouth, squinted at me through his glasses. "Jade Coffin! The guy who paddled a sea kayak up from Seattle, Warshington?" Haag smiled. *"Paddled a sea kayak all the way up from Seattle, Warshington! Jaaaaade Coffin!"* He coughed. "Very nice to meet you, Jade Coffin. Heard a lot about you from Victor. Lot about you! And, Jade, I got a lot of people here looking forward to seeing you fight tonight. Lot of people! 'Cause my fans, one thing they know is that when Victor Littlefield brings a fighter to Juneau, they're gonna see one hell of a fight!" Then Haag turned to Todd. "Todd Thompson! Dirty Dog! How the hell are you, Todd?"

Todd nodded, bobbing his head like a cobra. "Good, Bob. Good. Feeling good."

"Now, Todd!" Haag said. "Let me tell you something, Todd Thompson! Got a lot of people in here who think this is your year, man! This is the year of Todd Thompson! This is the year of Dirty Dog! You see what I mean, Todd? 'Cause when people hear that Todd Thompson's been working out with Victor Littlefield . . ."

A small Filipino man with a clipboard came up to Haag. Haag studied it, then shouted at someone else, then started pulling on guys to go this way and that way until all the fighters were in line in order of our bouts. Then he was gone, until moments later, when I heard Haag's gravelly voice explode across the barroom. "Ladies and gentlemen!" he barked into a mic. "Now who wants to meet the toughest bastards in Southeast Alaska?"

■

Bob Haag came up to the Last Frontier as a boy, when his mother, Frankie, packed him and his four brothers into a 1957 Buick station wagon and drove some four thousand miles from Missouri to Anchorage to see Haag's father, Leo, who'd come north to cash in on the post-statehood construction boom. As a young man, Haag saw himself as a "regular boxing encyclopedia": "You give me the year," Haag liked to say, "and I'll give you the heavyweight champion." He subscribed to magazines like *The Ring* and touted himself as the nephew of a 1930s Nebraska Golden Gloves champion. His heroes were not the clean-shaven ballplayers of the 1950s and '60s, but the hard-living backyard brawlers of Hell's Kitchen (a place he had never been, a place he would never go), guys like Jake LaMotta, Tony Zale, Rocky Marciano, men who fought their way from one backyard to another in search of who was the toughest guy around. But in postwar Anchorage, Haag found little in the way of boxing. Only after marrying his high school sweetheart, Sandy, and having four sons and a daughter did he start his first boxing club—an amateur outfit that, he promised Sandy, would expire as soon as his youngest son turned eighteen. Haag was doing a million other things—competing in bodybuilding competitions, building up a salvage yard, running a tow-truck business, flying planes—but deep in his heart, he knew that of all the things he'd ever done, the thing he did best was teach boys how to be upstanding young men through the sport of boxing. In the late seventies, Haag took a shot at hustling professional shows in remote small towns, at bars like Gussie L'Amour's (named after a famous prostitute), the Pines Club, and a bar in Sitka owned by his parents called the Kiksadi Club. However, because of various regulations—the cost of flying up fight doctors from Down South, the rules around how long a fight had to be, how much a fighter had to get paid—he soon determined that his dream of running boxing shows in the Last Frontier could only ever be a "break-even thing at best."

For the next decade, Haag and boxing parted ways. Then one afternoon he got a call from Earl Davis, the state athletic commissioner under Governor Wally Hickel. Davis wanted to know why boxing was a dead sport in Alaska. In Hickel, a man who had, in his younger years, boxed at the annual fur-rendezvous dogsled festivals, a man who was known as a wildly independent politician with a fighter's heart, Haag knew he had a sympathetic ear. He didn't mince words. "Too many durn rules!" Haag told Davis—few of which applied to the logistical realities of life in the Last Frontier. So Haag and Davis made up their own rules. This was Alaska, a land separated from the Lower 48 by some thousand miles of Canadian wilderness. What was the point of living in the Great White North if you had to play by the rules of a lesser world that people in Alaska referred to as Down South?

To eliminate the expense of ringside fight doctors, Haag settled on using local EMTs. To simplify weight classes to suit out-of-shape fighters, he invented three weight classes, with thirty-pound spreads. To make sure fighters who weren't in great shape could make it to the final bell, he shrank the traditional three-minute round down to a single minute. "The one-minute round is safer for the fighter and better for the fan," Haag often said. "And that way, you gotta get out there and impress them judges! Most fights these days, it's like going to church!" Then Haag started touring his Roughhouse shows around the state, to towns like Eagle River and Talkeetna, where most grown men had never had an opportunity to fight inside a ring. When "various members of the media" questioned whether a boxing show would make any money, Haag had a quick reply. "If me and you are hitting golf balls, maybe some people gonna stop and watch. If me and you are shooting baskets, maybe some people gonna stop and watch. But if me and you are knocking hell out of each other," Haag liked to say, in his gravelly, here-comes-the-punch-line promoter's voice, "then everybody's gonna stop and watch! Now that's Roughhouse boxing! It's a real sport!"

In the late nineties, Haag got a call from a Juneau man named George Wright. Wright was trying to run a small show in the capital city as a fund-raiser for a local amateur club. Various entrepreneurs in town had "run the numbers" but quickly gotten scared off. Wright, who had a suspect reputation as the manager of a charity bingo and gaming cooperative for various tribal and community organizations, had gotten word that Haag was the man to call. Haag was tentative—he'd seen his own failures over the years, gotten burned more times than he could count—but he made Wright a deal: if Wright could pitch in some of his charity gambling money to help out a gym in Anchorage, run by Haag's daughter, Jill, Haag would come down and help him run a boxing show. Deal.

In that first show, which Haag called King of the Ring, he expected to see six or seven fighters crawl out of local bars. But on fight night, more than forty men showed up. "That," Haag said, "is when I started to see a little bit of an opportunity." On his flight back from Juneau, he drew a map on a bar napkin that he still keeps in his briefcase. Anchorage, a town of nearly three hundred thousand people, had a weekly boxing show called Thursday Night Fights, at the Egan Center downtown. Most nights, the show sold out. For a city like Juneau, with a population of about thirty thousand, Haag figured he could get away with one show a month. But Southeast Alaska had something that the big city didn't: fierce rivalries between tribal nations and Native communities that went back decades, centuries even. To this day, such rivalries are just as heated as the rivalries between the bigger towns—Sitka and Juneau, Ketchikan and Petersburg. Haag called the year-end tournament the Southeast Showdown. The goal of the tournament: to determine who was the toughest guy in all of Southeast Alaska. In the run-up to that first Southeast Showdown, Haag told a reporter for the *Juneau Empire*, "I want everyone to know that every Friday in Juneau is Roughhouse Friday!"

The first writers of the *Juneau Empire* to witness the Southeast Showdown were charmed by the "special charisma" of Roughhouse boxing: Bob Haag, a "nostalgic and old-style promoter," wears a derby and chomps on a cigar, reminiscent of a modern-day P. T.

Barnum; the "lusty ring girls," who "strut on five-inch heels"; the screaming fans, thirsty for blood, foaming beer cups in hand. "But what the crowd witnessed," one writer said, "could hardly be called boxing." "Instead of fancy footwork, they charged like bulls. Instead of jabs, they dropped bombs," wrote another. One man called the fighters "local gladiators," more "unschooled" than "old school" and described one fighter's defensive tactic as "the windshield wiper." Haag described his boys as "the butcher, the baker, and the candlestick maker, a bus driver fighting a school-teacher, a fisherman fighting a cop. Sometimes, you just might be watching the guy next door." On more than one occasion, critics of Haag's show said that he was in the business of bully promotion. "I seen plenty of bullies who can't box!" Haag would say. His first champion was a quiet high school basketball player named Russ "the Dirt" Stevens—a man who'd never given anyone so much as a bloody nose. What Haag saw himself doing was giving guys who'd never had a chance to fight an opportunity to step into a ring and show the world what they were made of. "This is the Last Frontier," Haag often recited, "where a man stands up and fights, where stepping outside is still a way of doing business."

■

To the tune of "Eye of the Tiger," Haag stood in the middle of the ring, yelling the names of the night's fighters as they wove through the four-hundred-person crowd and entered the ring:

"He's a fifty-seven-year-old ivory carver from Juneau, Alaska, weighing one hundred and sixty-five pounds, fighting to buy his hunting knife back from a pawn shop . . . wants to be called Wayne 'Fu' Smallwood! Wayne Fu! Come on dooowwwnnn!"

Wayne Fu stepped into the ring in a pair of Coke-bottle glasses, a black beret adorned with eagle feathers, a heavy choker with a large animal tooth hanging from it. He held up his fist, bowed, did a spinning jump kick.

Behind him came a young black man in jeans and a white tank top; he was wiry and lean, like he'd gone through puberty that morning. Sometimes tables of supporters—work friends, family members, wives and cousins—exploded as one of their own entered the ring. Other times, the fighter stepped through the ropes into a stiff silence. There were twenty-one fighters in all—not including Roo, who was yet to arrive—for eleven fights that night. I was up right after the intermission. But as I stood watching the men in the ring, waiting for Haag to call my name, I had no awareness of why I was fighting beyond that my body was telling me to.

■

What made a Roughhouse fighter enter Haag's ring was something that the early *Empire* writers couldn't get their heads around either. "An inner need to test oneself," one writer surmised. "Something to prove." When the question was posed to the fighters themselves, they offered little insight. "I need to play, I like to play," one fighter said. Another: "I just wondered what it takes." Other fighters cited the crowd, the rush, the fun. But there were other ways to play, get a rush, and have fun besides stepping into a ring in a bar and fighting a stranger.

Some did it for the money: Mike "the Wrench" Morris was doing it for a new truck part. Guy Marble was fighting for extra Christmas money to buy presents for his kid. Donovan Brown, a Costco employee, needed the $150 to pay rent; Dani Hansen, to fix her car. Ryan Wong beat Norman "Thunder Punch" Flood so that he could buy more sushi, as part of his new health kick. Some men fought to settle grudges, like the two half brothers, William "Buddy the Hobbit" and Josh "the Unknown" Hintermeister, who'd been fighting at home but wanted to see once and for all who was tougher. Desiree Marble, Guy Marble's wife, was fighting three months after giving birth by C-section to prove to her husband that she could do it. A drywaller challenged a sprinkler installer on a jobsite grudge match. Several fighters cited their family as the motivation for getting into the ring. One man was fighting to win a title belt "for if I ever get kids, I can have something to show them." John "the Irish Indian" Smith, from Hoonah, who trained by running sprints up Dead Man's Hill, said that his grandfather and uncle had boxed, and he was fighting in their names.

There were more abstract spiritual reasons: Mike Vavillis wanted to get "the anger out." Sam "Wham Bam" Adams, a childcare provider, said she fought for the women who chop wood in the morning, work during the day, then keep house at night. Nathaniel Wirrkula said he was doing it for "world peace."

J. R. Diamond went home and cried after winning a lightweight belt. Lui Fenumiai, after losing a heavyweight title fight against Russ "the Dirt" Stevens, proposed to his girlfriend in the crowd just weeks before he was deployed to Iraq. Stephanie "the Cave Woman" Cave fought the current wife of her ex-husband in what Haag hoped would be a revenge match, but they found that their bout healed old wounds. Victor had once trained a forty-five-year-old man who had come to him after living a year on an island with only a rifle. He won the fight, retired from boxing forever, then took up chicken farming.

A young Haida man—who'd been commercial fishing since he was eleven years old, who trained by chopping wood and running between the Nugget Mall and downtown in his steel-toe boots, a distance of about nine miles, who said that fighting helped him with his ADD, who said his first fight was in a village in Prince of Wales against a Native-white boy, who maintained a diet of bear meat and tried to limit his salt intake because it drained water in his kidneys—laughed when I asked him why he fought.

"I'm Native," he said—followed by silence. Then he knocked out a man twice his age with a vicious flurry of body shots.

"A schoolteacher! Twenty-three years of age, one hundred and eighty-five pounds, with a perfect record of zero wins and zero losses! He paddled a sea kayak from Washington State to a little town called Sitka, Alaska, wants to be called Jade! The Stone! Coffiiiiiiiiiiinnnn!"

I stepped into the ring, peered out from beneath the hood of my sweatshirt, searching the shadows for a familiar face. Years from that night, I would look back through the accounts in the *Juneau Empire* in search of the reasons why I was fighting. But that winter—something to do with the Microphone Debacle, too much cigarette smoke, and unreliable relations with Haag—the *Empire* had ceased all coverage of the Roughhouse show, as if my season as a Roughhouse fighter had never happened.

∎

Victor was right: the boxing I'd seen in the gym was five times what I was seeing at Roughhouse Friday. The first several bouts were mostly unremarkable: one unfit, often pudgy fighter versus another, slapping each other for three minutes of sloppy, unrestrained, fast-burning rage. The most colorful bout was between Wayne Fu and his young opponent. After several wild, whirling haymakers, Fu connected a blind and looping right hand on the chin of his young rival, who flopped to the canvas as if he'd been unplugged. He convulsed for several electrified seconds, then hopped back to his feet with a suspicious jump start. In the second round, the same thing happened: pop, flop, convulsion, but this time, when a mulleted, potbellied ref in all black asked the young man if he wished to continue, the kid pulled off his gloves, shook his head, and called it quits. "Fuuu!" the crowd chanted. "Fuuu!" Fu bowed, martial arts–style, to each side of the ring before leaping into the air to perform a spinning jump kick. But he botched the landing.

"Ladies and gentlemen!" Haag barked from his ringside perch. "You can't see this on HBO!"

Todd stood in his corner, jaw clenched, cheeks rippling, one foot forward, eyes locked on his opponent, waiting to charge. His opponent was a commercial fisherman from Juneau named Jimmy Bennett. Bennett had never fought before, and judging by the panicked twitchiness in his eyes, he seemed entirely uninterested in going through with it now. Haag kept building up the fight as a clash between the old capital of Alaska and the new—"Sitka versus Juneau! Sitka versus Juneau!"—but by then the crowd was too drunk to make sense of anything beyond the clanging sound of the bell.

For the first minute, Todd did everything right: he asserted himself with a series of stiff jabs, then lobbed a few heavy right hands that landed flush into Bennett's nose. Midway through the first round, Todd dropped Bennett to his knees. After an eight count, Todd came out of his neutral corner to finish him off. Bennett, rather than face the assault, turned and ran, and for a moment it almost looked like the two men were playing tag. The crowd didn't like cowards, and, as the bell rang, they booed Bennett all the way back to his stool.

I stood in Todd's corner, as Victor, working inside the ring, sponged and watered him down. Todd was angry, fuming, so full of boiling turmoil that his eyes struggled to comprehend the smoky world floating before him. His breathing became quick, and no matter how many times Victor told Todd to relax, relax, Todd couldn't calm himself. By the second round, Bennett's nose was bleeding badly, down his naked, hairy chest, and for the first thirty seconds he stumbled around the canvas like a drunk chicken. But then Todd's nerves got the better of him. In the midst of a clinch, in a fury of unthinking aggression, Todd mixed a short kick into his punch combination. The kick landed right between Bennett's legs. Bennett hit the deck, rolled onto the canvas, holding his crotch with a puffy red glove.

It was a dirty move. Todd didn't mean to do it. But the crowd changed sides. They booed Todd, and the ref scolded him, and I watched as Todd's face became almost childish with shame. The little pilot light of sanity that he'd spent the past several weeks developing in the gym started to flicker and die. When Bennett rose to his feet, Todd, hands up, stood in the middle of the ring, hiding behind the padding of his gloves. He shuffled forward, took a few jabs to his face, shook his head before taking a few more shots.

"Punch, Todd! Punch!" Victor shouted from the corner, but Todd couldn't hear him.

Ding! Ding! Ding!

"How many people like this fight?" Haag barked into the mic. "We got somebody called Todd! Somebody called Jimmy! Two tough guys knocking the hell out of each other!"

Todd sat on his stool in a trance. Victor removed Todd's mouth guard, told him to breathe. Then Victor stood, calling the air into his lungs with both hands, telling Todd to do the same. He spoke to Todd gently, so that whatever broken thing inside of him rose out of his body. Maybe it was just that Todd needed to know that in the ring he was not alone; maybe he needed to know that in the ring he was more than just a crackhead. Either way, the third round ended the only way it could: with Todd and Bennett standing in the center of the ring, flat-footed, taking turns thumping their fists off each other's head. Todd was the stronger man and the better boxer, which allowed him to pound Bennett into a corner, until Bennett, woozy and bloody, seasick and pale, collapsed to his knees. When the final bell rang, Todd threw his hands over his head and screamed a low growl of joy. He jumped up and down, ran across the ring to Victor, hugged him, hugged me, climbed a few ropes, and screamed at the crowd. When Haag announced Todd the winner of the bout, he turned his affection to Bennett, hugged him, shook his hand, then hugged him a second time. Then Todd went to a small table in the back of the barroom, collected his check, put on his winter coat, and headed for the door.

"Where the hell you going, Todd?" Victor called out after him.

"Back to the hotel! Gotta call my mom!" His mom, back in Newark, was four hours ahead of Alaska time—by then it was likely past two in the morning—but she had promised Todd that she'd stay up for the call. "She won't believe it! I never won anything in my whole life!"

■

"Five foot eleven inches! Five foot eleven inches!" Haag said. Three women were running the round cards that night: a stiffly dancing tall redhead and two petite Hispanic women. Between rounds of each fight, to the banging chords of "Pretty Woman," Haag led them around the canvas, calling out their dimensions like an auctioneer at a 4-H show. "One hundred fifty-five pounds, right out of the bathtub!"

The ring girls had a long history at the Roughhouse Friday boxing show. Haag was known to recruit talent by sometimes approaching women in line at the Fred Meyer department store: "How would you like to make fifty dollars to dance inside a boxing ring?" Sometimes Haag was "slapped down" for his boldness. Other times, women were flattered by the offer. It baffled Haag that some of the most beautiful women in the world—his daughter, Jill, included—didn't like the rush of getting into a ring and being drenched with the attention of so many men. Such a conundrum led Haag to a theory about the human condition: there were two types of people in this world. "Egotistical giants" like himself, who liked nothing more than to be in front of a crowd; and everybody else. The first ring girls at Haag's show were women like Jamiann "Hi-Beam" Stevens, who, as the sergeant at arms at the statehouse, started out as a promotional assistant, then became a ring girl, then traded her bikini for boxing gloves. Though female bouts were rare at early Roughhouse shows, Haag had been impressed by girl fights he'd witnessed in other bars. Though Haag was a self-described chauvinist pig—in his house, "women warshed our dishes, the men pulled out their chairs"—he'd seen enough female fights to notice that "sometimes, women are just a little bit tougher."

During intermission, Haag engaged the crowd in a cheering contest, to see which of the evening's ring girls was "the hottest." First came the redhead—to mild applause. Then came the first of the two Hispanic women. One of them was named Paula. She wore a neon-green bikini with a neon-green sarong tied around her waist, her black hair falling down her back in a cascade of curls. She took bold, fearless laps around the ring, and as the crowd howled at her, she twirled to her right, untying the knot of fabric above her waist, revealing two glowing spheres, bisected by a thin line of fabric. The crowd erupted—louder than they had for any fight.

"How many of you expected to see that tonight?" Haag stuttered. "Hoot! Hoot! Hoot!"

The sound of the crowd got Haag excited, and he started chanting, "Show 'em your ass! Do it again!" Paula dropped her sarong a second time, but something was missing from the grace of the gesture, and she left the ring looking down at her feet.

Afterward, Haag held the microphone over each ring girl's head, told the crowd to scream for which one deserved the fifty-dollar prize. The crowd cheered for Paula, but Haag gave the prize to the other Hispanic woman. No one in the barroom seemed to care.

As the girls left the ring, a Native woman directed them back to their stools. The woman was very beautiful, dressed in tall leather boots and a red sweater. She observed the fights with a mix of bemusement and affection. I watched her for a while, convinced somehow that she understood the reasons we were all here. In the ring, I would learn later, she called herself the Wildflower.

7. THE NICE GUY

I sat backward in a metal chair, palms down, fingers wide, as Victor wrapped my hands in gauze, then tape, sculpting it over the contours of my knuckles. "Straight punches," he said, pushing on a pair of gloves. Then we started mitt work: light punches, repeating the limited combinations he'd taught me in the past three weeks. After I'd built up a sweat, I stood in the corner, hopping in place and shadowboxing, waiting for Haag to call my name. I wore my winter hat pulled down low over my eyes, had tightened the hood of my sweatshirt around my face so that I was nearly invisible. Beneath my layers of clothing, I began to sweat—so much that the sweat began to soak through my clothes. I got nervous that I'd dehydrated myself, so I drank a bottle of water. This made me have to piss, which made me worry that I'd dehydrated myself again, so I drank more water, which upset my stomach and gave me diarrhea, which meant that every five minutes I had to run across the barroom and fight my way through crowds to sit on the toilet before starting the cycle all over again.

Meanwhile, the Nice Guy stood next to a concrete pillar, punching the pillar with one hand while cupping a cigarette in the other. He winced after each drag, paused now and then to take a swig off a bottle of beer from a man standing next to him. He didn't look in shape—you could see the paunch of his belly pushing against the cloth of his T-shirt—but I had lost track of the scale of the danger of a fight, and the same swirl of fear and doubt and uncertainty that had first prevented me from accepting Victor's offer to fight now told me that there was some chance that the Nice Guy might kill me.

"I been watching him," Victor said. "Not a drop of sweat on him. He's dry." Victor nodded. "Run him, Jade. He'll go down."

"Jade Coffin! Mike Edenshaw!" Haag barked into the mic. By then his gravelly promoter's voice had devolved into a slurred growl. "Come on down!"

In the distance, the empty ring glowed neon, a thin swirl of smoke hanging above it. I took a step toward the ring, then turned away, into a corner of the barroom beneath a wall of dartboards. I knelt, lifted my wrapped hands to my chin, and closed my eyes.

The day I entered the temple, I sat in a chair in the middle of the temple grounds, shirtless and naked but for a *pakomaw* wrap, surrounded by perhaps forty members of my family. My mother stood beside me with a long pair of metal shears. She began to clip my hair. After several minutes, she passed the shears to my aunt. Then my aunt passed the shears to my uncle, until each member of my family had taken a turn. Then an old monk whom I'd known since I was a boy shaved the rest of my hair with a razor. He shaved off my eyebrows. My uncle led me into a room, where I dressed in white robes. Then he put a silk umbrella over my head and led me into the temple, followed by a parade of my family members. We walked around the grounds three times, chanting a prayer my uncle had taught me in the days before my ordination ceremony. I lit incense before the plots of my grandfather and grandmother, whose ashes were buried in the temple walls. Then I entered the temple and took my vows.

Now I chanted that same prayer. I had only a vague idea what the words meant—*nat mo tassa*—but I uttered them with the seriousness—*pakawat doe*—that I'd had on the day I first said them—*samma samphoot tassa.* I said the prayer three times, imagining a vision of my tropical god rising out of a steamy jungle, floating across the Bering Sea, ice fields, mountain ranges, and miles of wilderness into an upstairs barroom. Repeating the chant had always guided me back to that peace within myself like cultural sonar. But when I opened my eyes, all I heard was the thumping chords of "I Love Rock 'n' Roll."

"Jade!" Victor called out. "We're on, man! We're on!"

I stood up. Victor pulled my sweatshirt over my head. I followed him through the parting crowd as anonymous hands slapped my naked back. A drunk man with a mustache grabbed me by the shoulder, looked me in the eyes, and shouted, "Do it! Do it! Do it!" while pumping his fist.

Victor lowered the middle rope with his foot. I stepped through the hole and onto the canvas. Victor slapped Vaseline on my face, over my eyebrows. "Straight punches, Jade! Straight punches!"

The ref called me to the middle of the ring. I faced the Nice Guy. We did not look at each other. I knew nothing about him, nothing of his past or origins, nothing of what made him fight. The ref explained the rules—above the belt, no holding. The Nice Guy and I bumped gloves, and I returned to my corner.

Victor checked my mouth guard. "First round, Jade, just don't get hit."

Ding. Ding. Ding.

The Nice Guy shuffled out of his corner: hands low, head bobbing. We looked at each other. Then we started fighting.

■

At the dawn of the nineteenth century, in a village called Dadens, during the time of the first European contact with the Haida Indians on what is now the coast of British Columbia, there lived a leader of a tribe who went by the name Edenshaw. When this leader died, his position was given to his twenty-three-year-old nephew. Following a smallpox epidemic that wiped out some 60 percent of the Haida population, the young leader moved his village from Dadens to Kiusta. There, the young leader became known for his carving technique, and his particular skill at crafting ornate war daggers and shields. The leader went by many names: first Gwai-Gu-unlthlin, then Captain Douglas, because he believed himself a descendant of a man who had acquired the name from an English captain who had visited the Haida people some thirty years earlier. When missionaries arrived in Kiusta, Gwai-Gu-unlthlin, or Captain Douglas, became a Methodist, changed his name to Albert, and was among the first Haida to be baptized. English ship logs have accounts of Albert's keen work as a hired navigator, and he acquired a reputation as both a trusted ally and a double-talking traitor. Albert's English was known to be "excellent." Various accounts refer to him as "shrewd" and "intelligent." He dressed in a traveling cap and waistcoat rather than, as one European sailor put it, the "gaudy colors"—bold red, black, and yellow—of the "usual Indian style." One captain even compared Albert Edenshaw to Napoléon, or Peter the Great—"as subtle and cunning as the serpent." But the compliments only went so far: "Like all his countrymen," the same captain observed, "he has no perception of right and wrong, but only what self-interest dictates."

■

As I met the Nice Guy in the middle of the ring, I was so horrified by the shock of space surrounding us that I could not jab without bouncing backward in retreat. Once, I jumped back so quickly that I tumbled onto my ass. I flicked useless jabs, hopping in circles. Meanwhile, the Nice Guy remained almost still, waiting for me to get close enough to hit. The crowd began to boo. In the final seconds of the round, I ran at the Nice Guy, hoping to hit him once before the bell. His right hand caught my cheek: whack!

"You got hit!" Victor said. He took out my mouth guard, squirted water down my throat. "Look, Jade." Both his hands were in front of his face. "He's gonna drop his hands. I been watching him. Wait for it. When he does"—Victor lowered his hands— "Bang! Straight left." Over Victor's shoulder, the Nice Guy sat slumped in his stool, gazing at the tubes of neon lights. "He's gonna get tired, Jade." Victor popped my mouth guard back in, fed me more water. "He's gonna get tired. You're not."

Ding. Ding. Ding.

■

In Albert's time, a generation of European anthropologists— witnessing what they believed would be the imminent extinction of Haida culture—began to pay more attention to the art of the Edenshaw line. During this period, Albert Edenshaw fathered a son named Henry. Henry was among the first Haida to interpret the meaning of Haida art to the anthropologist John Swanton. Henry was also among the first of his people to drive a gas-powered boat, to move out of a traditional longhouse and into a two-story home. When Henry died, he left his carving tools to his sister's son, Charles. The tools were thought to be blessed: Henry had used them most effectively during visions inspired by hallucinogenic medicines.

■

By the second round, my nerves had burned off. I threw a left hand—it didn't land. I threw another one. Not even close. After several misses, I grew impatient and began to hunt the Nice Guy around the ring, until I found him in the corner. There, I hit him several times—nothing solid, just a few glancing slaps off his shoulders—but the pressure of the punches tipped him off-balance.

He took a knee. The ref sent me to a neutral corner and started a ten count. While the Nice Guy pulled himself to his feet, I lowered my head, closed my eyes, tried to gather my breath, find again that pool of peace behind my forehead. But it was gone. When the ref called me on, I charged forward, collided with the Nice Guy in a messy tangle of bad punches. The bell rang; I returned to my stool.

"You got sixty seconds," Victor said, kneeling before me as we prepped for the third round. "He's out of gas. Out of gas! You gotta pour it on. Everything you got, Jade! Sixty seconds. All your power!"

◼

Charles Edenshaw was born in 1839, in the island village of Kung. Charles's father died when Charles was still a boy, probably in the smallpox epidemic. As Charles moved to various fish camps in and around the villages of Masset and Skidegate, he became known for his extensive tattoos of frogs and sea wolves and whales and eagles. Though rumored to have been cross-eyed, Charles also developed a reputation as a carver with mystical vision, who could see the spirit of his subjects hidden within the wood. Charles's work earned the attention of the world-renowned anthropologist Franz Boas, who later wrote extensively on Edenshaw in his book *Primitive Art*. As Charles traveled with Boas to museums in Chicago, London, and Paris, the population of Haida, which once totaled thirty thousand, was reduced by disease to less than eight hundred. After the English in Canada enforced the Indian Act— an act that, similar to American Indian law, prohibited expression of traditional culture and language—Charles became a Christian. He changed his given name, Tahaygen, then married a third wife (his niece), who took the name Isabella, after the queen of England. While Isabella, a mother of five, worked in the fish cannery in Ketchikan, Charles moved from traditional carving to hybrid forms: Christian gravestones adorned with raven heads and crucifixes.

When Charles Edenshaw died in 1920, he was nearly blind. One story states that his last words before departing were "When I come back, I don't ever want to carve again."

■

The Nice Guy was tired. His punches came at half speed, which gave me time to think through the basic counterpunching sequence that Victor had taught me in the gym. I waited for the Nice Guy to throw his lazy jab, slipped to the outside of it, then drove my left hand into the narrow corridor between the Nice Guy's arm and chin. I saw the punch land. In the resulting clinch, the Nice Guy's right glove got stuck in my armpit, so that his head hung before me, waist-high like a floating balloon. I didn't understand the rules of boxing—that you can't use one arm to lock your opponent in position while you punch the back of his head with the other—so I started punching him in the chin and forehead. Through the padding of my glove, I could feel the hardness of his skull—a hardness that I can still feel in my middle knuckles whenever I recall that fight. I hit him six times before the ref pulled us apart. The crowd booed—they understood that what I'd done was illegal—but as soon as the ref cleared out, I chased the Nice Guy into a corner, showed him my head as a decoy. When he threw a looping, exhausted right hand, I slid under the punch and rose up with a left. The Nice Guy went down. I jogged back to the neutral corner. The ref began a second count, but the Nice Guy rose to his knees. I crossed the canvas, waited for him to offer a slow jab, then hit him again. This time he landed on his back, legs up, arms to the side.

The final bell rang.

"Yeah, Jade!" Victor said. I jumped into his arms. The crowd rose to their feet. Victor lowered the ropes and I climbed to the middle one, held my hands up over my head, pumped my fist. When I came down, the Nice Guy was standing behind me, one hand extended.

"Good fight," he said.

I shook his hand. "Thank you." Something warm filled my chest. My chin began to stiffen. "Thank you." What I did next surprised me: I bowed, lowering my head beneath him, as my mother had always taught me to do in the presence of elders.

We stood in the middle of the ring as Haag read the cards. "Knockout, round three, Jade! The Stone! Coffiiiin!"

The ref held up my glove. The Nice Guy held up the other one.

"Jade Coffin!" Haag shouted. "The Stone!"

Before I left the ring, I had an urge to say something to the Nice Guy. I was not sure what I wanted to say—just a feeling I wanted to communicate. "Hey."

The Nice Guy turned.

"I wish I'd fought you a long time ago." My intention was to tell the Nice Guy that, had he been my age, he would have been stronger and faster, and I might not have won the fight so easily . . . and . . . I don't know. It was supposed to be a compliment.

"Okay," the Nice Guy said. He climbed out of the ring.

Four years later, in February of 2008, I would read the Nice Guy's obituary in the *Juneau Empire*. He'd been diagnosed with brain cancer in the winter of 2007, not long after he'd lost a fight to another Sitka fighter—a coast guard swimmer named Matt Keiper—in less than twelve seconds. The Nice Guy's Roughhouse career did not include much in the way of victory. In the 2004–05 season, he fell to Scott Horne in forty-two seconds, then to Earl Wentworth in the second round. Edenshaw avenged his loss to Wentworth later that year—temporarily boxing under the name Iron Mike.

In the obituary, I learned that in addition to Roughhouse boxing, the Nice Guy's favorite hobbies were hunting, fishing, and volunteering at the Grandma's Club. He also had been a woodcarver, and many of his works could be seen around hotels in Juneau, although I could never figure out his exact relationship to the carving lineage that preceded him. When I looked up the meaning of his last name, I learned that the Haida name—*eda'nsa*—had originally come from a Tlingit word used to describe things that were melting away, like the ice of a glacier, until there was nothing left. I also learned that to friends and family he was not known as the Nice Guy. Rather, he was called Haida Mike.

One month before he died, Haag, at the last Roughhouse show of the year, presented members of the Edenshaw family with a plaque that read TO A GREAT BOXER, MIKE EDENSHAW, FROM ALL YOUR FRIENDS AT MARLINTINI'S.

■

Roo's flight had been held up by the storm, and he entered the Marlintini's barroom just twenty minutes before his bout, covered in snow. He dusted himself off, then changed into his boxing gear: black trunks, black shoes. Then he shadowboxed for several minutes before working the mitts with Victor. I admired the seriousness and efficiency with which he prepared himself to fight. When I asked him if he was nervous, he shrugged. "I reckon I still get a few butterflies."

His opponent was a large Filipino man named Lito Lumbab. He had inflated biceps and pectorals, which strained the fabric of his T-shirt. He outweighed Roo by thirty pounds. When Haag called them into the ring for the main event, Roo came up to Lumbab's chin.

The bell rang. Roo jogged out of his corner, led with a big right. The punch didn't land, but he kept coming behind it, driving Lumbab into the ropes, holding him there with his forearm and elbow as Roo threw hooks into his body and head. One of Lumbab's legs had gotten twisted beneath him, and his head snapped back through the ropes. The ref sent Roo to the neutral corner. Lumbab's nose and lips were already bleeding. At ten, Roo crossed the ring, tried to finish off Lumbab. Lumbab turned his back, ran for the corner, as Roo punched him in the back of the head. It was like watching a rat attack a dog.

"Rooooo! Rooooo!" the crowd chanted between rounds.

In the final minute, Roo feinted, lobbed a right over Lumbab's defense. Lumbab fell to his knees. Roo hit him there until the ref pulled him away, but before he could knock Lumbab out, the bell rang. Haag fell to his knees, as if in worship. The Wildflower threw her arms over her head. The crowd erupted.

"Fuck!" Roo said, as he came back to the corner. "Another minute, I would've finished him off."

■

The parking lot of Marlintini's was covered in snow. The sky was clear and full of stars. The mountains beyond the airport circled the city like giant concrete forms. As we crossed the Glacier Highway to the Travelodge, Todd danced in circles, shouting, "Dirty Dog! Dirty Dog!" Victor called out, "The Stone! The Stone!" Even Roo had stopped scowling.

Upstairs, Victor packed a bowl, smoked, passed it to Todd. Todd repacked the bowl and handed it to me. Growing up, I'd never smoked like my friends did—I always got anxious and couldn't sleep and just wanted the high to be over. But now it felt useful. I was so empty—of food, of feeling—that seconds after my first hit, all the cells in my body felt like they were floating, slowly rearranging themselves in a new order. I handed the bowl back to Victor.

"Used to be the only thing that could calm me down after a fight," Victor said.

We stayed up several hours, watching videos of our fights. We laughed at Todd's kick to Bennett's groin. We replayed Roo's forearm to Lumbab's teeth. But in watching my own fight, I saw a version of myself I had never known. My eyes were wide open with something like fear, or panic, in the first round. Then, in the second, they narrowed. By the third, as I pummeled the Nice Guy's head with uppercuts, my eyes were alive with . . . it was hard to say. Rage. Viciousness. Anger. An expression of something I did not know existed inside me. After I'd knocked the Nice Guy down in the final seconds, I did not even turn around to see if he was all right. As I pumped my fists and hugged Victor, the Nice Guy remained on the canvas behind me. He didn't get up for a full thirty seconds. Victor rewound the tape. We watched the punch sequence a second time: me slipping the Nice Guy's right hand, then popping up with a left. Violence. That's what it was.

For the next several hours, I lay in bed, forearms buzzing, staring at the ceiling as if still waiting for the fight. About three in the morning, I got out of bed, sat at the table next to the window, staring at the light of the streetlamps. Around 5:00 a.m.—9:00 a.m. back East—I went downstairs to a phone booth, dialed my father's number. As I waited for someone to pick up, I imagined a lonely farmhouse on the side of the road, surrounded by snowy white fields. Then I heard my father's voice.

"Dad."

"My son." He always called me "my son."

I narrated my way through each second of the fight, drawing a picture of the Nice Guy that made him sound like a more formidable opponent than he was. I wanted my father to know about the world I had entered, to see, too, the violence that had revealed itself during the fight. I must have talked for twenty minutes before I stopped to ask my father how he was doing.

"I'm good. I'm good." But his voice was drawn, hollow. He'd just come off another trip, to a military base in the Midwest, to debrief a group of guardsmen arriving home from Ramadi. "Was up at three in the morning, talking to guys about what it was going to be like to go from driving around the desert in a Humvee to driving around Enosburg Falls in a goddamn bread truck." He took a long breath. I heard in the exhale that same despair: the men at war, the heaviness of their pain, the truth of their suffering. Every conversation between us then had a way of spiraling into the same abyss. Real men were impossible to understand. Real men suffered. Real men were broken. Real men were alone. "You know," my father said, "the other day, I was rereading that passage from *The Sun Also Rises*. You know the one I'm talking about? Jake's up in his hotel room, drunk, after Brett's gone home with some guy? You know that passage? It's a good world to buy in?"

I knew the exact passage my father was referring to. After he'd shown it to me, I'd read it probably twenty times. The way that Hemingway broke down existence into an economic equation: You gave up something and you got something else. You paid in some way for anything that was any good. The world, as my father liked to say, in his various improvisations, was a good place to buy in. But hearing him say those words now, I could think only of the shadow of his conceit, in which Jake contemplates Brett's experience: "I had not been thinking about her side of it. I had been getting something for nothing . . . The bill always came . . . I thought I had paid for everything," Jake says. "Not like the woman pays and pays and pays."

Her side of it.

In my eyes, my mother was an autonomous figure, too fixated on survival to reveal its toll. For most of my life, I saw my mother as a somewhat lonely, distant figure, consumed by work. Only now that I had left her behind in Maine did I see for the first time how my father's life had created the terms of her existence. And now, talking to my father, the equation of his life appeared more clearly to me than ever: In going to war, he had made his payment. That he had met my mother, brought her back to the United States—this was the exchange of values. That she had given him a son, this was how he had gotten his money's worth. And when he had found the next thing he wished to buy—

another woman, another family, another life—he had made a final irredeemable transaction. It was a good world to buy in. But how the woman pays and pays and pays: first with her country, her culture and origin; then with her family, her life, her heart.

"Yes," I said, my hand tightening on the receiver. "I remember that part."

My father took a deep breath. Exhaled. "Wow. What a story. What a story."

Yes, I thought as I hung up the phone. It was quite a story.

8. RUNNING

"Fighting does weird shit to your body," Victor said as he dropped me off at my apartment. When I'd tried to open the door of his truck, the pain in my forearms made it difficult to pull on the handle. Before driving away, Victor told me to keep up my road-work, but to take a week off to let my body heal. We'd get back into training after the Thanksgiving break.

I spent the morning sitting on my couch, opening and closing my fists, trying to prove to myself that I had fought. The pain in my forearms told me so—what was it inside me that so badly needed to get out? The only other evidence I had of fighting was the check in my pocket: $150 was a lot of money for three minutes of work. I studied the puffy BIG H boxing logo in one corner. It looked less like a glove than a swollen heart.

I slept through the afternoon. It was nearly dark when I woke up. I rode my bike into town, to the harbor bridge. The snow was still fresh above the tree line, and the way it buried the broken ridges gave the mountains the appearance of being a single, unified shape. I remained on the bridge, watching the snowfields turn purple as the sun went down, until the white mountains glowed in the night.

■

I had no plans for Thanksgiving Day, but my coworkers at SNEP had invited me to a community meal at the ANB Hall at noon. I dressed in my nicest pair of khaki pants and a clean flannel shirt and rode into town.

Thanksgiving had never been a particularly important day for my mother and me; typically, I spent the day on my own, waiting for my mother to come home from work, when we would go to a friend's house, always late, to celebrate with the friend's extended family. I was often struck by the expansiveness of other people's families—the minivans full of various blood relations, all having driven up from suburbs of Boston or New York, the way they talked about their past as a shared story of how they had arrived at a common table. Sitting with my mother, people would sometimes introduce us as "like family"—an expression that made me flinch. Sometimes my mother would allow herself a little bit of wine— half a glass would do—then stand up and sing a Thai folk song, twirling her hands, dancing. Part of me was proud of my mother's performances—we did not speak Thai at home, did not celebrate Thai holidays, and her performances filled those absences—but sometimes she would see the way I watched her and it would make her stop. "Enough!" she'd say, her face bright red with alcohol. "Look at how I embarrass my son!"

One Thanksgiving during my college years, my mother came to pick me up in Vermont so that we could visit my father's mother in a nursing home in Burlington. For most of my life, my mother had cared for my grandmother as though she were blood. "It is differ-ent in the Thai culture," my mother once told me, when discuss-ing her devotion to my father's family. "When you marry into a family, you are always a family." My father and grandmother had a complicated relationship: she was likely bipolar and had been committed to institutions on several occasions, and for about ten years my father had refused to see her. When I was a boy, he would drop me off at the elevator of her twelve-story apartment building, press the button for the eleventh floor, then, several hours later, honk his horn from the parking lot when it was time to pick me up. But now I was beginning to understand that my mother's compassion for my father's mother was not merely about loyalty: it was her way of holding on to a broken past, staking a claim to the parts of my father's life that he had left behind.

The visit was brief—my grandmother, bedridden and often disoriented, could only stay awake for an hour at a time. But before my mother and I drove back to Maine, she called old family friends from the Champlain Islands, which led to an invitation to Thanksgiving dinner at their home. I remembered the family well: they had lived across the woods from our old house, and on many occasions I had slept on the floor of their living room while my mother and father must have been arguing. As we pulled up to their house, I had hoped to feel something like tenderness toward them—a warm recognition that we all had survived those years and come out on the other side. But it was an excruciating afternoon: I sat at their table awkwardly trying to make conversation to smooth over our unexpected arrival. But minutes into the meal, I became aware of something: these people had memories of me as a boy—Jeddy, they still called me—that I did not have myself. They had memories of my parents as a single unit. They had memories of my mother as she arrived in America, an odd figure in rural Vermont. And they had likely entertained the same questions I was entertaining now: What on earth was she doing here? As plates were cleared, I considered all the questions I would never ask, the answers our hosts would never offer. After a few hours, it was clear to me that, to them, the past was gone. It was clear to me that my mother's desire to maintain a connection to them was her way of proving to herself that the past was alive. The whole ride home, I did not speak. I was too angry that I was caught up in this reconciliation, too ashamed for what I did not know. Meanwhile, my father was having Thanksgiving dinner just thirty miles down the road with Martha's family, around a table where, each year, their clan grew bigger and bigger with every additional grandchild.

■

The ANB Thanksgiving spread was different from any I'd ever had: there was turkey, gravy, potatoes, and cranberry sauce, and also herring roe, canned salmon, and seaweed, served with moose gravy and fish oil, followed by watermelon-berry whip for dessert. Todd—he had no family in Sitka either—had also come alone. We spent the meal talking about our next fights as if dissecting the subtleties of a novel. We both felt good about our wins, but Todd wanted to do better next time: he wanted to be more aggressive, more disciplined, not lose his cool and kick his opponent in the nuts. I had things I wanted to work on, too: I had watched a tape of my fight several times and didn't like the way I'd so frantically jumped away after every punch. I wanted to dig in, stand toe to toe with my opponent, and trade shots without concern for getting hit. I was still uncomfortable with the version of myself that I'd seen in the last minute of my fight, but I felt that if I just kept training, I would understand its meaning.

After the meal, Todd and I took a drive to the end of Sawmill Creek Road, to see if we could get a deer. It was the middle of the rut, and the snow had pushed the bucks off the ridges, and Todd said he'd seen lots of tracks the last time he'd been out in the woods with his dogs. We drove several miles along the water, until we crossed the small creek where the hatchery road turned to dirt, where the shoulders of Bear Mountain banked into Silver Bay—a long sliver of water that lay between mountains like a narrow shard of glass. Todd drove an old tan Ford Ranger that Victor's father had sold him for three hundred dollars. The tailgate was rusted out and so was the bed, but you didn't need an inspection sticker in Sitka. His two huskies rode in the bed on a piece of plywood so they wouldn't fall through.

We pulled up to a metal gate and the dogs jumped out and we followed them into the woods. Walking through the forest, under a snowy canopy of spruce branches, was like entering a giant cathedral. Now and then, a branch would release and snow would explode through the light and then the forest would fall silent again. We walked for a mile or so, along the vague impression of a deer trail, until we came to a small clearing. Todd let me borrow his .30-06, and as we sat waiting, I felt a great peace moving inside me. I was tired of walking around the mountains with no purpose; hunting made me feel useful. Sitting next to Todd, I tried to imagine what it would be like to live alone forever, and whether that would be better than living with a family. The way Todd's eyes trained on the foliage, the way he whispered to his dogs, it made me wonder if he was any better or worse off than anybody else. He seemed to be doing all right. We remained sitting for another hour or so until the crisp visibility of the forest began to fade. At dusk, when it was too late to get a deer and dress it and pack it out, we followed Todd's dogs back to the dirt road.

On our way through town, Todd showed me where he kept his boat, in a slip at Old Thomsen's Harbor. It was a weathered green houseboat, not at all seaworthy, that sat low in the water. Under the deck, the narrow cabin was about the width of my closet, with a tiny one-burner kitchen. The only furniture was a foam pad and several woven blankets, and a space heater. With dogs in the cabin, it was "pretty cozy" during winter, Todd said. The windows were taped over with cardboard. As the sun set over the mountains on Kruzof, we sat on the stern, smoking a bowl, watching the light fade. The ocean was calm for November. There was something sad about being away from my mother on Thanksgiving—with my sister living overseas, I caught myself imagining my mother alone, in our house, singing by herself. But there was also something liberating about the distance. High, staring across the open ocean, life felt light and simple. Maybe Todd was onto something: if you cut ties with your past, you could have everything you needed right in front of you.

Later, Todd put my bike in the back of his truck, then dropped me off at my apartment.

"Nice place," he said, while parked in my driveway.

"It's all right."

As I got out of his truck, Todd said, "Hey, Jade, think I can borrow like twenty bucks? The guy who pays me to clean fish is out of town. Gotta buy some dog food."

I looked at Todd—it had been all of a week since our Roughhouse fight, but I guess the money hadn't lasted. I took a twenty out of my wallet.

"Thanks, man. I'll get you back after our next fight."

"Sure," I said, but I knew the money was as good as gone.

■

A message from Miss Mary was on my answering machine, inviting me over for a late Thanksgiving meal. After the Stardust Ball, I'd made a stern decision that I was done spending time with Miss Mary. This was partly because of the Goat, but also because I felt that spending time with a woman would be bad for fighting. I was 1–0 now. The last thing I needed was a girlfriend in my life to give me weak legs. And yet no matter how much I tried to validate my decision, I still felt something like loyalty to Miss Mary. We were both alone, both in need of each other's company and affection, and the coldness with which I had written her off because of her past with the Goat betrayed that delicate agreement, left me feeling as though I were somehow in debt to her. The debt had nothing to do with romance or physicality, but something more fundamental: a basic humanity that two people alone should take care of each other rather than turn away. It took me all of ten minutes of sitting in my apartment before I hopped on my bike and rode up the hill.

■

From the street, the windows of Miss Mary's apartment glowed with soft lamplight. The table was set. It looked warm inside. "Happy Thanksgiving," Miss Mary said as she opened the door. She hugged me. She wore a sweater and skirt and had done her hair. Over turkey and potatoes and stuffing, she asked me to tell her about my fight. I gave her the true version: how scared I'd been of getting in the ring, how that fear had transformed into something like anger. I was still piecing together exactly who I'd been as I pounded the Nice Guy into the corner, but I did understand that my desire to fight had little to do with inflicting pain on another person. Miss Mary listened patiently and asked questions. Whatever I'd felt for Miss Mary in the weeks before my fight—a crude combination of resistance and dependency—had vanished. In its place was something more honest: something that, in a certain light, resembled a version of friendship. For a moment, I saw us as who we were: two lonely people, trying to figure out what we wanted out of life by isolating ourselves in a place where we didn't necessarily belong. The "frontier woman" posturing that Miss Mary had offered me as part of her goat-meat stunt was no different from my heroic paddle up here. We were both just trying to prove to ourselves, and to each other, that we were tougher than the versions of ourselves that we'd left Down South.

It was a pleasant evening, but when I woke up in the morning, the fairness with which I'd regarded Miss Mary, the way I had come to understand our relationship, was gone. Instead, I felt myself grow cold and unforgiving again, resistant to her affection. Miss Mary had made waffles, and as we ate, she told me how it made her feel good to cook meals for a man. I nodded but didn't say anything.

"You know, Jed," she said, after I'd eaten several plates of waffles, "I'm very open to an arrangement like this. Even if it's just a few days a week." She was speaking very slowly. "This time of year women are just looking for someone to keep them warm."

I looked at Miss Mary. She wanted something from me—reliability, commitment, stability—that I did not possess. I wanted something from her—information about who I was—that she did not possess. It was a sad way to think of things—that between us was some equation of emotions that we could never balance. That, eventually, the bill would always come.

Miss Mary looked at me. She blinked a few times before speaking. "What about you, Jade? What are you running away from?"

I paused, trying to think of her side of things. Asked myself what, exactly, I owed her. When I think back on my younger self, think of how desperately I was searching for some definition of self, it seems sad that I needed other people—women, but men just as much—to help sketch my portrait. I needed to hurt people to understand my own weaknesses. I needed to offer tentative versions of who I was to test if they were true. I needed Miss Mary to listen to my stories so I could determine if they added up. By sharing those half-formed things with other people, I was offering them a bridge into my life, one that would never be fully constructed, one that was not made to last. All I knew in those years was that my commitment to solitude and autonomy was the only way to prove to the world that I was more than the sum of my origins.

I took another bite of waffle. "I'm not running away from anything," I said. I stood up from the table, thanked Miss Mary for breakfast. As I rode home, the sun was bright. Snow melted in the street. The water in the channel shimmered like a plain of silver light. I did jumps and skids in the snow—BMX tricks I'd practiced with my buddies in junior high—and for a moment, I felt like a boy again.

■

That Saturday was my twenty-fourth birthday. I went out drinking with a group of Filipino women who'd befriended me. I worked with one of them at the high school—her name was Lisa—and I think she felt that, being Southeast Asians, she and her friends had a moral or cultural responsibility to look after me. The women had all grown up in Sitka, the daughters of charter fishermen. They all lived at home with their parents, and some of them had children. They had beautiful names: Lotus, Evangeline, Priscilla, Angelica. When they found out my birthday was coming up, they took it upon themselves to get dressed up like they were heading out for a night at the clubs and made a plan to get me drunk.

It was a late, rowdy night that started at the P Bar and ended several miles out of town at a dive called Uncle Joe's. Before it was Uncle Joe's it had been Rookie's. Before Rookie's, it was the Kiksadi Club—Haag's mother's bar. The women called the bar Sloppy Joe's because it was where everyone went to hook up before last call. We sat at a table next to the dance floor. Lotus kept topping off glasses of Coke with a flask of whiskey she kept hidden under her shirt, and before long the girls had me dancing. It felt good to be drunk. It felt good to dance instead of fight.

The only person I recognized at the bar was the master bead worker, Paul. He was sitting at a table with several other SNEP employees. We shook hands, made small talk, chatted about work. He'd just had the regalia class that I'd seen him preparing for. He'd wondered if I was going to show up. When I told him it was my birthday, he shook my hand, bought me a shot, and then we returned to our tables. Later, I saw Paul leap up out of his chair. He started dancing: spinning, shouting, whooping, waving his arms. The entire bar fell silent. Everyone stared at him. Paul kept dancing. He was drunk—but no more drunk than I was, or any of the other white people were. Even wasted, I felt myself reading the moment: how Paul, by virtue of being Native, became a symbol to the rest of us, a sad signifier of our missing origins, a reminder of what past lived inside all of us, what truths we needed to bury to claim ourselves American. But instead of carrying that past evenly, instead of facing the absences in our own stories, we had asked Paul to carry it alone. So he kept dancing, until one of our coworkers put her arm over his shoulders and led him outside into the parking lot.

■

Sometime around two in the morning, the Filipino women and I all ended up at my apartment for an after-party. On my own, I had gotten used to the sparseness of my life. But with guests, I could feel how vividly my apartment appeared as the world of a single person. There was nowhere to sit. Nothing to offer my guests to drink. Nothing to prove to them that I was not a sociopath.

"You live here all alone?" Priscilla said.

"Yeah."

She looked at my empty walls. "Don't you get homesick?"

"Not really."

Priscilla shivered. "I like living with my parents. Free babysitting."

I tried to play a good host and took out some rice noodles and did my best to whip up something while the women dozed off on the couch. I didn't have the right ingredients, so I substituted maple syrup for sugar, apple cider vinegar for rice vinegar, soy sauce for fish sauce.

"Damn, Jade," Evangeline said. "This is gross. I thought Thai food was good."

She brought her plate to my sink, which was full of dirty

dishes. She laid it on the counter. Then she and the other girls went home.

■

I woke up with a splitting headache, shivering with a hangover. I stumbled around my apartment for a few minutes, still a bit drunk, fumbling with coffee, trying to get my bearings on the day. Something was off, something wasn't right. I sat down on my couch with a jug of water, stared at the cinder-block walls, tracing the grid of lines between them as if it were a crossword puzzle. So this was what it was like to be twenty-four.

When my father was twenty-four, he'd just graduated from Middlebury, ROTC. The year was 1968. He, and many of his friends, were well aware that they'd likely be going to Vietnam. American soldiers were dying in dozens by the day, and every story my father had ever told me about that period of his life felt laced with death. The night before he'd reported for basic training, he went on a date with the daughter of a family friend, to see the opera in New York City. As they parted, the young woman offered to be with him—a gesture that, rather than exciting my father, filled him with something like dread.

The day he landed at Fort Gordon, Georgia, my father had eaten a delicious, enormous peach from a wooden crate in the back of a truck. It was just a simple memory—what could be more mundane than eating a peach—but the taste of that luscious, precious fruit had stayed with him. There was the first meeting with his fellow lieutenants—one from Puerto Rico, another from Ohio—who, upon learning that my father was from Maine, had looked at each other and asked him, "Then why you fighting in the American army?" That summer, a private came to visit my father's platoon with a book of assignments—every one of which began with a V for "Vietnam"—then made a joke about an opening for an unglorious position in a small village of Panomsarakram, in central Thailand, with the 809th Engineer Battalion. My father, breaking every rule of informal military protocol—*never volunteer for anything*—asked for the assignment, thinking it might be a way to keep himself alive. His close friend and fellow frat brother—an all-American athlete named Bayard "Bye-Bye" Russ—had volunteered for infantry and come home dead three weeks into his deployment. The night before my father shipped out, he spent a single night in San Francisco, at a Chambers Brothers concert with a flight attendant he'd met that evening, listening to a thirty-minute psychedelic rendition of "Time Has Come Today."

Two days later, my father landed in Bangkok. He spent a week killing time in a hotel room, until an unspeaking officer in a jeep drove him fourteen hours to a military base in the remote province of Sakon Nakhon, on the border with Laos, where the 809th had been relocated. There, he was charged with managing a communications unit patrolling radio wires along the Mekong River. In the first week of duty, while my father was trying to get some radios repaired at a nearby outpost, a jeep—maybe driven by a North Vietnamese sympathizer, it was unclear—tried to run him off the road. His own jeep flipped over, throwing his arm out of its socket, leaving him unable to draw his weapon. He was rescued by Thai rangers. He spent a week in a military hospital, doped up on morphine, thinking he was being attended to by an African American nurse who he later found out did not exist. In honor of my father's sacrifices, he was given a front-row, wheelchair-only seat at a Bob Hope concert, where he got kissed by Miss Universe and Ann-Margret. He could still recall how, up close, the women's faces were masks of exuberance concealing utter exhaustion, how the smooth voice of Bob Hope was like a song of death. "That," my father once told me, "was when I realized that nothing good was going to happen here." On any given day, he saw choppers returning from ten-minute reconnaissance missions, watched them crash-land in a ball of flames as men—concussed, disoriented—stumbled out. Sometimes he heard the broken dispatches of failed missions, the panicked voices cutting out, followed by radio silence.

Over the years I had learned to imagine that period of my father's life like the beginning of a fable—a tale of the American innocent, delivered into a world of political corruption and Southeast Asian absurdity, my father as a lost and wandering antisoldier, like Yossarian in *Catch-22*. The frames of this story ran fluidly in my mind, backgrounded by steaming jungles and smoke, until the film began to flicker and trip. While teaching English to Thai civilians, my father met a young Thai woman who had come to Sakon Nakhon from Panomsarakram. She worked as the manager of the officers' club, drove a motorcycle, played pickup basketball with American GIs in a skirt and high heels. He loved the way she liked to sing Elvis songs in front of all the soldiers who patronized her club. Her favorite song, my father once told me, was "Your Cheatin' Heart"—although a part of me always wonders if I am making that up.

What was missing from the film: my mother's side of the story. In the mid-1960s, the 809th Engineer Battalion—a convoy of tanks, bulldozers, backhoes, and dump trucks—had rolled into her village of Panomsarakram to build a military base. They paved the old dirt roads, built up communications infrastructure, put the locals to work—for high American wages. My mother, the eldest of five, was working as a teacher, trying to support her siblings following the death of her own mother. The money she could make working for the U.S. government was better than any money she could make as a teacher. When the 809th made plans to relocate north, my mother followed the money. She did not consider the larger implications of what it meant that Thailand had allied itself with the anticommunist sentiments of the West. Her concerns were not global.

In Sakon Nakhon, my mother enrolled in an English class. My

father was the teacher. I have seen pictures of him then: in an olive drab military uniform, a lean and mustached six foot one, he is a stunning portrait of the beautiful lie that is American masculinity. In his image, perhaps my mother saw a figure of formidable strength, someone who might help her achieve her goals of a more lucrative life in America. The day they were married, my mother wore a pink silk gown, her hair in a beehive. My father knelt next to her, their heads joined by a blessing string, their hands over a bowl of blessing water. "I married your mother," my father once told me, when I asked him why, "because she was the strongest woman I'd ever met." I had always held on to my father's recollections of my mother as a way to make sense of how two people who had been through so much together—a war, nine years of marriage, a vicious divorce—could hardly stand to be in the same room.

But not everyone in my mother's family was sold on her marriage to a white man. One aunt had given my mother a bracelet, made of gold, for a wedding present. "When your marriage fails in America," she told my mother, "sell the bracelet for a plane ticket home." My mother still had the bracelet: hidden in her closet, inside a locked safe.

I put on my running shoes, started jogging down Halibut Point Road, down Katlian Street. By the time I got to the ANB Hall, the hangover started to burn off. The rain felt good on my face, the air fresh in my lungs. As I ran through Indian Village, I saw Paul sitting on a seawall, drinking coffee from a paper cup. He looked groggy from the night before. But I hadn't forgotten my feeling of admiration for him. How heavily the past lived in all of us. At least Paul had the courage to face it down, to give it life.

"Hey, Paul," I said, as I ran past him.

Paul looked up. "Hey." He waved.

I waved back. I kept running.

9. THE HOONAH HOOLIGAN

The arrival of winter brought a wave of new fighters to the gym. Chad, whom I tutored during the school day, showed up a few times with his older brother, Tyler, a senior whom all the girls were crazy about. The boys came from a wealthy fisherman's family and often arrived at school wearing bright white T-shirts that still showed the crisp lines of their mother's ironing. One night, their mother came to watch her sons work out. Tyler—everyone called him Pretty Boy—didn't last a round with Victor and gave up before the sparring even got difficult. Chad, on the other hand, proved everyone wrong: he couldn't box much, but even after the front of his white T-shirt was speckled with blood, he didn't give up, despite the look of horror on his mother's face. Chad never came back to the gym, but every time I saw him walking the hallways of Sitka High, he walked with a little bit more authority.

Another night, a Native boy who'd recently moved south to Sitka from Fairbanks came into the gym, dressed in a pair of blood-spattered white trunks, with his name—JUNIOR—printed across the belt. When Victor asked Junior if he'd ever had a fight, Junior nodded. "I got the silver medal. Second place." All of us—Victor, Roo, Todd, and me, the high school boys—looked at one another, unsure if Junior was joking. Victor spent a few rounds working with Junior on the mitts, but every time Victor tried to push him, Junior would stop punching. He only wanted to spar. Ethan was happy to spar with Junior. For the better part of two rounds, Ethan tagged him with every punch combination he'd ever dreamed of landing on his brother and Richie. Victor let it go on until Junior could barely stand. We never saw him again.

There were also several grown men who came to the gym, interested in fighting at Roughhouse Friday. One night, Richie showed up with a friend of his older brother's named Donny. Donny was about six foot, lean as a sapling, with noodle-like posture and sallow skin. He looked like he'd just crawled out from under a boat. "You ever do any fighting?" Victor asked him. Donny shrugged. "Mostly street fights." Victor showed Donny how to stand, how to use his legs to generate punching power, how to keep his hands up. Then Victor held the heavy bag for him and told him to punch. Donny reached back, whacked the bag a few times, shaking his head menacingly as it swung on its hook. Four punches later, Donny had trouble breathing. "I'm good," Donny said. "I gotta quit smoking." A few weeks later, in the single Roughhouse fight of Donny's career, he showed up to Marlintini's drunk, then pounded a pudgy short white man for three rounds before collecting his money. He'd named himself Donny "Hang 'Em" Lowe because, he said, he had "huge balls."

Another night, Richie brought his cousin to the gym, a former marine named Randy, who had just come back from a combat tour in Afghanistan and was visiting Sitka because he was trying to figure out what to do with his life now that he wasn't a soldier. Randy had the tight jawline, gelled-up short hair, and barbwire biceps tattoos of a bodybuilder. He probably weighed about two fifty and stood well over six feet. Victor worked the mitts with Randy for one round before pausing to call Haag, to tell him to put Randy on the next Roughhouse card—against anyone. In his single fight, Randy dispatched his opponent in about thirty seconds before disappearing with a woman from the crowd.

It was odd to see how fearlessly guys like Donny and Randy came into the gym totally prepared to fight after I had spent weeks unable to make up my mind. It was hard to put a finger on what separated them from me. Perhaps it was a matter of social class: they had spent the past several years of their lives working on a commercial fishing boat or serving in the Marines—two occupations in which physical danger was guaranteed—while I had spent those years wandering around a college campus in brooding detachment. I had often considered that detachment an act of defiance—a way to hold on to something about myself that made me different. Whenever teachers accused me of being cynical or overly philosophical or too deconstructive in my thinking, I held my ground. To buy in, to be positive and hopeful, to engage earnestly and fully with the world, betrayed some precious thing inside me that I didn't want to let go of. Some days, I worried that my loyalty to that precious thing would leave me hollow and lost. For a while, I buried myself in books—lots of French philosophy and literary theory, ancient Buddhist scripture—in an attempt to understand its origins, to give it a name. Entering the temple, I knew now, had been my attempt to trace that thing back to its source. But even the quiet discipline of meditation had not led me any closer to it. The stillness of my breath allowed me to see that thing for what it was, but it did not allow me to tear it apart, to study the pieces, to understand how it was made so that I could rebuild it on my own terms, retool it with proper adjustments for American life.

But now, declaring myself a Roughhouse fighter made me feel, perhaps for the first time since I'd left home, a new certainty about who I was, and how I should spend my time. I showed up to the gym every afternoon without the slightest doubt that what I was doing—training to become a barroom fighter—was of the utmost importance. I began circuits of exercises—a cycle of push-ups, sit-ups, burpees, heavy bag, followed by line work, mitt work, and sparring—as if partaking in the rituals of an ancient culture. It did not strike me as weird that something so arbitrary as stepping into a ring with a stranger for three minutes could be the great organizing principle of my otherwise formless twenties. But I had bought into Victor's story of personal realization through fighting, had seen in Kid Roo an image of total autonomy and self-possession that represented the man I wanted to become. It was so different from where I had been just a year before, when I had left Maine with little notion of where I was headed, lamenting my lack of direction, silently seething with murky feelings of disconnection. Roughhouse Friday gave me a name, a purpose—something, I suppose, to fight for.

The next Roughhouse show was in mid-December. Haag couldn't find an opponent for Roo because no one wanted to fight him; Todd's opponent was still unknown, but there was no shortage of inexperienced lightweights. Haag had decided that I was ready to fight with "the best guy in town": a Southeast Alaskan high school sports legend from the Tlingit village of Hoonah who called himself the Hoonah Hooligan. The Hooligan had already won two fights by knockout, in a small-time start-up show run by Haag's former assistant Jamiann "Hi-Beam" Stevens. Our fight was going to be the big draw, Haag said, because everyone in Southeast Alaska remembered the Hooligan from his decorated career as a wrestling and basketball star. Because the Hooligan was taking classes at the University of Alaska, Haag was publicizing our fight as "Teacher versus Student."

"You don't have to take the fight," Victor said, after explaining all of this. In offering me a way out, he was showing his hand: with just five weeks of training and one fight under my belt, a good argument could be made that I was getting in way over my head.

I asked Victor what he would do.

He paused, took a deep breath through his nose, and nodded to himself. "If you want to be the fuckin' man, I think you gotta fight whoever wants to fight."

■

The Marlintini's barroom sparkled that night: Christmas lights and paper snowflakes hung from the ceiling, and the ring girls—there was a new one, a lean blonde named Gabby—strutted around the canvas in Santa Claus hats. Haag wore a red-sequined tuxedo vest with a matching bow tie and derby, and a big white beard. The Hooligan stood in the middle of the barroom, surrounded by a crowd of men who looked like they might be his brothers or cousins. When the men shifted position, I caught a glimpse of the Hooligan's face. He looked as much like me as anyone I had ever seen: black hair, shaved head, thick eyebrows, and round face. According to Victor, the Hooligan was my height and weight exactly.

"Heard this kid's pretty tough," Victor said.

I watched the Hooligan from across the barroom, tried to get a better look at his body when the men who surrounded him shifted. But all I could see was his face: his eyes staring into space, his brow lowered. He was scowling. Later, I learned that while I was riding pine as a third-string point guard for the Brunswick Dragons JV squad, the Hooligan was averaging 24 points per game for the Hoonah Braves, leading them to what would be remembered by one Southeast Alaskan coach as "the greatest championship game of all time." What he was doing fighting me, in a bar, was his story to tell.

The night got off to a bad start. Todd's opponent hadn't shown up, and the only man who'd volunteered to fight him was the lip-ringed fight doc. Before the bout, the doc kept telling Todd, "I ain't fought since I was a teenager!" but then the doc put on a pair of worn leather boxing shoes and started shadowboxing, and it was clear that he was no rookie. For three rounds, while Todd tried to find his rhythm, the doc kept dancing away, sliding off the ropes, mocking Todd's efforts to hit him. Between rounds, the doc, rather than rest on his stool, made a big show of dancing with the ring girls in his corner, then chasing them off the canvas. The crowd loved the performance, but it rattled Todd's confidence, and he was never able to recover. When Haag announced the decision in the doc's favor, Todd stormed out of the ring. "Fuckin' horrible," he said. "Horrible!" Then he disappeared for the rest of the night.

After Roo's performance in November, no one in Marlintini's was interested in fighting him. But later that evening, a Filipino man named Anthony Manacio III came into the ring—to square off against Sean "the Comeback Kid" Baird—and asked Haag to introduce him as "the man who will beat Kid Roo!" The crowd swooned with interest. Manacio nodded, raised his fist. But then Roo, who was standing ringside, shouted into the ring, "How 'bout now, mate?"—and Manacio changed his mind.

■

"We have a schoolteacher fighting a student! Teacher fighting a student!" As Haag made laps around the ring, trying to rile up the crowd, I stood in my corner with Victor, watching the Hooligan warm up. He jogged backward, threw flurries of short half punches. He wore a Hoonah Braves basketball jersey, black shorts, black sneakers. His legs were lean, with bundles of muscles in his calves—the kind of legs made for quickness. My legs were thick like my father's—good for endurance, but maybe not the best legs for a three-minute Roughhouse fight.

As I watched the Hooligan move, I found myself copying him, embarrassed that I didn't have my own style of preparation. Later, I found out that the Hooligan had been a Division I wrestler in college and had seen this kind of action many times before. I jogged in place, tried to invent an advantage for myself, tried to call up a small beat of confidence. Then I heard the chant. "Hoo! Nah! Hoo! Nah!"—a slow-rising incantation. Then the chant became louder—"Hoo! Nah! Hoo! Nah!"—until the entire barroom was shouting the name of the Hooligan's village. The Hooligan raised his glove: a single black fist that glistened in the neon lights.

Victor, slapping Vaseline on my face, paused. He looked at the Hooligan for a moment, then he looked down at my gloves—puffy and blue, the padding and leather deflated and wrinkled from use. They'd been handed to us by one of Haag's assistants. "We got the wrong gloves," Victor muttered to himself. Then he turned to Haag. "We got the wrong fucking gloves!" Victor shouted. He marched across the ring, inspected the Hooligan's gloves. They were brand-new, the padding taut and hard, the leather shiny. They were sixteen ounces—a full two ounces lighter than mine. On any given punch, such a difference in weight could be the difference between a hard blow and a knockout punch.

I couldn't tell if Hi-Beam or Haag had anything to do with the mix-up, but they acted as confused as Victor. Meanwhile, the crowd, thinking that I was complaining, started booing. Victor pulled off my gloves, called for a new pair. He slid them over my fists, then smacked the padding off my knuckles. "Someone just tried to fuck you over," he said under his breath—I could tell that he'd taken the slight personally. "Now you fuck them up." But in his voice I heard what he was thinking: that to everyone but him and me, my role in this fight was not to win, but to help Haag create his new champion.

Ding. Ding. Ding.

"Hoo! Nah! Hoo! Nah!"

At the time of our fight, all I knew about the village of Hoonah had come from reading John Muir's *Travels in Alaska*, in which Muir chronicles the years he spent exploring the waters of Southeast Alaska with his dog and a missionary sidekick, Samuel Hall Young (an acolyte of Sheldon Jackson's). In the central episode of the book, Muir and Young hire a Tlingit guide from Hoonah to take them north in a canoe, into the sacred fishing waters of Glacier Bay, in bad weather and during the worst time of the year, much to the tearful opposition of the guide's wife. Muir's account of this episode documents not only the rapturous hours he spent frolicking among a meadow of turquoise glaciers, but also his various encounters with noble savages, who often make grandiloquent fireside speeches about their luminous conversions to Christianity. Thirty years later, in the final year of his life, Muir recounted these experiences in a book that would be read by circles of New England intellectuals during the grand age of Arctic exploration. These same readers would go on to become the first wave of steamship passengers to travel to Southeast Alaska as tourists.

"Hoo! Nah! Hoo! Nah!"

The Hooligan came at me so quickly and with so many punches that I could barely keep my eyes open. For most of the first minute, I chased him around the ring, hands out, groping for a clinch, while he slid backward, and away, pummeling my head from above. Even in the chaos, I could hear his fans chanting. In the last seconds before the bell, the Hooligan wound back with a right hand that was intended to knock me out. And yet, the little bit of extra grind on the punch slowed his fist down just enough for me to see it coming. I ducked, felt the Hooligan's fist soaring over my head just as the bell rang.

"What do I do?" I asked Victor between rounds. I hadn't landed a single punch; I hadn't even been able to get my arms around the Hooligan enough to slow him down.

Victor shook his head, as mesmerized by the Hooligan's speed and aggression as I was. "He's a banger. He's a banger." I waited for Victor to offer something else—a game plan, advice, a secret combination—but he was still staring across the ring. "Kid's a fuckin' banger," he said to himself. "A banger."

"Hoo! Nah! Hoo! Nah!" chanted the crowd.

"Schoolteacher versus a student!" Haag barked over the mic. "Teacher! Student!"

Several thousand years ago, the Xunaa.kwan Tlingit had likely settled in this region of Southeast Alaska as descendants of northern Athabaskan people, who had likely migrated into interior Alaska across the Siberian land bridge. After several centuries subsisting in Glacier Bay, the Xunaa.kwan Tlingit resettled on a small horn of land on the south coast of Icy Strait. In the traditional story of the Xunaa.kwan exodus from Glacier Bay, a young girl, in a moment of hubris, taunted a massive glacier. As punishment, the sentient glacier began to advance upon the girl's village. While residents of the village packed their canoes in retreat, the girl's grandmother offered her life to the glacier as settlement for her granddaughter's transgressions. The story captures not only the natural history of Glacier Bay—it is well documented that glaciers did in fact advance in the past three centuries—but also underscores the moral values upon which Xunaa.kwan culture is founded: the danger of hubris, the importance of respect, the virtues of sacrifice and honor in the name of one's family and community. In time, the new Xunaa.kwan settlement separated into subclans—the Wooshkeetaan, Chookaneidi, and Takdeintaan. As Europeans arrived in Hoonah during the decades of the fur trade, they brought with them churches, a post office, and fishing canneries, and for much of the twentieth century, the Xunaa.kwan continued to make their living as fishermen, still harvesting salmon and seal from the bay, which they considered their spiritual grounds of sustenance.

"Hoo! Nah! Hoo! Nah!"

In the second round, the initial shock of the Hooligan's speed had worn off by a few degrees—just enough for me to wrestle him into the ropes after our first exchange. In the clinch, I lifted the Hooligan off his feet and threw him to the canvas. It was less an act of malice than a desperate attempt to assert myself. The crowd booed—I knew they would—and the Hooligan threw up his arms in protest. He wasn't impressed by my dirty tactics, but it was Roughhouse boxing, not prizefighting, and I shrugged at the ref, pretending that I wasn't sure what I'd done wrong. In that little exchange, I discovered the only edge I had in the fight: the Hooligan had much faster hands, better coordination, and was by all accounts a more talented athlete, but I, a bit bulkier in the chest and shoulders, a bit thicker in the legs, was a little stronger.

By the time I returned to my stool after the second round, I was losing the fight on every card, but I no longer felt that the outcome of the fight was inevitable. Victor sponged down my neck and head. He was trying to think of something to say, some bit of advice to offer me. But what I knew remained invisible to even him. "Victor"—I tried to catch my breath—"I'm stronger than he is."

Victor paused. Nodded slowly. "Okay." He squirted water down my throat. "Then you gotta be the more aggressive guy."

Just before the bell, Roo came into my corner. Up to that point, he'd never so much as offered me water, never mind advice. But something that he'd seen in the ring interested him. "Mate," Roo said quietly, "when you get close in like that, don't wrestle with him. You're wasting your strength. When you get close, throw an *appakat*!"

"A what?"

"*Appakat*! Throw an *appakat*! Like this, mate!" Roo dipped his shoulder and raised his fist in a straight upward line, nearly punching himself in the chin. "It's there every time. Trust me, mate. *Appakat*!"

I nodded. It was unlikely that I'd be able to learn a new punch on the fly, never mind against a better opponent. But I told him I'd give it a shot.

"You ain't gonna run out of gas, mate! He is! *Appakat*!"

"Hoo! Nah!"

In the decades prior to 1980, there were roughly 150 fishing permits held by Hoonah fishermen. After 1980, when Glacier Bay was declared a national park, that number dropped to 30. By 2000, Glacier Bay was closed altogether to fishing and hunting—even subsistence hunting done by Tlingit. Unemployment in Hoonah rose to 15 percent, twice the average rate of Alaska. Like many villages in Southeast Alaska, the local Native corporations looked to tourism: Huna Totem Inc., one of the hundred Native corporations created under the Alaska Native Claims Settlement, invested in a cruise-ship port near the old cannery at Point Sophia, with plans to construct a traditionally themed Tlingit village. By then, the number of fishing permits held by Hoonah locals had dwindled to four.

Just as you could trace the journey of the Glacier Bay people from the sin and sacrifice of the young girl and her grandmother, I suppose you could trace the emergence of the national park to John Muir's travels in Alaska. In a 2007 USDA report on the sociocultural effects of tourism in Hoonah and Glacier Bay, one resident said, "Hoonah used to be Glacier Bay. The Feds took it away. They took our food—our strawberries, our seal, our goat, and our seagull. They stopped us from trapping. We should have subsistence in Glacier Bay. We're not going to rape the country." In the same report, a Tlingit interpreter reflected on the meaning of John Muir as "the biggest story for the National Park Service," but considered it a case of "selling white history." One clan leader, who worked as a cultural interpreter in the park, said, "You know what? John Muir was a neurotic and obsessive person who was relentless and demanding. He went to Glacier Bay with two Chookaneidi seal hunters who were his guides. They left him onshore with a dog. They left him there so that he could discover it. After a while, they decided to go back and get him. Because they have respect for all living things, they went back to get him, even though they didn't want to."

"Hoo! Nah! Hoo! Nah!"

I took a volley of punches in the opening seconds, then waited until I felt the weight of the Hooligan's body resting against me. As we came apart, I imitated the motion that Roo had shown me in the corner: dipping my shoulder, digging my fist through the Hooligan's elbows. At the end of my fist, I felt a smooth, clean bolt of connection. When I looked up, the Hooligan stood in front of me, gloves down, confusion on his face, as he stumbled back into the ropes. I was just as perplexed by what had happened and paused before chasing after him with two more lefts. Both punches landed. I kept punching until the Hooligan stumbled forward. We spun across the canvas, into the ropes and then through them, our tangled bodies smashing onto the judges' table. The table tipped forward and the judges cleared out, and while I lay upon the table, pinned under the Hooligan's body, I looked up at several people standing above me. The ring girls had fled, but the Wildflower remained ringside, hands cupped over her mouth, laughing. I wanted to ask her what she saw, if the violence I felt inside me had found its way to the surface. But before I could get an answer, several hands lifted the Hooligan and me back into the ring. Delirious with exhaustion, we smashed together one last time before the final bell.

I drunk-walked back to my corner.

"Now that was a fuckin' fight!" Victor said. "Fucking gnarly!"

"I got hit a lot."

Victor nodded. "You did. You did."

The crowd was still chanting, "Hoo! Nah!"—but now some of the voices seemed to be cheering for me, too.

"Ya worked for that one, mate!" Roo said. "Just like I said! *Appakat!*"

Before the decision, the Hooligan crossed the ring to shake Victor's hand. "Your kid's tough!" The Hooligan turned to me. "Good fight, man."

"Good fight." As I shook his hand, I could tell by the confidence in the Hooligan's grip that he was certain he'd won. Then we stood in the middle of the ring as Haag read the scorecards.

"Twenty-nine to twenty-eight, in favor of the red corner!" Haag shouted.

"Hoo! Nah! Hoo! Nah!"

"Twenty-eight to twenty-nine, in favor of the blue corner, Sitka!"

"Booo!" went the crowd. I didn't blame them.

Haag paused for dramatic effect. "Final card reads . . . twenty-eight to twenty-nine . . . for a fighter from a little town called Siiiiitka, Alaaaaaska, Jade! The Stone! Coffin!"

A deep moan filled the barroom, as several empty Solo cups flipped into the ring. The Hooligan threw his hands up, pushed his way past Haag, appealed to the barroom in protest. The barroom whistled and booed.

I followed the Hooligan back to his corner. "They fucked it up!" I said. "They fucked it up!"

The Hooligan wouldn't hear it. He tore off into the crowd of men waiting in his corner.

"Fuck 'em, mate," Roo said over the noise. "That's the right call. You did what you had to do. Those last fifteen seconds, I reckon. Just like I said: *appakat!*"

But I found it hard to agree with Roo. I had gotten my licks in in the final seconds, but getting beat on like that in the opening rounds had taken something away from me. I could still feel its absence as a shameful hole in my chest.

Victor didn't seem all that convinced either. He just looked at me, shrugged, put his foot on the middle rope to let me out of the ring. As I stepped through the ropes, I felt a hand on my shoulder.

"Jade!" Haag was standing in the corner, his derby tipped back, a sheen of sweat glistening on his forehead. I was expecting him to offer some rationale as to why I'd ended up with the heavier pair of gloves, as to how it had nothing to do with me winning or losing the fight. Even years later, trying to unravel the source of that mystery, I always found myself baffled by my own hypotheticals: that Haag had given me the heavier gloves so that the Hooligan, a more marketable figure than me, would have faster hands and harder punches en route to becoming his new champion. Or that I'd been given the gloves as a decoy, so that Haag had a reason to tell Hi-Beam that her fighter had an advantage, when he'd known all along that he was going to give me the decision to get back at her for starting her own fight show. But all this was just my own speculation; trying to trace Haag's motivations was like trying to capture the whorls of smoke that floated over the fight ring: the moment you saw them one way, they changed shape and went somewhere else. In the Roughhouse world—a world invented on a bar napkin—nothing that happened in the ring was traceable to any one motivation. And that, I would later realize, was exactly why I kept coming back to the ring. Whatever was making me fight was so mercurial, so many-faced, that searching for its cause would always leave me empty-handed.

But that night, in Haag's red face, in the bark-growl of his gravelly voice, I recognized something earnest and honest that made all those theories feel irrelevant.

"Jade Coffin," Haag said, his eyes suddenly clear, "you're going to remember that fight for the rest of your life."

I suppose he was right.

■

I spent the rest of the night camped out in the shadows of the barroom, trying to make sense of how I'd somehow ended up the winner of a fight I'd lost, but mostly hoping to avoid any confrontation with drunk and disappointed fans who wanted to call me out. The Hooligan and his entourage had been kicked out of Marlintini's for making a scene, but I still felt like the villain.

And yet I couldn't deny the thrill of landing my first uppercut, of smashing through the judges' table, of being guided by that wild spirit that carried me through the final round.

As I watched the main event—which featured a heavyweight called Walter "the Showstoppah" Brown, whom Haag introduced as "two hundred pounds of bent steel and sex appeal," and who, before the bell, kicked his legs onto the top rope so that he lay suspended horizontally, one hand under his ear, like a chubby reclining Buddha—I took stock of the Roughhouse world. On the surface, it was a circus of graceless violence, but at least here, in Marlintini's, the hidden violence and rage and anger people felt inside them was being laid bare in the ring—free to swirl across the canvas, to bounce and career off the red, white, and blue ropes, to stutter and flop beneath the naked glow of neon light. I still did not know why I was fighting, but even after a dubious victory, I was beginning to realize that the value of such a question was not in the answer but in the asking. Wrong-size gloves, botched scorecards, suspiciously earnest words of encouragement from Haag—the flawed, sloppy world of Roughhouse Friday was exactly the world I had, in leaving home, been searching for.

Between rounds, as the DJ played "Who Let the Dogs Out?," the Showstoppah got on all fours and chased after the ring girl Paula like an excited puppy. But early in the final round, the Showstoppah took a soft punch to the chin and flopped to the canvas with a heavy thud. There were worse ways to make fifty bucks.

After the fight, Haag led the ring girls through a dance competition. Each girl had about a minute to dance by herself to "You Shook Me All Night Long." Then Haag threw several dollar bills onto the canvas, so that they had to bend over to pick them up. After so much fighting, the crowd loved the performance, and the ring girls—likely drunk by now—seemed to be enjoying themselves. At least I hoped they were. I studied the faces of the women as they danced, watched their eyes as they cheered one another on. Maybe for the ring girls, too, the Roughhouse ring allowed them to forget about their lives outside Marlintini's. Beneath the lights, even beneath the hungry gaze of lonely men who called out to them, the curse of winter disappeared.

■

Before we left Marlintini's, the Hooligan and his entourage came back into the barroom. They were looking for me. I searched for Victor and Roo, but they were already standing by my side.

One of the oldest men held out his hand to Victor. "Good fight, man." Then the man came up to me. "Our boy, he's not in shape right now, see? Over Christmas, we're gonna work on him. He's a wrestler. He's used to diving in." The man motioned a diving action, then straightened himself. "He's gotta learn to stand up and fight. Over Christmas, we're gonna get him trained up. Get him ready."

The Hooligan came forward. He had two beers in his hand. He gave one to me. "Sorry about all that. All my people, they came all this way to watch me fight. They just wanted me to win. They aren't mad at you." Then he looked around the barroom. Behind us, several of the Marlintini's staff were disassembling the fight ring, clearing the dance floor, hanging a disco ball from the ceiling. The men at work, the blinking lights, it all reminded me of watching carnies setting up the bazaar in my hometown every summer.

The Hooligan shrugged. "Everybody in here, they all been saying our fight was the best Roughhouse fight they ever seen."

■

Back at the Travelodge, there was no sign of Todd—just two fist-size holes in the wall above his bed, and a small pile of Sheetrock rubble on the floor. Victor studied the holes, then threw his bag on the ground. "Fuck, Todd." Victor shook his head, looked at me. "Who the hell does he think's gonna pay for this?"

10. BACK EAST

I flew back East for the holidays, but when I landed in Boston, rather than catch a bus home to Maine, I boarded a Greyhound to Vermont. I had not seen my father in over a year. As the bus moved through the snowy foothills of the Green Mountains, I expected that I would feel all the same emotions I had always felt when coming to see him: a mix of nostalgia and familiarity and fondness, a sense of freedom at being under the care of my father, all wrapped up with a quiet longing for a place I had left behind. But as I got off the bus in Burlington, the tight air of winter felt more cruel. When I saw my father standing outside the bus station, he looked vulnerable and cold, an exile stranded in a city where he didn't belong.

"My son," my father said, hugging me. He slapped his hand on the back of my neck. I looked at him, studied his face for my features. Then we got into his car.

As we drove thirty miles north along the highway—past glimpses of the frozen lake, over the long stretch of the sandbar, snowdrifts blowing across the bridge—I told my father about my last fight. He was intrigued by my association with the boxing club, with men like Victor and Roo. As much as my father admired such men, he was not cut from the same cloth. My father often said that the thing he was best at was talking to men—alcoholics, veteran soldiers, adolescent boys—about their feelings. But as we made our way to the Birches, I felt a silence lingering between us, an unspoken question neither of us knew how to ask.

When I arrived at the Birches, I stood in rooms full of stepsiblings, their wives and children, my father and Martha, scrutinizing the terms of our relation. While my father did his best to generate meaningful conversation between the disparate people in his family, Martha busied herself with her usual Christmas routines: baking cookies, making cups of tea, singing along to Joan Baez records while decorating a tree. But now, beneath those charming rituals, I detected a hidden layer of embarrassment, and guilt, and shame. As I watched her, I found myself recalling a Christmas nearly fifteen years earlier, when I had sat with my father and Martha around the tree, each of us revealing what we wanted for Christmas. "I wish we could all be together again," Martha said. She looked at me. "Your mother, too." At the time, the comment had not struck me as all that strange—it was her way of recognizing that I had another life in Maine. But now I heard her speaking those words again, and it occurred to me that not once since that night, and never in all the times that I had come to this house, had my father, Martha, or any of my stepsiblings and I ever spoken about my mother's position in this family. I looked at my stepsiblings; the source of the awkwardness that had existed between us as children now wandered through the living room like a vengeful spirit. Not once in twenty years had any of us ever so much as nodded at its presence.

At night, as I lay awake in a bed I had slept in since I was a boy, I asked myself why I felt so devoted to my father's life in Vermont, so intent on proving to him that the past played no role in the landscape of the present. To recognize the truth of that past would have forced me to rewrite entirely the boyhood fantasy I held of him as a powerful and forthright man. To lose that vision would leave me with no mythology to fill in the blind spots of all the memories I didn't have.

As the headlights of cars speeding down Route 2 moved through my windows and ignited the walls with bright white, the past became alive. My mother had once told me a story about the Christmas after I turned two years old, when my father had come home with two bouquets of flowers: one for my mother, the other for Martha. A month earlier, he'd missed my second birthday, apparently because he had gone with Martha to New Hampshire to see if they were actually in love. During this period, my mother would sometimes call Martha's house in the middle of the night, asking her to send my father home. "He's a grown man," Martha would say. "He can come home when he wants to."

Right outside the window of my bedroom, across the yard and through a stand of cedar trees, was a cemetery where my mother used to park, with me buckled into my car seat, to gaze upon the farmhouse in search of my missing father. For years I had played in that cemetery—stolen American flags from gravestones to use as spears and arrows, raced BMX bicycles around the long gravel loop, played hide-and-seek and kick the can. I looked out at Route 2, at a strip of front yard where my mother used to park her car when she would pick me up from vacations with my father. She never came inside. She never called. She merely waited on the gravel shoulder until I came running out to meet her, a sleeping bag under my arm. I imagined myself on the road, ashamed of the boy I saw, his willingness to play along.

The next morning, my father drove me back to Maine. As we left the Champlain Islands, the snowy horizon of the Green Mountains, once the majestic gates of my father's kingdom, now appeared meek and artificial. Compared to the rugged mountains of Sitka, which rose from the dark waters like monoliths of some craggy broken truth, the lower vision of my father's world whispered to me what I already knew: that the plates of the past were shifting beneath me, and that I was changing, too.

■

It had been twenty years since the first time I'd made the trip between Maine and Vermont. That morning, my mother had driven three hundred miles from the Champlain Islands to Brunswick, in a Dodge Omni, alone, to pick up my paternal grandfather's mint-green F-150 long bed. She then drove the truck back the way she'd come and loaded up the bed with all of our things. I stood on the porch, watching her work, while a man named Joel—the father of a family that lived down the road—helped her tie down the load. Afterward, Joel picked up a piece of rope, coiled it around his elbow. Then he uncoiled the rope and showed me how to do it. For years afterward, whenever I coiled a rope—climbing mountains, working on a fishing boat—I thought with a mix of fondness and rage of Joel guiding me through that process.

In the bench of my grandfather's truck, I sat between my mother and my sister for the next five hours, a bowl of goldfish on my lap. (Their names were Hop and Pop. They would not survive the journey.) Before us, the turnpike glowed with red lights, the day fading to dusk as we arrived at our new home. On the front steps of an unfinished apartment building, beneath a single light, stood my grandfather. He was built like my father: tall, broad, athletic. But the two men were on difficult terms. My grandfather had been an electrical engineer, served on an aircraft carrier in the Sea of Japan during World War II, owned a small house on an island in Casco Bay, which he maintained on his own, with tools from a shop, each drawer of his red Craftsman toolboxes marked in all-capital letters. He'd left my grandmother for his secretary not long after my father returned from Thailand, leaving my father to care for his mother by himself. Even then I sensed that my grandfather's mechanical ability—and my father's lack of it—had something to do with the uneasy terms of their relationship. My grandfather addressed real-world problems—bungled circuits, finicky heating systems—with concrete solutions. He was a man of the Greatest Generation. My father, who could not read a tape measure, brooded over invisible problems with no solutions. He was a man of the Lost Generation of Vietnam. My grandfather admired my mother's work ethic, her old-world toughness. For that reason, when my parents separated, he extended his loyalty to her as if she were his own daughter. We would still pay rent.

That night, I saw concern on my grandfather's face as he spoke to my mother about our new life. The way he moved his hands, as if baffled by their sudden ineptitude, told me that he was worried I might not be okay.

My mother shook her head. "He is a very tough boy. Very tough."

I pretended I hadn't heard her, rolled into the dirt, then sprang to my feet like a ninja—to prove to my father's father that what my mother said was true.

■

That first year, my mother spent her free time driving confused loops around southern Maine, trying to make sense of our new life. She did not know how to read a map, so navigated the town by our proximity to the Androscoggin River.

She did her best to celebrate our new life. My first birthday in Brunswick, my mother arrived at my preschool in a clown costume—a striped one-piece she'd sewn herself—and a rainbow-colored wig, and full face paint. On the Fourth of July, our first since leaving the Champlain Islands, she wrapped my Knight Rider bike in red, white, and blue crepe paper, and we rode around Main Street, an empty, sleepy strip with no parade. Sometimes she brought me to McDonald's, with a friend, to eat Happy Meals on the playground; other times we had picnics on the banks of the

Androscoggin, beneath a steel footbridge, in the shadow of a derelict mill, where we swam in the foamy brown water of upstream runoff. It was impossible to separate my memories of my mother on those afternoons, wading in the shallows, her skirt hitched up past her knees, from memories of her in her village, wading in the canal where her family washed their dishes and clothes. We went often to the Maine Mall, some thirty miles away, in Portland, the first city she had lived in upon arriving in the United States. She always drove with music on; we listened to a lot of Wham! on the way there, spent the afternoons wandering around department stores and snacking in the food court, then drove home at night, past the lonely lights of hotels and apartment buildings, singing along to Lionel Richie. My mother's favorite song was "Stuck on You." I knew the lyrics by heart, but the chorus confused me: The man singing, was he leaving on a train? Coming back? Who was stuck on whom? And what had caused him to leave?

I have a single memory of my mother expressing the anger she hid from me and my sister during those first years. It was winter—cold outside, already dark. For some reason, we had returned to Vermont for a single night—perhaps to retrieve something we had left behind. Our old house was being rented to someone else, and we were staying at the home of a neighbor down the street. My father had gotten wind of our return and came to the door. "Let me see my children," he said, through a small opening. My mother shook her head, pushed the door closed. "Let me see my children!" he said, forcing the door back open. From the living room, I watched them battle: my father's massive form—six one, 220 pounds—against my mother—a foot shorter, half his weight. Her face became violent, seething. She screamed nonsense—maybe something in Thai. Then she squatted, and with a final thrust, the door slammed shut. Through the window, I saw my father's face. He looked sad and pitiful as he shook his head, plumes of breath rising up around him. Then he turned away and disappeared into the night. Minutes later, my mother, tears in her eyes, came to my sister and me, unrolled our sleeping bags on the floor. She seemed to be both laughing and crying. "Okay," she said, as if to herself. "Go to sleep now."

Otherwise, my mother somehow maintained an impossible gentleness toward the world. One afternoon, my sister and I found a wounded pigeon in the driveway of our apartment building. It hobbled uselessly in the sunlight, its eyes still, determined to move forward in some arbitrary direction, if for no other reason than to prove to itself that it was still alive. The trail of blood left behind on the pavement was as bright a red as I had ever seen. A dead pigeon was no major loss, but my sister and I could not bear to see the bird die, so we woke my mother from her afternoon nap—a sin, we knew—to show her what we had found.

My mother shuffled out of her room. Blinked several times, then inspected the pigeon groggily. "Oh, the sweetheart," she said, squatting next to it. She went inside, came out with a shoebox and a small towel, gathered the pigeon in her hands, and placed it inside the box. Then she went back to sleep. For the next hour, my sister and I watched the bird die. Even as it bled out in the box, its eyes did not blink. A part of me wanted to see the pigeon suffer, to show in great detail the full range of its pain, to reveal to me, finally, the brokenness of its spirit—but the bird didn't flinch.

■

Slowly, my mother made progress. She bought a car—an unreliable red Ford Escort, a model recommended by my father—and we moved to a proud colonial in the old college neighborhood of town, a short walk from the elementary schools and the hospital. There were pillars out in front; the garage had a basketball hoop. For the next several years, in the hours before the night shift, my mother stayed up sanding the floors, wallpapering all the rooms.

Then she got rid of the Escort and bought a used Volvo—an inde-structible emblem of the middle class. On nights when our baby-sitters didn't show, my mother brought my sister and me to the hospital, laid out our sleeping bags on the floor of a conference room, and woke us up the next morning in time to drop us off at school. Sometimes, at night, my mother played a game with me in which she would close her eyes, clasp her hands together, and challenge me to pull them apart. She told me that she would en-vision a steel bridge and insist that as long as the image of that bridge endured, she would never lose. I laughed at her—what a silly idea, such a small woman professing such physical strength—but she was right: no matter how hard I tried to pull her hands apart, her will was iron.

In 1987, the year I turned eight, my parents finalized the terms of their divorce. In the division of assets and custody, my father got a 1985 Triumph motorcycle, a rental home next door to our former home, and visitation rights every other weekend. Once a month, he sent me into our house with child support checks for about eight hundred dollars. In addition to this money, he was obliged to pay half the price of our trips to Thailand every two years. My mother's side of the deal: our old house in Vermont, and all the possessions of my parents' former life, with particular stip-ulation, in writing, for "elephant tusks" and "gold jewelry."

■

As I arrived back in Maine, my mother's home looked less like a place of origin than a vault: rectilinear and cold, unadorned and overly simple. And the vision of my mother, now having occupied the home for nearly as long as she'd ever lived in Thailand, only made her solitude more stark. As soon as it was dark, I fled to a bar with my high school buddies, drinking and smoking and carry-ing on until two or three in the morning, when we stumbled down the sidewalks of our past to the neighborhood where we'd all grown up. I was glad to be home, proud to brag to kids I'd gone to high school with that, yes, the rumors were true, I was a barroom boxer in Alaska. In many ways, telling that story justified a missing variable in my life, clarified an unspoken recognition that the story of my family was different, and that out of that story something beautiful—and dangerous—might grow. Even girls I'd known since kindergarten regarded me with tender caution: hands on my cheeks, they said, "But your poor face . . . ," in a way that made me feel like a soldier coming home from war.

But no matter how banged up I'd gotten at the bar the night before, I still managed to get up and run every morning, to keep up with sets of push-ups and sit-ups. Eventually, when I showed my buddies the tapes of me fighting at Marlintini's, they cracked jokes about how shitty the fights were and how clumsy my style was, but I could tell they were afraid of what they saw in the barroom, stunned by what they saw in the ring. All but one of my friends was white; they knew, without us ever talking about it, that when I came back from Thailand as a boy, I had seen things—dead puppies in the street, the open-air cremation of my grandfather, the poverty of rural Southeast Asia—that existed far beyond the limits of what we experienced in small-town Maine. Fighting filled in that difference, in a way that no explanation, no language, ever could. Fighting told its own story: that no matter how murky my origins, no matter how unspoken my past, my journey to this town was driven by forces that they would never understand.

Eventually, after some goading, I convinced my friends to give me rounds inside a ring that we made by clearing the snow off a friend's back deck, using laundry line and chairs as the ropes and corners. My buddies were mostly working office jobs in cities, where they had to wear suits and stare at computer screens all day, so it wasn't hard to line them up, four or five in a row, and beat on them until they could barely stand. Half consciously, I suppose I was re-creating in my own life the stories Victor had told me about his fighting past: sparring with his buddies in his father's machine shop, driven by a desire to be more than just another Native kid who slipped through the cracks. And yet, after a few afternoons of backyard brawling, my buddies started to look back at me with their heads cocked sideways. "We done?" I asked several times when, after an hour or two of sparring, when everyone had gone inside to watch football, I stood on the porch, glaring through the window into the living room, finally catching the image of myself in the glass: standing alone on a deck, drenched in sweat, steam rising off my shoulders, looking for someone to fight.

As for my mother: I didn't see much of her that December. I spent Christmas Day as I'd spent many Christmases: running on the beach—a seven-mile jog along pitch-pine forests, buffered to the south by the open ocean. When she came home that night, we sat on the couch together and I showed her a video of my fights. My mother was embarrassed by what she saw, but also intrigued. "Hmm . . . ," she said, over and over. Dismissively at first, as if seeing me fight in a ring was no better than having me go back to Thailand to work in a rice field, and then with an undertone of curiosity. I knew that the uncompromising, unsurrendering self that had found the strength to remain in America understood what I was searching for in that ring. But like many other things during that period of my life, we passed over such matters in silence.

I went upstairs to my room, waited for my friends to come by so we could go out drinking again. But I could still feel her presence in the air. The tension between my mother and me—as mother and son, as two people committed to a life that had befallen us somewhat by accident—seemed only to emphasize how powerfully alone we were in this country, how little else was keeping us here besides each other.

II. REDEEM

The middle of winter was a bleak time for my students. It was dark when they arrived in the morning and dark when they left, and most days it rained so hard that you could hear it beating on the roof. Because my classroom had no windows, my students and I sometimes didn't see one another by the light of day for several days in a row—just by the bright neon glow of the ceiling lamps, which seemed to make their vulnerabilities all the more apparent. Like any teenagers, they were always so sleepy, so hungry, so gloomy. But I also sensed that some other force was at work, even beyond the visible difficulties—divorce, alcoholism, financial stress—of their complicated lives at home. Something else was holding them down, something that, I felt, if I could just dig deep enough, I might be able to understand. Meanwhile, my job was to convince these young people that they should do their homework: solve algebraic equations for empty variables; conjugate Spanish verbs that they would likely never use; write papers about English dramas that took place hundreds of years ago, in kingdoms they would never visit, detailing experiences they would never have. It was a hard sell.

Many of my students had gotten into the daily routine of eating lunch in my room, so that some days I had a dozen or more students sitting at desk tables. At first I made my room available to only the students I worked with directly—Peter and Donna, Danny and Nathan, Carrie—but then these students started inviting their friends in, and soon their friends invited their friends, and before I knew it there were thirty kids sprawled out across the floor like they were staging a sit-in. Donna asked me if she could bring in a CD player, so that she could listen to music—a favorite song that year was the Petey Pablo single with that "Take your shirt off, twist it round yo hand / Spin it like a helicopter!" refrain—and eventually the kids started to mess with the controls for the black curtain that hung over the drill team's practice mirror. Then they figured out how to turn the red, blue, and green lights on. Soon, for thirty minutes a day, my room was transformed into a stage, upon which they could perform better versions of themselves.

Many days, and often without knowing it, I gazed across my classroom, watching my students perform, looking for a version of myself. At fifteen, I had been a small boy, clothed in the hybrid rap-grunge wardrobe of the mid-nineties: baggy flannel and denim, and basketball sneakers. I was always sleepy, always hungry, always horny. I played on sports teams every season (soccer, basketball, baseball), and my heroes were either athletes (Jordan, Nomar Garciaparra) or music icons (Eddie Vedder, Snoop). I spent my days with my buddies, riding bikes around the trails and woods beyond town, to abandoned quarries, exploring old mills full of rusted-out machines. I also spent a great deal of time in front of the mirror, with my shirt off, examining my muscles, willing them to get bigger.

By my junior year of high school, the muted preteen detachment I held toward the world gathered into something more coherent and cynical. On weekends I began taking longer walks in the woods, wandering through networks of ravines and blueberry fields, a blanket roll over my shoulder, imagining myself a modern Kwai Chang Caine, or a Navajo scout. While many of my friends had started smoking weed and fading strangely inward, I was in search of something more important, an idea I sometimes called "truth," which I'd read about in my English class, while studying Thoreau and Emerson. I often sat in the back of chemistry drawing chiseled cyborg angels in my notebook, their metal wings spread wide as they ascended through the clouds. I spent long periods in art class painting overly muscled men bound in chains, breaking free from some vague spiritual imprisonment. My art teacher would sometimes look over my shoulder at my portraits of hyper-muscular, somewhat sexually charged heroes and utter, "Mmmm . . . interesting," before reminding me that the assignment was to paint a bowl of fruit. But even my still lifes came out too dark and too bold, the outline of shapes too heavy, the colors smudged in all the places where I'd pressed too hard.

My father, sensing that a change was taking place, started sending me audiocassettes of lectures on masculinity: *Men and the Life of Desire. Iron John: A Book About Men. The Naive Male. Rediscovering Masculine Potentials*. I listened to the tapes at night, while blowing off homework. The lectures were long, full of song and drumbeat and storytelling, told by middle-aged white men who spoke like they were addressing not an auditorium but a tribe of warriors in a cave. I did not really understand what the lectures were about, but over the phone, my father helped me focus on the simple ideas: the importance of "showing my sword," as a metaphor for revealing my strength; the importance of entering the forest, as a symbol of the unknown. We discussed at length the meaning of the wild man who lives in the bottom of the lake in the *Iron John* story. The young boy's great head of golden hair—that was his masculine potential. It was exhilarating stuff, sometimes difficult to apply to my life in small-town Maine, but between my father and me we developed a code of manhood that felt all our own.

The most important lesson of all, however, was "stealing the key from my mother's pillow." The key could unlock the cage of the forbidden wild man. I understood such a metaphor as an elevated form of cutting the apron strings, a way of turning away from my mother and toward my father. Even metaphorically, I didn't really understand the idea: my mother worked, a lot, and after ten o'clock at night, I was free to leave the house, wander town until 7:00 a.m., when she came back home. I spent entire days with my buddies—from first light to sundown—riding bikes down forgotten logging roads, cooking hot dogs over fires on the banks of hidden streams. When my mother asked what I'd been up to, I could just shrug and mutter, "Nothing," without further interrogation. And yet, slowly, my father's urgings began to influence the way I observed my mother. All the things that had been necessary to her survival in this town—her relentless work ethic, her furious obsession with financial security, her careful curating of all the various emblems of the New England middle class—disgusted me. While I was blasting Nirvana, rapping along with Warren G, I was trying to send my mother a message: that all the sacrifices she had made in my name were useless to the American life I planned to live. Robert Bly, my father told me, had a name for my rebellion: "laying in the ashes."

The morning of my high school graduation, my mother and father took me out to breakfast. Dressed in a poorly fitting suit jacket and necktie, acne faced and sleepy, I sat with my parents at a small table, surrounded by other families. My sister was overseas, and without her there to roll eyes with, I sat between my parents in a fuming silence. They'd learned not to argue, which only meant that they didn't talk. Before we paid the bill, my father cleared his throat, told me that he wanted to read me a poem he'd written. The poem ran ten pages of yellow legal pad, was a long confession about the joy of raising me, of watching me come into the world, of bearing witness to my evolution as a young man. Midway through his reading—by then, nearly every stoic Mainer in the restaurant was eavesdropping on his performance—he burst into tears: long sobs and barely controlled weeping. He continued reading, right to the last page. When he was done, he put his hand on my shoulder. "I love you, my son."

My mother scoffed. She called the waitress over and paid the bill while my father continued to cry. "Jesus Christ, Jonathan," she finally said. "Enough."

As a graduation gift, my father presented me with a book: *The Hero with a Thousand Faces* by Joseph Campbell, which outlined in specific detail the journey a young hero must take to discover his purpose in life. He inscribed the book with a letter, explaining how he'd discovered Campbell's writing "in a very lonely and wild time in my life" and how it "gave me a place. I hope and believe you will not only find a place, but also a star to seek. My love to you." I spent the entire summer reading *The Hero with a Thousand Faces*, taking notes on all the various stages—departure, refusal, and the ultimate boon, return—of my imminent manhood. Not once that summer did I pause to consider what my father had been referring to as the "very lonely and wild time" in his life; not once did I wonder why his story included no return.

■

After my school day was over, I always had a couple of hours to burn before my evening training session. But now, the middle of January, it was too dark to do anything outside, so I spent all my time reading. I read with a newfound patience, a searing intensity, as if under a spell. I read more books that single winter than I had read in the past four years of college. Even now, I can recall not only every book I read, but where I was in my apartment—couch, table, floor—when I read certain passages. My purpose in reading came from some primal place that was neither academic nor for entertainment. I had often been told that the point of reading was to take you away from your own reality, to create a universe into which you could disappear. But I was not reading to escape.

Murakami's *Norwegian Wood. A Heartbreaking Work of Staggering Genius* and *You Shall Know Our Velocity!* by Dave Eggers. *For Whom the Bell Tolls, The Complete Short Stories, A Farewell to Arms*, by Hemingway. *Cannery Row* and *The Long Valley* by Steinbeck. *The Sound of Waves* by Mishima. Whitman's *Complete Poems*—"Song of Myself" and "A Noiseless Patient Spider." Jack London's *Martin Eden. The Unbearable Lightness of Being* by Kundera. I underlined passages that moved me, dog-eared pages that spoke to feelings I had within me but couldn't express, scribbled stars and notes to myself beside sections that felt as if they'd been lifted directly from my mind. I would never feel so deeply connected to books ever again, but at that point in my life, when I felt as though the world I knew offered me no models of how a person like me could exist, I read books as if I were pressing their pages against the rough form of my body, grafting their meaning onto my own emerging story.

Then one afternoon, I was sifting through a box of discarded magazines when I found a short story called "What You Pawn I Will Redeem," by Sherman Alexie, in a tattered *New Yorker*. I had never read anything by Alexie. I had never heard of him. I knew only that the way he talked about his cultural past—as a Spokane man—was frank and clear, light and heavy at the same time. Jackson Jackson, the protagonist of the story, had found in a pawnshop a blanket that had once belonged to his grandmother. He tried to buy it, but ended up spending all the money he hustled up on alcohol. Finally, the pawnshop owner gave him the blanket and that was that. To celebrate his spiritual victory, Jackson Jackson began to dance. But as I read the final lines, I looked up from the page, some fundamental insight unfurling inside my head. The world seemed on the verge of showing me something that my mind was unable to comprehend.

The only stories I had read about Native experience, mostly passed down to me from my father, were written by men pretending to be Native. I remember sitting around a woodstove as my father read Forrest Carter's *Education of Little Tree* out loud, all of us wiping tears from our eyes in the final chapters (we had wept the same way at the end of *Dances with Wolves*). Shortly after that, my father gave me a copy of *Watch for Me on the Mountain*, also by Carter, about the Apache warrior Geronimo. ("Geronimo was a great man of his people," my father wrote on the first page. "I hope that you, too, can become a great man of your people.") Witnessing the tragic loss of another person's culture had become an empathic form of cathartic entertainment. For Christmas one year, I had even given my father a framed drawing of an Indian man in a headdress, shooting an arrow at a full moon.

I spent the rest of the afternoon reading back through the story of Jackson Jackson, searching for some minor detail to illuminate what I was feeling—to reveal to me what, exactly, had been pawned and what, now, demanded redemption. As I rode down HPR, along the harbor, down Katlian Street and through Indian Village, I looked into the foggy windows of the old clan houses, studied the mint-green facade of the ANB Hall, pedaling along the narrow street in search of an answer. But I was too concerned with the world in front of me to recognize that what I was looking for had nothing at all to do with the Native people of Alaska. Their stories were their own; I, like so many Americans, was borrowing their story to illuminate the absence of my own. The Indian stories of my father—stories that, even after learning that they were false, I would still, in some irrational and emotionally confused way, continue to believe—were the surrogate creation myths of his American experience. That winter, I read in search of my own.

■

It was good to be back in the gym: working out with Victor and Roo and the high school boys got me out of my own head, made me feel like I had a place to be. Focusing on my next fight gave each month its own shape, each week its own purpose. Typically, I took it pretty light for the first week after a fight, to lick any wounds and give myself time to recover. Then I dug in during the middle two weeks, sparring extra rounds, doubling up on sets of push-ups and sit-ups, sprinting by telephone poles as I ran home from the gym each night.

There was still no sign of Todd: after he'd punched two holes in the wall of the Travelodge, he'd apparently decided he needed a break from boxing and found work on a rockfishing boat for most of January. Haag had told Victor that it was going to cost three hundred dollars to fix the holes but had offered to let Todd fight off his debt—two wins, Victor said, and they'd be square. But Todd wasn't interested and, I suppose as a matter of pride, wanted to pay Haag back with fishing money instead. Victor wasn't convinced: "I've known Todd for a long time, and the day he gets back to town he'll blow all that fishing money on drugs." But I could tell that what disappointed Victor the most about Todd's absence was that he had walked away from the relationship they'd developed as fighter and trainer. This told me something important about Victor's devotion to his fighters, a group I could now lay claim to: that once you stepped into a ring under Victor's guidance, his loyalty remained unbending.

The first week back in the gym, Haag came to town to visit his mother and had told Victor he'd stop by during practice. I was still uneasy about having won a fight that four hundred people thought I'd lost. Victor had tried to convince me that boxing was a judged sport, and that the fight was close enough to go either way, but somehow I still felt that I was to blame for the Hooligan's loss. Or else that Haag was to blame, and that I had taken the brunt of his error.

I was working the heavy bag when Haag marched through the door in a bright red NASCAR jacket, his derby on his head, his arms full of duffel bags and boxes. Inside the boxes were brand-new boxing uniforms, blue and white and black Adidas tanks and trunks adorned with a Sitka Boxing Club logo. The bags were full of new sparring gloves and helmets, the padding crisp and the leather shiny. Haag's mother, Frankie, had bought the equipment for the high school boys, so that they could look decent in the Fairbanks tournament that March. But Haag also wanted Todd and Roo and me to wear the trunks in the Roughhouse ring because Haag liked to build up rivalries between towns and figured that the more we labeled ourselves Sitka fighters, the more the Juneau fans would come to Marlintini's to see us lose.

While Victor talked with Haag in the corner, I pretended to work the heavy bag while trying to listen to their conversation. During a break, Haag pulled me aside. "Now, Jade, what I'm going to do is, I'm gonna give you a chance to make up for that fight. See, I got a lot of people looking forward to seeing a rematch between you and the Hooligan. I got a lot of people think you lost that fight. I'm gonna give you a chance to *redeem* yourself, Jade, prove to them what kind of fighter you really are. I think you can win that fight fair and square, Jade, no two ways. I really think you can. I think what I'm going to do is have a little tournament between you two, see if we can't figure out who's the *toughest guy*. The teacher or the student, student or the teacher. Jade, I got a lot of people wanting to know. Lot of people, Jade. That's just how boxing fans are. They want to know certain things, and I seen the way you two were getting at each other, and I was thinking the same thing: 'I just want to know.'"

The beeper sounded and I got back to work. Haag nodded and stepped away. Out of Marlintini's, without the lights and the ring to elevate him, without the tuxedo and the ring girls and all his drunken fans, Haag was just a little man who talked too much.

A few days before my fight, I showed up to the gym early, only to find Victor dressed in full boxing gear. He was wearing boxing shoes, laced up high, shorts with THE SAVAGE across the waist. He wanted to spar.

"You all right?" I said.

Victor shrugged. "Miranda ain't doing so well."

I didn't ask any questions—I was awkward in this kind of exchange, but also wasn't sure how much Victor wanted to share with me.

"Got out of work, was losing my mind. Got home, grabbed my old gear, and came right to the gym. I needed to fight."

He tapped the beeper. We circled for several rounds. Typically when Victor and I sparred, he built his power over time. When he hit me too hard, he'd lay off. But this time, he pounded me. He was quick and slick, and after several minutes I was bloodied. I felt an obligation to take the beating, to stay in front of him. It was the language of what pain I should have absorbed through talking. "Thanks, man. I needed that."

On our way downstairs, Victor had something on his mind. He took a deep breath. "Over the holidays, Miranda had some health stuff. She's been dealing with it since we had a baby. We have to go to Seattle for some tests." Victor was sure it was nothing. "I'm so sorry, man. I talked to Roo. He'll go over with you." I told Victor not to worry about it—if I couldn't go into a ring and win a fight on my own, then I probably didn't deserve to be in the ring in the first place. Victor nodded in agreement, but I could tell that he was disappointed to miss my fight, that in some way developing a fighter was a surrogate for fighting himself. On our way out of the gym, he held up his fist. "Hey, Jade. Crush skulls, steal souls."

I held up my fist. "Crush skulls, steal souls."

∎

I was wearing the new blue Adidas trunks that Haag had bought for our club. It was no small thing to enter the ring with Sitka's name on my uniform. With Todd gone, and Roo unable to find an opponent, I was the sole representative of my new town, and I had never felt so proud to be from somewhere as I did in Marlintini's that night. I remembered the morning of my first fight, the way the man in line at the airport had told me to kick some ass for Sitka, how I'd felt like such a fake, a poser when promising him I would. Tonight, I felt none of that doubt.

I came out in the first round much too confident. When the bell rang, I started circling the way I'd seen Ali do in old fights: hands low, ripping jabs off his front foot, slipping punches by leaning backward. It was a great approach for a fighter with hand speed and otherworldly talent—all things that I lacked severely. When the Hooligan saw how open my defense was, he stepped in and hit me in the neck, right above my collarbone, twice. I fell back into the ropes and shelled up, and he hit me twice more in the chest. Then he hit me in the head: three fast punches. But I stayed calm in the flurry, and when I felt the Hooligan's punches fading, I grabbed him around the shoulders and pushed him into a corner and unloaded a flurry of my own shots. I kept punching until we fell into a clinch. Behind us, sitting outside the ropes, the Wildflower and the other ring girls were cheering us on. I knew I was in control of the fight, and I wanted to look good in front of them, so I tried to stay calm and look cool when I should have kept attacking the Hooligan like a rabid dog.

"You had me worried, mate," Roo said, sponging my neck. "I thought we was losing you after that first flurry. Ya got to keep your hands up. None of that dancing around shit. *Appakats*. He likes to dive in. I'm telling ya, mate. *Appakats*. They're wide fahkin' open."

Over the next two rounds, the Hooligan's punches lost their pop. When he dove in low, I tried to hit him with uppercuts. Haag kept shouting, "The teacher! The student! The teacher! The student!" But the fight wasn't as good as the first one. The crowd wasn't chanting "Hoo! Nah! Hoo! Nah!" The Hooligan's entourage was gone. When the final bell rang, the Hooligan was huffing in his corner, his elbows on the ropes. He looked exhausted, alone. In just thirty days, we'd traded places: I had the advantage, and the Hooligan looked like someone who'd shown up at Marlintini's by accident. By my estimation, I had myself winning on all three cards, three rounds to none.

"The winner!" Haag shouted, as we stood in the middle of the ring. "From a little town called Hoonah, Alaska! . . ."

The crowd booed. I looked at the Hooligan.

"Crazy." He was laughing. "You won that fight. I won the last one, but you won this one."

We shook hands and went back to our corners. I expected Roo to be as surprised as I was, but he just shrugged. "I reckon it was that first round that got you. Could have done more. Can't leave it to the judges. But that's boxing, mate."

■

The ring came down. The disco ball went up, and women from the crowd danced onto the floor with drinks in their hands. I sat at a table with Roo and Nicole, who'd flown over with Roo so they could spend the weekend in Juneau. They were clearly in love. Roo flirted with women in the crowd, Nicole laughing, secure in his loyalty. Maybe I was just drunk, but I was sure that whatever existed between them was better than anything I had ever known.

Every few minutes, someone from the crowd came up to me, shook my hand, said he'd been pulling for me, said that he felt I'd won. Most of the fans were drunk, but it still felt good to have their confidence. Then a small old Native man came up to me, spoke in a voice so quiet I could barely hear him. He was spinning his hands at his side. He looked so much like one of the old men in my mother's village that I was almost sure that we had met before. "You gotta jump rope more," he said, skipping.

"Thanks."

He nodded. "Jump rope." Then he wandered back into the crowd.

Then Haag came over. He was sweating, worried, his hat tilted far back on his head. "Very close fight, Jade! Very close fight! Could have gone either way! Lot of people saying it was right down the middle. Right down the middle, Jade." He chattered on for several minutes about all the plans he had for my next opponents, how I was the best fighter he'd had, how I reminded him of the Goat, how having a trainer like Victor Littlefield was gonna be the best thing that'd ever happened to me. Then he took a wad of cash out of his pocket, put it in my hands. "Jade Coffin, you deserve that money. I like to say, you *fought* for that money. And now what I'm going to do, Jade, is I'm gonna give you two a chance to settle the score. I know a lot of people in this barroom who just want to know who's gonna win that third fight. It's going to be a real old-fashioned *rivalry*. Just like in the old days. A real crosstown rivalry. A backyard brawl. Toughest guy from one town, against the toughest from another town. You ever heard of Hell's Kitchen, Jade? I never been there, but back in the old days, guys like Jake LaMotta, Tony Zale . . ." Haag kept talking about the rivalry for a while longer before fading into the crowd. I slipped the folds of bills into the waistband of my trunks. It was a strange world—where the fights you won were the fights you lost, where the fights you lost were the fights you won, where redemption had nothing to do with winning. I could feel the alcohol making me philosophical, softening the edges of defeat. You won some, you lost some. Everything you got was paid for in some way. It was a good world to buy in.

Then from across the dance floor I saw three women looking toward our table. One of them was the ring girl Paula. She'd changed out of her bikini and was wearing a blouse with a rose on it. She walked over by herself and leaned forward, her hair falling onto my shoulder, a faint smell of perfume. "My friend, she wants to talk to you." Paula pointed across the barroom. "She wants me to introduce you, but she's shy."

The girl was hiding behind several other women, pretending not to watch.

I looked at Paula. "What if I like you?" The words just came out. I never talked that way to women—so directly, so honestly. I usually coded my desire in all sorts of indifferent posturing that rarely made its way to the surface.

Paula stepped back. She had a drink in her hand. "No! My friend! She will be mad at me! She will think I tried to steal you!" Paula was drunk, too. She looked at her friend. She looked at me. "You want to dance with me?"

Paula knew what she was doing. Once a week, she taught Latin dance at Marlintini's Salsa Thursdays. I bought us another round of drinks. It felt good to be with someone, to have another person next to me. My basement apartment felt miles away. Sitka felt miles away. My life back East was just a dream. Even the fact that I'd lost my fight seemed irrelevant now. I'd blown the extra cash Haag gave me on drinks—all of it.

After last call, Paula and I walked out into the parking lot together, arm in arm. The night was clean, silent—the stars bright, the air fresh in my lungs. After all the noise of the barroom, the world suddenly felt peaceful and still. On our way into the Travelodge, while we were waiting for the elevator, Paula saw the swimming pool. She was laughing. "I want to swim." She opened the door to the pool and began undressing. Then we went into the elevator, and when we entered my room, she fell onto the bed and was still laughing, as if everything—the fights and the dancing and the darkness—were all just a big joke.

■

I woke to pale light seeping through the blinds, the air in the hotel room dense and stale. Paula was still asleep. I got out of bed and opened the shades, then opened the window to let the cool air in. I stood at the window for a while. In the distance the bases of the mountains spread out under the clouds. In the muted daylight Marlintini's was cloaked in the same ashen pallor. I stared at Paula for a moment. It made me sad to see her there, lying in a hotel bed, her shiny black hair splayed out across her pillow. I didn't know the first thing about her. She didn't know the first thing about me. Several hours earlier, drunk and buzzing with the energy of the night, none of that had made a difference. But in the daylight, the strangeness of Paula in an empty bed made me feel lonelier than waking up in a room by myself.

The single piece of advice my father had always given me about how to treat women was "Remember, that's somebody's little girl." It was a strange bit of wisdom. My father's intention, I think, was to remind me that every woman I interacted with had once been a child. Had been loved like a child. Had come into the world innocent and beautiful, and that her parents had loved her with all the hopes of what a good life might bring.

Yet it had been entirely lost on me that, by this logic, the reason I should treat women with respect was out of honor for the father. That a man should honor another man.

My grandfather, my *khundtha*, was as good and as honest a man as I knew. He had trusted my father to bring his daughter to a different country. He had trusted that my father would treat his daughter, once there, with the kind of respect and loyalty she deserved. That my father had betrayed that trust entirely was only exacerbated by his never having had to face my grandfather, to explain to him what he had done. The two men lived thousands of miles apart. They did not speak the same language. They came from profoundly different worlds. My mother, perhaps as a point of dignity and pride, had concealed her divorce from her family, at least, as far as I knew, until her father died. But that had never stopped me from imagining a meeting between those two men, in which my *khundtha*, sitting on a wooden bench next to a canal, scrutinized my father. I could even see the smooth mahogany skin of his ancient face crinkling as he searched for evidence of the better man he'd mistaken my father for.

I woke up Paula. She rolled over and groaned. "I have a headache."

I wanted to say something back—something decent, something kind, something to tell her that, outside of Marlintini's, I understood that she had her own life, was more than just a ring girl, just as I was more than just a fighter—but I only felt guilt. Guilt that she had bought into a version of me that was false, and that this false self had invited her back to a hotel room. I looked at the clock. "I have to catch my flight."

Paula nodded. She dressed in the corner, then called a friend for a ride home. We walked downstairs to the lobby together, trying to make conversation. But we had nothing to talk about. I stood with her outside in the parking lot until a car pulled up. Paula got in. I watched the car disappear onto the Glacier Highway, then I went back up to my room.

She was somebody's little girl, too. As if that had ever made a difference.

12. THE BANANA

"Losing fucking sucks," Victor said, my first night back in the gym. "First time I lost a fight, I went back to my hotel room and cried. Good thing Miranda was there, else I would have gone out and embarrassed myself in front of all my friends." I could tell that he felt my first loss was partly his fault for not being in my corner. I refrained from telling Victor about spending the night with Paula; I didn't want him to think that I was the kind of person who had one-night stands. As much as I would have bragged about it to my friends, Victor held himself with a level of dignity that made such bragging come off as shallow. He had a wife and a child at home. Instead, I told him that Haag had given me an extra hundred bucks after losing the fight, and that a lot of people had actually felt that I'd won. But Victor wasn't convinced: "When you go to someone else's town, you can't leave it up to the judges."

To make sure that I wouldn't lose again, we doubled down on training. We had decided that my most powerful punch could be a left hand to the body—basically an uppercut to the lower ribs—the same punch Victor had depended on. We practiced the punch over and over, Victor passing a right hand over my head, me using the rising motion of my legs to generate power. At night, I repeated the motions in my apartment. I threw the punch at school between periods and practiced the motion while riding my bike no-handed down the hill on Monastery Street. Slip, dip, up, and bang! In reality, to put together this kind of combination with any precision, in the real time of a fight, was so far beyond my ability that practicing it was probably useless.

After practice, I sometimes spent my evenings watching a box full of old fights Roo had loaned me. He wasn't totally sold on Victor's approach to fighting—it was too aggressive, too rowdy, not technical enough, too Roughhouse—and Roo said that I'd learn just as much watching professional fighters as whacking the mitts the wrong way for five rounds. I took his advice quietly, but stayed up late at night studying the fights, mimicking the boxers' movements, translating their stories onto my own.

The great Zab Judah's bloody show of mercy to the young Cory Spinks. The three battles between Micky "the Irish" Ward and Arturo "Blood and Guts Warrior" Gatti. Oscar "Golden Boy" De La Hoya's brutal defeat of the legendary Julio César Chávez and his later domination over Fernando "El Toro" Vargas. Lovemore N'dou's lean South African style, the way Kassim Ouma, a refugee boy soldier from Uganda, came into the ring without a shred of fear. The Latin fighters, light welterweights like the Cuban Joel Casamayor, the wild man Diego Corrales, who came back from two knockdowns in a single round to batter Castillo, only to die two years later after he flipped his motorcycle. Sometimes I stood in front of my little VCR, in the blue glow of my dark apartment, shirt off, mimicking the boxers' movements, from the way they punched to the seriousness and focus with which they entered the ring. Each fighter seemed to know exactly for whom they were fighting and where they came from, as if their cultural identity were as endemic to their violence as their punching power or hand speed. But I knew better: I'd never have Judah's Brooklyn swagger. I'd never be able to claim the Southie Irish toughness of Ward, any more than the slick Italian viciousness of Gatti. A few weeks earlier, a friend had sent me a hooded sweatshirt, joked that I should get HALF-THAI MAINE THUNDER written across the back. I entertained the idea, but I couldn't bring myself to do it.

Roo's favorite fighter was a Korean Russian by way of Australia named Kostya Tszyu. As I began to study him—his strong, steady, honest attack; his patient, almost predatory ring generalship—he became my favorite fighter, too. One night, Victor invited Todd and Roo and me to his house, to watch a pay-per-view bout on Showtime between Tszyu and an American named Sharmba Mitchell. With Todd coming back into the fold, and Roo soon heading out of town to visit his mother in Australia, and Victor possibly headed back to Seattle with Miranda on a moment's notice, our evenings together—even in the gym—were few and far between.

Todd picked me up on the way out Halibut Point Road. Victor lived in a small ranch at the top of a steep gravel road, named Little-Byrd Way, after his and Miranda's last names. There was a dog chained to the porch—a young German shepherd–husky mix— and a skiff parked in the driveway. We found Victor in his garage, lifting weights and working the heavy bag. We took turns at the bag, then at the bench press. "I'm gonna start training again," Todd said after a few rounds. He said he was ready now. The time on the rockfishing boat, away from the drug scene in Sitka, had done him good. Victor nodded, but he didn't appear all that hopeful.

Inside, it was almost bedtime for Victor's one-year-old son, Hunter. Before Miranda took him off to his room, Victor held up his hands. "One-two, Son," he said, and Hunter hit his hands with a left-right combo. "That's my boy, my little warrior." Victor lifted Hunter to the ceiling. "How you make a big man small, Son?"

Hunter mumbled something along the lines of "Kick him in the nuts."

"That's right."

"Victor!" Miranda said—but as little as I knew about parenthood then, as little as I knew about what it meant to raise a child, I could tell that she and Victor loved each other just as much as they had since they'd started dating in junior high.

While we waited for Roo to show up, we went out to the back deck to smoke. Then Victor took me inside his room, where, in a glass case above his bed, hung his two Southeast Showdown belts. Miranda had gotten them framed as a gift for Victor's retirement from fighting. The other thing she'd given him was a scrapbook, filled with all the articles and photographs of Victor from local papers. On the cover of the album was a picture of Victor—a glamour-shot studio portrait—lean and trim, with his wrapped hands up near his chin, his shirt off, scowling at the camera. He was wearing his trunks—SAVAGE across the waist. Above it, Miranda had labeled the album "The Fighting Career of Victor 'the Savage' Littlefield." While waiting for Roo to show up, I sat on the couch, flipping through the album, fantasizing about what it would be like to be able to look back on my past as a fighter, to have someone in my life who could help me understand my story, and where I came from, to keep that story in an album, in a glass case over our bed. Then Roo pulled up, and we settled in for the fight.

As Tszyu entered the ring, there was some discussion as to where he was from: he had grown up in Russia, but his grandmother was Korean, but he later had moved to Australia to train. He even spoke broken English with an Australian accent. I watched the fight in a haze of muted feelings: Tszyu's menacing persistence, throwing Mitchell to the canvas over and over, Mitchell's spirit slowly being broken by the punishment. But a moment from the introduction of the fighters had caught me off guard. As Tszyu was called into the ring, he was followed by his father, who had spent his life working in a smelting plant in rural Russia. When the announcer called out Tszyu's name, his father proudly held up Tszyu's WBO belt. I was too baked to understand what feeling was tugging inside me, but I knew that it had something to do with my not being able to imagine myself getting into a ring with my father in my corner. On paper, I had no reason to doubt his loyalty: he'd told me, hundreds of times, how much he loved me. In early grade school, he used to come into my classroom a few times a year, spend an entire day sitting next to me at my desk, just so I would know that, during those first years of my parents' separation, he had my back. Several years later, my father had shown me a drawing he'd made at some kind of humanistic psychology workshop, in which he'd channeled an image of himself in a past life: a lone horseman on an empty plain, adorned in flamboyant jewelry. The Outrider, he'd called himself, and for a while he signed off letters to me with "Your Outrider." At times, his loyalty struck me as ridiculous—more about his own self-image than my needs. But then, my senior year of high school, he'd driven to every single one of my soccer games, ten hours round-trip, eighteen games in a row. Some of my teammates' parents, who lived five minutes from the field, didn't make half as many games that season.

"Kostya Tszyuuuuu!" the announcer belted, and as his father raised his son's belt, a single thought went through my mind: No. To go into a ring, one needed total trust in the man in your corner. If you did not have that total trust, he did not belong there. It was as simple as that. For the next five rounds, the fight passed before my eyes. I felt like I was right there at ringside, watching Tszyu through the ropes.

"Yo, Jade." Victor tugged on my arm. "Wake up. Fight's over, man."

■

In addition to the Native kids who were assigned to my classroom, I started working with non-Native students, too. There was a group of Filipino kids: Divina Casalucan—a fun, distracted spirit who, whenever I told her to stop goofing around with her friends and get to work, sighed, "Awww, come on, Jade! We were having fun!" And Alex, who wore his hair in full shiny curls, who dressed in pink polo shirts and white pants, who danced around my classroom trying to incite gossip. I remember watching him one afternoon, as he was being teased by a group of boys in logging boots and baseball hats and Carhartt jeans, and thinking that he had something important to teach me about toughness that I'd never learn in a boxing ring. It wasn't just his willingness to dress the way he wanted to dress, to carry himself in a way that challenged the gruff but posturing masculinity of his male peers. Rather, it was that even the slightest comment, the quietest utterance of a homophobic slur, would be met with Alex's unrestrained fury. Sometimes, he'd call out his aggressors by name, tell them that the only reason they made fun of him was because they were jealous that Alex would never suck *their* dicks. Other students would sometimes look at me, expecting me to punish Alex for his language, temper his fury and aggression, but I just didn't have it in me. This was his fight, in a much more dangerous ring, and I felt he deserved a chance to show the world how tough he was.

There was also Mari, a young woman who worked as a checkout clerk at the grocery store and who came to me for help on a report she was writing about how to become a nurse's assistant. Her English was limited but precise, and whenever she asked me for help translating her homework, I often found myself imagining my mother's journey through nursing school. I had vague memories as a boy of sitting in the back of a chemistry class, at the University of Vermont, playing with LEGOs while my mother sat at a desk several feet away. My father had often told me that many times my mother had struggled with nursing school because the language barrier was too difficult to overcome, and that one of the few things he did right in their marriage was to help her study, so that she could earn her degree. No matter how many times he'd recited that story, though, the portrait of his devotion was always tainted by the ending. Because of that ending, those extra hours I spent with Mari, translating multiple-choice questions about various kinds of hygienic practices, never felt wasted.

I also started working with many white students—which, at first, I resisted. The purpose of SNEP was to help Native students, not the white students whom the school system had no other place for. But while the Native and Filipino students often had large family networks to give their lives context, the white students were a unique brand of exiles. Melissa was the daughter of a fisherman who was never home. She was vague about the whereabouts of her mother—who was often back in Tennessee, leaving Melissa to hang out at home alone for weeks on end. Gradually, Melissa came to school wearing less and less clothing and more and more makeup, effects that concealed the growing sadness of her face. She spent periods drawing pencil sketches of fairies and sprites weeping crystal tears, inside of which were snow globes of another, happier world. Sometimes, Melissa would rip the pages out of her notebook and pin them to my wall, so that other students could see her drawings and perhaps understand the feelings she held within herself.

I had another student, Trisha, who, because of her weight, told me her nickname back home was Miss Piggy. Trisha spent most of the period writing poetry in looping cursive, which she cataloged in a binder that she carried under her arm. On the cover of the binder were pictures of her two-year-old cousin, who was a professional baby model, whose parents dressed her up in makeup and bows and fancy clothing. "Isn't she pretty?" Trisha said, gazing at the pictures for minutes at a time. Once, when Trisha learned that I liked literature, she asked me if I would read her poems. Page after page of sadness and longing and heartbreak, written in singsongy rhyme, directed toward a mysterious lover.

Days later, Trisha asked me if I'd had a chance to read her poems. I told her I had.

"Did you like them?"

I looked at Trisha: her eyes looking up at me, a sadness in them that told me that her entire worth was riding on the next words. "Really good."

Trisha smiled. Laughed nervously. "Really, Jade?"

I nodded.

She beamed, walked into the hallway hugging her binder like a teddy bear.

I also had a blind student named Michael. He was confined to a wheelchair, but had a braille computer that allowed him to type. Michael was generally uninterested in his schoolwork. I offered him extra sympathy at first—but he'd seen my type before and quickly disregarded me as someone who just felt bad for him. Michael held a dark and cynical attitude toward life, and the thing he hated more than anything was writing. I tried everything: framing writing assignments as personal essays, trying to get him to tell his story in his own words, sometimes letting him talk while typing for him. But the more I tried to help Michael, the more he would disappear down a rabbit hole of solipsism, cross-examining my motives, trying to get under my skin. When I'd had enough, I finally gave up on Michael, told him he could come to my classroom as long as he wanted to, but that I was done helping him with homework. Then one afternoon another student brought a guitar to my room. She strummed a few chords, sang a few songs, lost interest. Michael asked her if he could play it. "I can only play one song," he said. He laid the guitar in his lap like a harp and slowly began picking the opening riff of "Nothing Else Matters," by Metallica. Everyone in the classroom stopped what he or she was doing and listened. The way his fingers moved across the fretboard resembled nothing like typical guitar technique. To find the frets, he slid his fingers up and down the neck, creating an otherworldly slide sound. I could not claim to know what it was like to be Michael, but the beauty and sadness of the song helped me understand why he never felt like doing his homework.

The only student I couldn't get along with that year was Johnny. He had bright blond hair and was built like a bulldozer. I didn't like the way he talked to girls; his coercive, pathetic baby voice begged their sympathy but also messed with their emotions. Whenever I told Johnny to mind his own business, he'd stand up, put his arms out to his sides, and shout, "I ain't doing anything!" When I told him to get his homework done, he'd shout, "Give me one reason!" and make a big performance in front of the class. He knew what I knew: that somehow, the world had turned its back on him, and that doing his homework would not make a bit of difference in his life. Once, after another such exchange, he came right up to me, breathed in my face. When I told him to sit down, he didn't move. I knew that he wanted me to hit him. I knew he wanted his own blood smeared over his cheeks, wanted to know that I'd had enough of him. I did want to hit him. But I also knew that I was the last stop on his journey. He'd come up from Down South—Washington State, I recall—to live with his father, after his mother remarried. He spoke highly of his father, said they had a great time playing "grab ass" around the house. I could send him to the guidance office, and then he would go to the principal, whom he would probably tell to fuck off. Then he would end up wandering around town with nowhere to go. He was just waiting for someone to press the final button. I walked away. "That's what I thought," Johnny said, snickering at his table.

"Feel for the kid," said the guidance counselor, after learning about Johnny's behavior. "Can you say ADD?" She exhaled, shook her head. "And his dad, I saw his name on the sex offender list. That's gotta be tough."

I nodded, but I still could not dig up the kind of sympathy for

Johnny that I offered my other students. The shimmer of his blond hair, the almost luminescent whiteness of his skin—it set something off inside me. He looked like the young Mordred in *Excalibur*. I felt myself drawing a hard moral line in the sand, which Johnny stood on the wrong side of. If he ever wanted to grow up, he'd need to free himself from his father's legacy.

■

Haag advertised the fights that month as the Valentine's Day Massacre, because the show fell on Friday the thirteenth and because he needed a good name to drum up some enthusiasm because of the flagging attendance at Marlintini's. Victor and I flew over to Juneau in the evening, in the middle of a building snowstorm that was only supposed to get worse as the night wore on.

Most of what occupied my mind that night was whom I'd be fighting and whether I'd cross paths with Paula again. The latter had been revealed the minute I'd arrived in the barroom and saw a string of ring girls, but no Paula among them.

Haag had, on his own dime, flown my opponent down from Anchorage. He came into the barroom alone, in black sweats, his head hidden entirely by the hood of his sweatshirt. I watched him warm up in front of the pool tables. He kept one eye on the action in the ring while throwing a series of short, quick jabs. The immediate difference between him and the other fighters in Marlintini's was his ability to box. His footwork was sound—better than mine, which wasn't saying much—and when he took off his sweatshirt, he wore a boxing tank and black trunks with white trim, and respectable Nike boxing shoes. He didn't have bulky gym muscles but rather the long smooth biceps of a fighter; he was not bigger than me, but he was lean and trim.

When I asked Victor about how I might approach the fight, he wasn't all that worried. "You hear his name? Calls himself the Tanana Banana!" Victor laughed. He told me that when he was at electrician's school in Anchorage, some guys from Tanana used to snowmobile into town along a river because their village was otherwise inaccessible by road. But "the Banana"? "I mean, who the fuck calls himself a banana?"

I watched the Banana warm up, his mop of brown hair bouncing on top of his head like a houseplant. But his name was throwing me off. Partly it was the goofiness of the image of fighting a banana in the ring—like some kind of game show where I should be dressed as a pumpkin. But it was also the word—*banana*—that got stuck in my brain. On more than one occasion, I'd heard people use the word *banana* as a name for Asians who acted white. The Asian version of an Oreo. People were mostly playful about the term—it was little more than a reference to becoming American, I suppose, to allowing the process of ditching your immigrant roots. I understood that, yes, I had a white father, so I was already mostly a banana, but something about accepting the full quotient of my white blood called up a rage that I could never just laugh off with a nickname.

In the minutes before our fight, I grew increasingly agitated with the mystery of who my opponent was: Why had Haag flown him down here just for three minutes in a ring? If he was in fact from Tanana, then he was probably Native, but he looked more white than me. And was he a boxer, or just pretending to be a boxer? As I climbed into the ring, as Victor slapped Vaseline on my face, I decided that the only way to dissolve this ambiguity was to hit him with everything I had. My previous three bouts had been prefaced with prefight fear that over time evolved into anger, rage, and finally something like violence; the night of the Valentine's Day Massacre, I entered the ring with a singular desire to hurt someone.

The Banana hopped out of his corner, light on his toes, flicked a few jabs in my face. They landed but they didn't hurt, and in the clinch, I decided to counter his first right hand with the body punch Victor and I had been practicing in the gym. It was almost too easy: when his punch came, I bent at the knees, let the Banana's fist float over my head, then rose up, driving my fist into the small pocket of unprotected skin under his ribs. The contact was clean. I saw the punch land, saw it collapse into his flesh, and saw the Banana step back, pause, then fall. The speed with which he hit the canvas, then lay there, on his belly, facedown, was surprising. What also surprised me was the speed with which he rose to his feet, just as quickly as he'd gone down. The ref called us together again, and I shuffled out of my neutral corner and waited for the same right hand. When it came, I slipped it just as I had the first time and drove my glove into the same opening under his lower right rib. The Banana dropped to the canvas again. When I stepped back, he was lying on his face as if balancing his entire body on the tip of his nose.

Between rounds, Victor complimented me on the punch. "Man! You fucking nailed him!" I agreed: something important was coming together with my body and my brain—a basic ability to fight and think at the same time. To synchronize my physical self with the murkiness of what it felt like to be me.

The second round was almost identical to the first. The Banana hopped forward again, flicking short, peppery jabs, then threw that looping, soaring right. I repeated what I'd already done, landed the same punch, in the same soft area of his torso. He lay on his face, robotically still. But as I waited for him to rise, I felt myself growing impatient with his display of pain. Somehow, even after landing the most powerful punches I had ever thrown, I was still convinced that the Banana was faking it. In our next exchange, I loaded my uppercut to the ribs with the full force of my legs, threw it into his body as if trying to pull out his insides—as if trying, it occurs to me now, to steal his soul. I watched my fist sink into his body, watched him go down. The Banana lay at my feet, groaning a little. Why I felt such malice, such anger toward a stranger who'd flown six hundred miles to fight me for three minutes did not cross my mind once.

While sitting on the canvas, the Banana looked at the referee and, with an almost indifferent shake of his head, told him that he was done. Then he got up, hugged me, and hopped out of the ring.

"That uppercut to the ribs," Victor said. "That was some fuckin' punch."

"I saw it go in," I said. I had seen my blue glove connect with the Banana's ribs, then sink an inch deeper. But even with that as evidence, I still found myself doubting that the Banana's pain was real.

"Some fucking punch," Victor said, and in his eyes, I saw something I hadn't expected to see: a recognition that if he and I had met in the ring, it would have been a pretty good fight.

■

Later, I sat with the Banana up by the pool tables. He was already dressed, drinking a beer, enjoying the fights of the evening like a spectator. "You're a good fighter," he said. "Good work to the body." He began a long riff about his gym in Fairbanks, about some job he didn't like, about a trainer who'd screwed him over, about his difficult relationship with his father. He went on and on and on, talking without pause, and after about ten minutes it occurred to me that he'd keep talking forever. I excused myself, still preoccupied with my own thoughts about our fight, still trying to invent a line of logic by which to justify my suspicion about the outcome. Maybe, I imagined, Haag had flown the Banana six hundred miles just to take a dive, so that he could pad my record with a reasonable win. But that didn't make any sense: Haag could just as well have used a local fighter and saved the five hundred bucks. Maybe the Banana, after feeling the impact of my first body shot, figured the best way to survive the fight was to hit the deck early and often, pack it in until the final bell.

But as I stood in the shadows of the Marlintini's barroom trying to build a story to explain my doubt, what I was searching for wasn't the final truth of Haag's logic (a logic that probably not even Haag himself understood), nor was it the validity of the Banana's performance in the ring. What I was searching for was a final reconciliation with the boy I had once been: a boy who, on more than one occasion, had faked physical pain to avoid confrontation with his feelings.

Then Paula entered the barroom. She was wearing her restaurant uniform. She came over, put her hand on my arm. "I'm sorry I missed your fight. I couldn't get time off." She looked down at herself. "I have to change." She disappeared behind the small door into Haag's back office, where the ring girls changed outfits every few rounds, and a few minutes later came out in a different outfit—white sweater, painted-on blue jeans—with her hair styled as she wore it in the ring. She looked beautiful. I ordered us a round of drinks, then quickly ordered another.

By last call, we were stumbling outside, into a foot of freshly fallen snow. The night hung over the mountains, vast and silent. Paula had driven to Marlintini's from her job in the valley, and I offered to move her car to the Travelodge parking lot so that she wouldn't get towed. I didn't make it far. As we crossed the Glacier Highway, the blue lights of a police car began flashing behind me. I pulled into the Travelodge.

The policeman looked at me, didn't ask if I'd had anything to drink. "You forgot to turn your lights on," he said, flashlight in my face.

"It's not my car," I said—a pointless, nervous rebuttal. Paula sat next to me, hidden in the darkness, perhaps hiding her face. I was not sure of her reputation in Juneau, although by the way she was looking out the window, it didn't appear that she wanted to have anything to do with the cops. I got out of the car. "Just didn't want to get towed."

The policeman nodded, asked me for my ID. I took my wallet out of my pocket, pulled out my ID, but dropped it on the ground. The policeman shone his flashlight on the ground and I got on all fours, searching for my face in the snow. He pointed the beam of his flashlight to help me search. There it was. Jade "the Stone" Coffin, looking back at me, dusted in white.

"Maine?" The policeman held my license. He scrutinized the card for several seconds. "What are you doing up here?"

I looked at the policeman. I was too drunk to feel the gravity of what it would mean to get a DUI. I looked around the parking lot. I looked at the streetlights glowing across the Glacier Highway. I looked into the windows of Marlintini's. "I'm a Roughhouse fighter." Describing myself that way gave me new confidence. I pointed across the street. "I fight in that bar."

The policeman shone the light in my face. I looked at him sternly.

"You win?" he said.

"Dropped him in the second round."

The policeman nodded. "I think I saw you fight around Christmas. The Hoonah Hooligan, right?"

"That was me."

The policeman laughed. "That was some fight. One of the best fights I've seen. You guys put on quite a show." He looked at Paula for a moment, looked at me. "She with you?"

"Yes."

He handed me my ID. "Don't go anywhere else tonight."

■

I asked the woman at the front desk of the Travelodge for a room at Haag's rate—seventy-five bucks. I'd dropped at least that much on drinks at Marlintini's, which, in addition to the hotel room, meant I'd spent about $150 on the evening. It was a good world to buy in: three minutes of fighting for a break-even night.

Paula and I stayed up for several hours, talking like old lovers. She told me about her life back home, in Ecuador, about her father, for whom she didn't much care, and how she was living with her stepmother, in a house in the valley, while her father was supposed to be working out of town but was actually visiting his mistress. It was nothing she was proud of, she said. I asked her if she liked being a ring girl. "At first it made me feel good. But then I don't like the way Haag treats me. He doesn't respect me." To dance around in a bikini, to show drunk men her ass in a thong, to pick up dollar bills off the canvas, all for seventy-five bucks—she wanted to quit. But she had to work almost a full shift at her restaurant to make the same money. She shrugged. "I like to work. Everyone speaks Spanish there." When I asked her how she'd ended up in Juneau, she looked away. I told her that whatever her reason, it was all right with me.

Paula paused. "I am married."

"You're married?"

"Yes." Her husband, she told me, was an American. He spent all his time playing video games and riding his skateboard, and he was not kind to her. She had married him for love, but also to stay in Juneau, so that she wouldn't have to go back home. But now she wanted to get divorced and was just waiting for the papers to come through. "I'm sorry I did not tell you."

I wasn't sure what I was supposed to feel—anger, betrayal, surprise. But when I looked at Paula, I felt none of those things. All I felt was . . . sorry. Not pity, not sympathy. I was just sorry that she'd had to go through what she'd been through. That it had led her to Marlintini's, that it had led her here. That life in America had been less than her expectations. That now she had to decide whether to stay or go back home.

"It's okay." I tried to think of a better way to say it, but I couldn't. This whole time I'd assumed that I'd been using Paula to fill my own void; that I, as a fighter who flew into town for a night on someone else's dime, was getting the better deal. But maybe we were both here for the same reasons.

Paula pulled closer to me. "Thank you," she said.

13. MIXED BREEDS

The Monday after my fight with the Banana was Elizabeth Peratrovich Day. Elizabeth Peratrovich was a mixed-blood Sitka woman who, in 1945, worked with her husband, Roy, and the Alaska Native Brotherhood and Sisterhood to pass the Anti-Discrimination Act through the Alaska Senate. When Americans had first come up to Sitka in the late 1800s, they'd classified Russian mixed-blood children like Peratrovich as simply Russians, which placed them one rung above the Tlingit "savages" in the caste system. Even at the time of Peratrovich's activism, one state senator had commented that "mixed breeds are a source of trouble," and that "certainly white women have done their part to keep the races distinct. If white men had done as well, there would be no racial feeling in Alaska." Another senator remarked, "It is the mixed breed who is not accepted by either race who causes trouble; rather than being brought together, the races should be kept farther apart. Who are these people barely out of savagery who want to associate with us whites, with five thousand years of recorded civilization behind us?" Peratrovich stood before the all-male Alaska State Senate and declared, "I would not have expected that I, who am barely out of savagery, would have to remind the gentlemen with five thousand years of civilization behind them of our Bill of Rights." Later that evening, after the Anti-Discrimination Act passed, Elizabeth and her husband—the son of a Czech fisherman and a Tlingit woman—danced in the ballroom of the Juneau statehouse, where hours before a sign reading NO NATIVES had hung.

To celebrate the day, many of my students had been given writing assignments to reflect on Elizabeth Peratrovich's legacy. I read their work with great interest. Donna wrote a beautiful essay about what it meant to be Native, about not wanting to be seen as just another stereotype of a broken Indian. Many of the most interesting stories came from students who I hadn't even known had mixed blood. Kim, a six-foot-tall basketball player who always came to class in sweatpants, explained that her grandfather was Native and spoke Tlingit at home, and oddly, the moment she said this, my perception of her face began to shift: suddenly I was able to see another face beneath hers, rising to the surface. The same thing happened with Hank, a wrestler, who had jet-black hair and a Russian last name.

And then there was Tayla. She was blond, green eyed, narrow featured, and much smarter than she let on. While I was helping her revise her paper, she mentioned that her grandmother was from the Aleutian Islands—but nothing more. When I pushed her on the topic, Tayla explained that all she knew was that her grandmother had come to Sitka during World War II—apparently as part of a relocation program. The history was otherwise fuzzy. When I asked Tayla if she had any memories of her grandmother, she said she could remember the way she talked, then dropped into an Aleutian accent that sounded like another person had possessed her body. She laughed bashfully and switched back into her daily accent. That's when I saw Tayla's features, too, shift and morph into a new face. I would remember her face many years later when I would see my own daughters' faces carrying the hidden evidence of my mother's blood.

In the story of Peratrovich's courage, I saw the power of a single voice to speak up on behalf of her people, to illuminate a better way forward some twenty years before the Civil Rights Act passed into federal law. But I also noticed that I didn't have clear convictions about mixed blood. A reluctant and confused part of me could understand why people from two different races might be well served to, as the senator said, "be kept farther apart." Such a belief was based not on principle but merely on feeling. Sometimes, I daydreamed about versions of my alternative selves, in alternative universes unchanged by the force of war. In those worlds, my mother remained in Panomsarakram. She married a man—a Thai man—from a nearby city. Perhaps he was a doctor or a farmer or a teacher. Together, they remained in her village, created a son who grew into a dutiful, respectful young man surrounded by generations of family. With them as models, he understood exactly his place in the world.

In my father's universe, he graduated from college on the eve of no war, remaining free to consider the terms of his future. Perhaps he married his old high school girlfriend, Sarah Lowry—from Wellesley—and together they settled in the area, happily unaware of the complicated world beyond their suburb, content to watch their young son grow into a vision of themselves. Nowhere in the boy's life did there exist some shadow of other origins; nowhere in his imagination did he consider the morass of worlds that separated his parents. Had they divorced, the separation could have been ugly or civil, it did not matter. Each side of him would mirror the other. The choice of where he might direct his affection would be based on simple emotions of love and loyalty, tethered only to a single common universe that his parents would always share between them.

It was a stupid, fruitless thought experiment. But sometimes my mind went to those possibilities with a primal curiosity. What fascinated me was the possibility of total certainty—that in those other visions of me there existed some beautiful core of uncompromised self: pastless, historyless, simple and free. Hitting another man in the head, feeling the bones of his skull through layers of skin and padding, told me that such a self did exist—if not in me, then beneath the skin of others.

But the optimism of Elizabeth Peratrovich Day was short-lived. Later that week, Laura called all SNEP employees into her office for a special meeting. She'd gotten some bad news: the school board was holding a vote to decide whether to cut SNEP funding by some one hundred thousand dollars, which in turn meant that many SNEP positions as cultural educators might also be cut. Paul, as the master bead worker, Karen Williams, driving the bus, Donna's grandmother—their jobs would be defunded. My job would likely go, too, but that was the least of my worries. The memo from the school board brought up larger questions: What was an education? While my Native students were getting plenty of Shakespeare and algebra and Spanish, they were getting little education in a language that was once spoken by people up and down this coast for ten thousand years, and which now was spoken fluently by fewer than two hundred people. They weren't learning the stories of their people in school. Maybe this was supposed to be stuff they learned at home—but the division was clear, and so was the message: that Native life was on the margins of town life, that Sitka was an American, Western community first.

None of this went over well with the SNEP staff. Dionne Jackson, a SNEP employee and cultural liaison, wrote to the *Sitka Sentinel* defending the use of the money for SNEP, which did not "sit there" (as one school board member had described it) but was "used to pay the already woefully low salaries of those people who fill the unique role of teaching the traditional songs, dances, artwork, and language to the Native youths of Sitka." She defended the role of SNEP in providing "positive self-identity" and asserted that without the money the town would see the eventual "demise of the cultural education of our youths in Sitka." The district couldn't offer such an educational resource without SNEP. Limiting the work of SNEP in the community, Jackson said, would cause "irreparable" damage. She signed off her letter "Gunalcheesh," Tlingit for "Thank you." The next day SNEP ran an ad in the *Sitka Sentinel* outlining all the ways SNEP improved the community—it offered classes in regalia, language, traditional songs, dancing, and drumming, offered tutoring and preschool and transportation to every kid in Sitka, Native and non-Native—encouraging people to show up to the school board meeting in full regalia. A few days later there was a long list of Native people who had graduated from SNEP's cultural programs and who had gone on to become important figures in the community. Halfway down the list I saw a familiar name: Victor Littlefield.

■

Once I'd watched all of Roo's fight tapes about a dozen times, I got into the unhealthy routine of watching movies until late at night, sometimes until three or four in the morning. When I realized that I could get through a school day on four or five hours of sleep, take a nap in the afternoon, and still be fresh for training in the evening, it was a hard routine to break.

I rented the movies from a store downtown. I started out with films my father had quoted scenes from—brief performances that he often prefaced with the disclaimer "One day, my son, when you're a little bit older, maybe you'll have a look at . . ." or which I tacitly associated with his generation of American men. *Five Easy Pieces, Rebel Without a Cause, The Champ, Cool Hand Luke, Butch Cassidy and the Sundance Kid, Easy Rider*—the titles hung in my memory like the appendix of my father's young manhood. Yet, like in so many of the books I read that winter, the heroes of these stories—disillusioned white men unable to make sense of the world, tormented by some spiritual disease, willing, eager even, to die in the name of freedom—appeared to me as caricatures of men, as little more than comic book heroes. Their souls were too simple in sentiment, too vacant of substance, too unaware of the delicacy of their own claims, to offer me the convincing model of masculinity I had been hoping for.

Then I started watching movies I'd watched as a kid, amazed that films that had once seemed so sinister could now be so benign and silly. *Pale Rider, Tightrope*—when I tried to picture my father and me sitting on the couch, eating ice cream while Clint Eastwood stared gravely into the sun, I could only laugh. The biggest shock, though, was watching *Excalibur* a second time. Though the movie was about ancient Camelot, it was really about the eighties. The metal soundtrack, the goofy dancing women, the highly sexualized male friendships—that I had watched this movie with such intense concentration, in a living room in rural Vermont surrounded by my stepfamily and father, made me cringe for my younger self.

Then I got on a kick of movies about Vietnam. *Apocalypse Now, Full Metal Jacket, Hamburger Hill, Platoon, The Deer Hunter*—movies that once had offered me visions of tragic antiheroes laughing in the face of absurdity, of heroic young men facing their hearts of darkness in a Southeast Asian hell, now appeared only as the artifacts and relics of some bankrupt civilization. Every quotable joke, every quip, every betrayal, every single death—all of it disgusted me. One night, after I'd stayed up until nearly dawn watching, back-to-back, both volumes of *The Deer Hunter*, I turned off my twelve-inch television set and stared into the darkness trying to make sense of the heat in my eyes, the confusion boiling inside my chest. The men coming back from war, the wounded souls. The psychedelic horror of Southeast Asia, set to a butt-rock soundtrack—I hated it all. I sat on my couch for several hours, the images of those films scrolling through my mind's eye. The story they told of the war that had brought my parents together—I wanted a better one. One that was more complete, one that told me something about . . . her side of it. The only time I'd asked my mother about how she understood the war was during my senior year of high school, when I was studying Vietnam in my U.S. history class. As a woman from Thailand, what, I wanted to know, was her opinion of America's involvement in Vietnam? It seemed an innocent enough question—one that carried with it no extraneous longings or baggage. My mother paused, raised her eyebrows—as if surprised that anyone, ever, would care for her opinion. "I think maybe Americans, they underestimate the Vietnamese people. They think they're small. Maybe weak." My mother nodded to herself, almost proudly, and I could hear in her voice a tone of gathering conviction. "But Americans, they don't know how tough those people are. That they will do just about anything to survive."

But the movie that affected me the most that winter was *The Passion of the Christ*, the Mel Gibson–directed film about the life of Jesus. The downtown theater was playing the movie for the beginning of Lent, on Ash Wednesday, and with some sixty Christian churches in Sitka, the arrival of the movie cooked up a fervor in town. I knew little about the story of Jesus and had never felt drawn in any way to Christianity, especially in Alaska, where the work of missionaries was so obvious and explicit when juxtaposed with a landscape of such powerful wilderness. You didn't have to be a scholar of Alaskan history to recognize how closely linked the enforcement of American rule was to the arrival of the Christian faith.

The theater that night was so packed that I had to sit in the very front row. The lights went down, and for the next two hours the theater was completely silent. The movie was as bad as I thought it would be. Jesus never held any doubt in his heart that what he was doing—basically, walking to his death—was the right thing. The violence of Jesus' crucifixion was overly gory and gruesome: all the whips and chains and torn-up flesh—it made the Vietnam movies look innocent. Compared to the story of the Buddha, the story of Jesus had always seemed to me to be so unnecessarily brutal. Why torture yourself in the desert when you could sit under a bo tree and meditate instead? In the final scene, as Jesus hung on the cross covered in his own blood, the subtitles at the bottom of the screen flashed like a ticker tape. "Father," he said through cracked, bloody lips. "Why have you forsaken me?"

The words swirled around my brain, faded with an echo. I wanted to stand up and scream at Jesus. He was bleeding out on a fucking cross in the desert, and the best he could do was ask his father why he'd abandoned him? I looked around the theater for some confirmation of how I felt, thinking I might see at least the expression of confusion on a few faces in the rows behind me. But everyone in the theater—I mean everyone—was bawling their eyes out. Grown men. Fishermen. Their wives. Children. Their faces shone with tears, as if they hadn't known what was coming. I got up from my seat and left the theater just as the boulder was being rolled away from a cave.

■

The night before the school board meeting, I went to the gym early, so that I could get in a short workout. With Victor Down South with Miranda, Roo in Australia, and Todd nowhere to be found, the high school boys worked out on their own time, and I did, too.

By then I had been training for six months. I was strong and had endless wind, but I was also growing more certain about what kind of fighter I wanted to be. I was never going to be fast or slick. But I knew I could think and punch at the same time. Victor sometimes told me, "Boxing is the art of controlled aggression, of asserting your will over another man," and when I thought of those principles, and how they applied to me, I began to gain confidence in my limited gifts. If I had slow hands, then I would make up for my lack of speed with persistence and punch rate. If I didn't have natural snappy, quick-twitch power, then I'd have to have better wind, to outlast that power with endurance. What was most astonishing about my training was that I didn't even need Victor there to keep me focused. I had my own goals that drove my hands into the bag. I moved through the silence of the room, repeating the sequences of punches, eyes closed, imagining the attack of my opponent. I did not care who he was. I did not care where he came from. It had nothing to do with the other man. In fighting, I was creating a language—a physical, silent tongue, each punch a word, as complex with mood and feeling as any vocabulary.

I got to the meeting a few minutes late. I sat down in the back row, still sweating, just as the SNEP Gajaheen dancers were performing in front of a packed hall. Donna was dancing, and her little sister was beating a drum. The other kids were dressed in construction-paper hats and felt robes, singing a song in Tlingit while propelling an imaginary canoe with wooden ceremonial paddles. Paul, the master bead worker, was dressed in full regalia, guiding them through the song. Laura sat with her daughter in the front row.

The meeting started with welcome greetings from the presidents of the ANB and ANS, who each introduced themselves in Tlingit, and in traditional fashion: first by identifying their matrilineal clan and house affiliations, then their ancestors and grandparents, until, finally, they gave their given Tlingit, and then English, name. Then it was time for testimony.

One of the first men to speak was Herman Davis. He wore a vest with a frog crest on it, had a long white beard and white hair. He spoke about the power of culture to give a person values and identity, and how important it was to pass this gift on to the young. Ronald Dick cited the low graduation rate of Native students: "It's embarrassing. The people who are responsible should be ashamed. You don't deserve our money. We're doing a better job with your money than you can." Bob Sam said that his life had improved since SNEP was created. "Old people got together because of my generation. It was critical. They realized there was something missing in our lives, and that was culture." One after another, members of the Native community—old, young, alone and in pairs—came to the mic, appealing to the school board to maintain funding for SNEP. The school board members nodded after each testimony, but it was hard to say whether the stories were influencing their opinions.

Earlier that week, Laura had asked the few non-Native SNEP employees if we'd be willing to speak up as well. As I sat through the meeting, I tried to think of how I would introduce myself: "I am Jade . . . of . . . Maine . . . and . . . my grandparents . . ." I didn't even know my grandmother's last name. Sa-Lit, my mother had once told me, in some project for family heritage in elementary school. But I wasn't even sure that was how you said it. My mother liked to believe she was Chinese—Chinese, good with money!— but I wasn't convinced of her claim. My grandfather was a medicine man, who apparently had Lao blood. But I didn't know the meaning of his last name—Muncharoen—and for most of my life, despite the fact that it was my middle name, I'd spelled it wrong.

My father's bloodline was a bit more familiar. My last name, Coffin, filled up two pages in the phone book, but I did not know a single one of them. When I'd fished on a lobster boat, men at the dock used to say, "A Coffin! Uh-oh!" as if I was supposed to understand what that meant. The only time my father spoke explicitly about our heritage was when he referenced the Coffins of Nantucket. I'd never been there, but my father sometimes told me about a memorable trip he'd made to a whaling museum, where he'd seen old whaling-ship figureheads: carvings of women, gazing out across the sea. The statues had moved him. "Brought me to tears," he liked to say. But what had impressed him most about the history of whaling was the way the men used to disappear for years on end. "Out to sea," my father said, over and over. "Out to sea. That's just how it was back then. Our ancestors, they just went out to sea, sometimes didn't see their families for seven years. You imagine that?" He shook his head, in admiration and awe of such a burly class of men. But something about the sound of his voice as he told that story made me feel that he wasn't telling it to illuminate the days of whaling ships but to justify to me, to himself, why he'd done the same thing.

One of the final speakers at the meeting was Paul. He walked to the microphone, but started to tremble and had to pause for a long breath. Several of our coworkers stood up next to him for support. Paul looked at the audience, introduced himself in Tlingit first, then English. He began to cry. The room was silent for a long time before he spoke. "My culture"—Paul took a deep breath—"is my life." He remained in front of the microphone for a moment, then sat down.

It was late. I knew that if I was going to say something, now was the time. But perhaps by then the school board had heard enough. Perhaps my voice was irrelevant. When I tried to muster the courage to explain my own relationship to the story unfolding in the ANB Hall that night, I had no words—only feelings. Then, just when I was about to raise my hand, a woman from the United Kingdom walked to the microphone and spoke about her ancestors, and the loss of the ancient Saxon language, and how losing another language was destroying the richness of our world. When she was done, everyone applauded. I sat in my metal chair, searching the noise for the sound of my voice.

14. THE ICEMAN

The White Elephant held odd hours, but if you showed up early, waited in line on the sidewalk, you could get first dibs on some pretty good stuff. Foul-weather gear and old fisherman coats, retired camping equipment and strange tools, silverware and pots and pans, old western novels. One night, while digging through a box of musty clothing, I found a navy-blue sweatshirt made of a rugged thick material. When I held it to my chest, I almost had to sit down. Across the front, in dignified tall white varsity letters, it read MIDDLEBURY COLLEGE.

I never planned on going to the same college as my father. Despite decent grades, I spent a lot of my junior year of high school arguing with my mother over my desire to spend my twenties wandering the world. My mother, who'd attended college part-time, and who'd spent her entire life saving for my sister's and my education, was baffled by my hoboing ambitions. ("Someday," she liked to say, "maybe you show up in the psychiatric unit just like one of my patients!") In a year, my sister would graduate from Saint Michael's College in Vermont; sending a second child to college proved to my mother that she'd achieved an impossible American dream. "Do you know how lucky you are?" my mother often said, shaking her head. A part of me liked that I was throwing a wrench in her carefully laid plans. It was my way of proving to myself that I was more than just another overachieving son of an Asian mom. Ours was a strange but probably inevitable standoff of wills, pitting my mother's relentless aspiration against my philosophical remoteness. When I finally wore her down, my mother, in a rare instance of parental coordination, asked my father to intervene.

He suggested I apply to Middlebury. His best friend taught there, and though my grades weren't up to snuff—I had average test scores, and I was barely in the top 10 percent of my class of about two hundred students—I had done some interesting things, and I wasn't white. As I understood it, my father had gotten into Middlebury based on football rather than grades. He spent his years there living in a frat house—Delta Upsilon—until his junior year, when he was put on academic probation and graduated a year late. Then he shipped out to northeastern Thailand.

I filled out my early-decision application, sent it in, and a month later the process was over. That September, my mother drove me to campus in a brand-new Volvo sedan that she had bought—"Straight cash!"—the day before. I hated that car. Nothing made me angrier than my mother's efforts to imitate the upper-middle class, and I read her desire for mobility as little more than a desperate message to my father that, on her own, she had achieved all the things he had promised her—and more. My parents, on individual salaries of roughly seventy-five thousand dollars, and with help on a third from my grandfather—had decided to pay for my tuition out of pocket, which made me feel both rich and guilty. But as my mother pulled up in front of my dorm, I saw something that would begin to shape my understanding of the world I was about to enter: a young blond man, in a pink polo shirt, standing in front of his own brand-new car. The car was the exact same green as my mother's. His was an Audi A4.

I spent the next four years with a chip on my shoulder that only increased in size with each passing semester. I found campus life to be profoundly uninteresting. Even dreadful. Nothing was more depressing to me than waking up on a Saturday morning, walking into a cafeteria full of hungover twentysomethings in their pajamas, being served by a cafeteria staff, eating as much food as I wanted, finishing with dessert. Class was not that hard—it was easy just to show up, say a few things, bullshit your way to a standard B. My body pulsed with a desire to experience something difficult, something scary, something that would reveal to me what I was made of and who I was; yet so many things at college felt like a process of pacifying, of numbing that mysterious vigor, of deconstructing those primal sensations with reasonable, measured thought. Sometimes I would sit in my dorm room on Saturday nights, watching people dressed up for a party, or on their way to semiformals, or I'd see the artsy kids wearing all black, smoking butts, wearing trucker hats, or I'd see the kids in outdoor gear, going camping for the weekend—and I would find myself so disgusted by what I was becoming, disgusted by the subculture I was part of, that I would sleep until noon the next day. The irony was that my life had never been easier.

To keep my distance, I tried to make friends with people in town, who reminded me of the people I'd grown up with. I got a job working at a sandwich shop, for which I would ride up the hill from the other side of town, enter the glowing kingdom of campus, and deliver sandwiches to dorm rooms full of kids funneling beers. I could feel the dark absurdity of our royal station rising up around me like a slow tide. And yet, because I didn't have the courage or inventiveness or initiative to come up with a better plan for how to spend these years of my life, I moped around campus like an angry court jester. Sometimes my friends gave me a hard time about being so negative and brooding, like I was out to spoil the party. But this contrarian stance was the only way I could feel like I wasn't selling out. My bravest moment of rebellion came one afternoon when I—who'd never skipped a single class—staged a one-man protest during a nature writing course I'd enrolled in. The professor was a thoughtful, gentle-voiced man beloved by students, many of whom had spent their junior years studying abroad in developing countries, returning to campus adorned with the artifacts of their journeys. I found their adoration for the natural world, their affection for simpler people to be both precious and patronizing. (I lacked the courage to admit to myself that in many cases, I shared their sentiments.) I wasn't even sure what I was standing up against—a feeling more than a principle—but as I sat in my room, watching the minutes go by, racked with guilt for wasting an hour's worth of tuition, I was sure that I was doing the right thing.

Eventually, I started looking for fights. In intramural sports, I used to single out the biggest, bulkiest football players and deliberately cheap-shot them, just to see what their reactions might be. Mostly, they seemed astonished that a five-foot-eleven Asian-looking kid on a shitty freshman squad would have the audacity to offer such a challenge. Predictably, nothing ever came of such confrontations, except for uneasy looks from my friends, who had no interest in covering my ass should a fight actually break out. Then, about the time I organized the John Keats Club, I somehow found myself at a basement frat party, standing awkwardly in a crowd of football players. I knew no one there; I rarely went out on the weekends, and I had nothing at all to do with Greek life.

I felt a hand on my face, pinching my cheeks together, like a parent grabbing the face of a child. The hand belonged to a massive white kid who looked like he spent his summers eating ice cream and lifting weights. He had the square jaw and broad forehead of a New England man. He was smiling. "Well, aren't you cute," he slurred, his lips quivering into a grin. A small crowd formed around us—mostly his friends. For a moment, our eyes met. He wouldn't let go. But I couldn't move. Then he laughed, pulled his hand away, and went back to his fellow brothers.

I remained where I was, staring at the boy's back, imagining alternative endings to our confrontation: a swift kick to the nuts, a punch to the gut, a knee to the face, and an escape out the basement window. My hands tingled; I could feel my body screaming to act. Instead, I wandered upstairs, outside, walked across campus, muttering judgment at the droves of kids dressed up in goofy costumes, headed to an eighties dance.

At the White Elephant now, I tried the sweatshirt on. A perfect fit. I paid three bucks for it and walked out. On the sidewalk, I took out the jackknife I kept in my pocket and cut off the sleeves. I didn't like that someone with my educational background had come to Sitka, probably with similar aspirations to my own. It challenged the novelty of my journey, made me feel that perhaps my quest was less original than I'd thought. But I was willing to bet that the previous owner of the sweatshirt hadn't been a Roughhouse fighter.

For the next several days, I wore the sweatshirt to the gym like a piece of armor. No one in the boxing club had heard of Middlebury—to most people, wearing a sweatshirt adorned with the name of your college was likely not all that different from wearing a hat with your dentist's name on it—but as I shadowboxed in the reflection made by the big window on a far wall, I sometimes looked at the letters, reading them backward as if deciphering a secret message: Y-R-U-B-E-L-D-D-I-M—Why Are You Be Led Him? My mind had a way of fixating on syllables and sounds as I worked the heavy bag, but as I repeated the cryptic message in my head, I couldn't crack the code.

■

The last days before my fight, I still wasn't sure if Victor was coming to work my corner or if he had to stay in Seattle with Miranda.

Then, after school, I got a call from him: he was planning on flying up from Seattle direct to Juneau on Friday evening. Victor had talked to Haag about who our opponents might be. Todd was going to fight Sean the Comeback Kid Baird. They were an even matchup, but Haag thought Todd was the favorite—probably for financial reasons, as Todd still owed Haag money for the damage to the walls of the Travelodge. I was fighting Chuck "the Iceman" McCracken. The Iceman was a veteran Roughhouse lightweight; he'd done some boxing in the army and had even beaten Kid Roo by controversial decision. The good news, Victor said, was that the Iceman was out of shape, and therefore overweight, and because of that he was being forced to fight as a middleweight, which left me as the bigger man. The bad news: Haag had told Victor that he was flying the Goat back to Juneau, to fight in the main event. It had been several months since I'd talked to Miss Mary—enough time, I thought, to clear up any hard feelings between the Goat and me.

Friday afternoon, I packed my bag for Juneau. I had begun to take great pride in folding my Sitka Boxing Club uniform into my backpack—it made me feel like a warrior going into battle. Before I rode to the airport, I pulled my Middlebury sweatshirt over my head.

■

It was raining when Todd and I landed in Juneau. We met Victor in the Travelodge lobby, then followed him to the Goat's room. When we knocked on the door, a quiet voice on the other side said, "Come on in." The room was dark, shades drawn. Victor entered first, then Todd. I followed quietly behind them and remained in the shadows, behind the door.

The Goat was sitting on his bed, wearing a hunting shirt and jeans. Next to him was a duffel bag, a waist belt, boxing shoes, and sparring gloves. He was polishing his helmet with leather juice. The boxing gear, the Goat's ruddy face—handsome as Paul Newman's—the moment reminded me of a mash-up of scenes from *Cool Hand Luke*.

The Goat looked up at Victor. "How you doing, old buddy?" The Goat even looked like a goat. He had a pointed chin with a tuft of hair growing off it, and his bangs flipped up in the front in a cowlick.

When Victor introduced me, I came out of the shadows and shook the Goat's hand.

"I hear you been doing a little boxing?"

"Yeah," I said.

The Goat nodded. "That's good, man. That's good." He kept polishing. "You play some banjo, I hear, too?"

"A little bit. I just started."

The Goat continued to rub his gloves. "That's good, man. That's good. We got a lot in common, you and me."

Victor was looking at the floor. The Goat kept polishing his gear. I waited for him to ask about Miss Mary.

"You ready to kick some ass tonight?" Victor said.

The Goat nodded. "Yeah, I guess I'm looking forward to it."

Victor and the Goat talked about his opponent. The Goat had fought the Razor before and beat him, but the Razor was an experienced boxer. He'd trained in Boston as a young man and had over a hundred fights. "Should be a good dance," the Goat said. But the Goat was acting like he already knew the outcome.

Later, when we all walked across the Glacier Highway to Marlintini's, the Goat looked at the mountains for several seconds, then at me. He laughed. "Hey, man, Miss Mary was my girl. But you know what? I treated her like shit." He shook his head ruefully. "I ain't mad at you. I was just mad at . . . myself. I was in a bad place. I was living in that big city, didn't have any friends, didn't know what I was doing with my life." The Goat shrugged. "Training in Philadelphia with pros is fun and all, but . . ." He laughed to himself, threw a few punches in the air. "Nothing worse than being lonely."

■

The mood in Marlintini's was as lively as it had been the first show of the season. A lot of that probably had to do with the return of the Goat—and now that I'd met him and witnessed his cool charisma, I could understand why Haag had flown him all this way for a victory lap. As he stood in the barroom, fans came up to him, shook his hand, patted him on the shoulders. The Goat, without even fighting, was his own kind of show.

A few weeks back, I'd gotten an e-mail from Paula, telling me that she'd finally decided to stop coming to Roughhouse shows because she didn't want to work for Haag any longer. She'd offered to come visit me in Sitka, but the idea of bringing someone from the Roughhouse world into my private life felt too bare. I wrote her back with a bullshit explanation about how I was going to be out of town. Somehow, I was more willing to see myself as a jerk than reveal to someone who I was when I wasn't fighting. To compensate for my guilt, I convinced myself that a married woman didn't need to be hanging around with a guy like me, anyway.

My fight with the Iceman was after the intermission. The Iceman was shorter than I was and had a smaller frame, but he was out of shape and we probably weighed about the same. Haag introduced me first—"He paddled a sea kayak from Seattle, Warshington, to Sitka, Alaska!"—the same line as always. As I circled my corner with my glove raised, I saw a young woman sitting at one of the ringside tables, watching me. I looked at her and threw some overly stylized punches, then returned to my corner. "He's a military veteran, works at the Greens Creek Mine! Chuck! The Iceman! McCracken!" The Iceman had probably been awake since 4:00 a.m. and had worked a full day underground. He also had three kids under the age of ten. His wife was somewhere in the crowd. In most cases, those facts would have been enough to make me feel something like sympathy for the Iceman—who would want to physically harm a hardworking family man?—but without knowing those details at the time, I saw him only as an opponent.

The bell rang. The Iceman hopped in front of me, feeling out the fight. But I had no patience for half-cocked confrontation. I chipped down the distance between us with jabs, then, when I was just a few feet away, I threw a left into his defense. The punch landed. The Iceman bounced back into the ropes. I followed him there, kept punching until the Iceman's gloves came apart. A strange energy filled my body that night—a refined substance that burned freely, without the fear and doubt of my earlier fights. For the first time, I didn't wait to get hit to start my assault. When Victor shouted at me to push forward, I continued dropping lefts into the Iceman's guard until he slid to the canvas. I stood over his fallen form, gloves at my sides, begging him to get up, until the ref pushed me back into the neutral corner.

The same thing happened in the second and the third rounds: the Iceman worked the outside of the ring, moved off the ropes, but I kept cutting down his angles and pounding on him in the corners until he fell to a knee. I knocked the Iceman down three times that fight. It wasn't even close. When the bell rang, I found myself looking beyond the ropes, into the shadows of the barroom, yearning for someone else to step in.

"Holy shit!" Victor said as he pulled off my gloves. "That was wild, Jade." Apparently, Haag had put me against the Iceman thinking that it would be a good challenge: a necessary step up. Victor shook his head, almost regretfully. "Jade, you're the fucking man now."

I felt like the fucking man as I walked through the barroom. The anger that ran through me in the fight still pumped through my veins. I felt like I was glowing. When I went to the back of the barroom to pick up my money, the check was written for two hundred dollars. I asked the woman at the desk if it was Haag who had tipped me extra. She shook her head. "It was Chuck. He came over to my table with his wife after your fight and said you deserved the money more than he did."

I took the check, folded it into the waistband of my trunks, and went looking for Victor. "You see this?" I handed him the check, explaining why it was made out for more money.

Victor raised his eyebrows. "Fuck, Jade."

I found the Iceman on his way out the door. His wife was beside him. I put my hand on his shoulder, asked him if I could buy him a drink.

"Sorry. Got to get home to the kids." Then he held out his hand to Victor. "I don't know what the hell you're teaching in Sitka, but this guy's a fucking animal!" Then the Iceman followed his wife down the stairwell.

"You hear that, Jade?" Victor said. "He just called you a fucking animal!"

An animal. I liked that. Even more, I liked that the Iceman had given equal credit to Victor.

A year from that night, the Iceman would be deployed to Iraq, to work construction in the Green Zone. The first thing he did when he came back from his tour was return to his work in the mines and get back into the Roughhouse ring.

■

The Goat and the Razor fought in the main event. The Razor had the kind of delicate floating footwork that didn't fit in a Roughhouse fight. He never lost his balance, never sacrificed power for control. In one exchange, the Razor zinged the Goat with a perfect hook and the Goat stumbled forward as if someone had pushed him from behind. I thought he was about to go down, but while he was in the clinch, he looked at Victor and winked. Between rounds, while I was helping Victor work the Goat's stool, the Goat winked again, at me. "You think I was going down?" Then he laughed. "I almost did."

It was a close fight, made sloppy by the Goat's street-fighting tactics, and when the bell rang, the two fighters stood in the middle of the ring, both of them raising their hands in victory. The crowd started chanting, "Goat! Goat! Goat!" The Goat pumped his fist in rhythm to the chant, even though from his face I sensed that he didn't think he'd won the fight. Then Haag read the cards. The Goat got the split decision. The Razor shook his head, laughed to himself, and on his way out of the ring said something to the Goat. The Razor probably knew that the Goat, as Haag's favorite, held an advantage.

"Good fight," I said to the Goat, as he stepped through the ropes.

The Goat shrugged and out of the corner of his mouth said, "You got to learn how to fake it sometimes, Jade."

■

I was standing at the bar when the young woman I'd seen sitting ringside appeared next to me. She had dark hair, slight epicanthic folds between bright round eyes. I'd seen that face a million times, looking back at me in the mirror.

"Nice fight," she said. "But that other guy was too small."

I bought her a drink and we tried to talk over the crowd but couldn't hear each other. Then she took my hand and led me onto the dance floor. Every few songs we stumbled back to the bar for another drink. At last call she asked me to come home with her.

It was snowing outside, a real blizzard. She drove a pickup truck. Her name was Katrina. She was from a village up north, but she had moved to Juneau to live in the city. She didn't ask me where I was from and didn't seem to care.

We pulled up to a small house, right on the channel across from downtown Juneau. Her driveway was heavy with snow, but she pounded her truck through the banks and then backed it out and did it again before parking with the bed uphill so she could get out in the morning. She kicked the snow off her steps and pushed the door in with a shove. Her apartment was clean and warm.

"Why don't you take a shower?" she said, but it was more of a command. She didn't want a dirty brawler in her house. When I came out, Katrina was sitting on the couch, watching television. She didn't seem the least bit ruffled to have me around. We started talking with a casualness that made me feel like we'd met before. She leaned on me, laid her head on my shoulder, changing the channels. We were drunk, but not so drunk as to justify acting like a married couple.

"What was your name again?"

"You don't remember?" I said.

"Sorry. Oh well. Who cares."

We went outside to the deck to smoke. You could see the lights of Juneau across the channel. The black water lapped at the shore, melting back the new snow, taking it out with the tide. Spruce branches hung heavy with white, craning over the water. There were two fishing poles and two chairs on the deck and some old beer bottles. I almost asked about them—it was obvious there'd been another guy around—but it was no use ruining the evening.

Later, as we lay in her bed, her head on my chest, it was so quiet and peaceful that you could almost hear the snow falling outside. "Why don't you stay for the weekend," Katrina said.

I told her I had a flight to catch the next morning.

"Right." Then she closed her eyes and fell asleep.

In the morning I woke up with my heart pounding. It was always like that the morning after a fight, as if, even in my dreams, my body remained in the ring. Katrina hadn't woken up yet. I got out of bed, walked through her living room, looking at framed pictures on her wall, of people I figured were her family members. I walked out onto the deck overlooking the channel, watched the smoke rising out of the chimneys downtown until I felt calm again. Like I'd flushed my system of anything bad in it, and my body was left to float. The new snow made the air crisp and clean. I took a deep breath, felt it move through my lungs.

When I went back to Katrina's bed, she was awake. "I don't usually let random people spend the night with me." She looked at me for a moment with her head turned sideways, as if sizing up a piece of furniture, determining whether it would go well in her home.

"I gotta catch my flight."

Katrina nodded. "Let me give you a ride."

I told her I'd call a taxi.

"No. I want to drive you."

The mountains in the Mendenhall Valley glowed blue and white, the Glacier Highway a wide dark line unfurling before us. I'd spent all of seven hours at Katrina's house, but I felt like we were leaving each other under more pressing circumstances. Before I got out of her truck, we exchanged numbers on a ripped-up bar tab. The careless way she slipped the piece of paper into her pocket told me that I'd probably never hear from her.

■

Victor and the Goat and Todd were eating breakfast in the airport diner.

"You find a place to stay last night?" the Goat said.

"Yeah." I didn't know whether to brag or pretend it was nothing.

The Goat nodded. "You're having a good time being a Roughhouse fighter, aren't you?"

I wanted to tell him that it wasn't as it seemed, that I was driven by loneliness just as much as lust. That after releasing what was inside me during a Roughhouse bout, I didn't like being alone. It was too empty, too hollow. But I had no words to describe that experience, no way to explain how closely tied that loneliness was to fighting.

The Goat looked up. "That's good, man. That's good." He paused. "You put on quite a show last night. Victor told me you were pretty tough, but I didn't believe him. You got some rage in you, man. I can see it. You got some anger. Anger's good for fighting."

I looked at the Goat, thought of the footage I'd seen of him back in November—beating a man as he had—and how I'd been in awe of his viciousness. That he had seen the same thing in me . . . I looked at my hands. There was nothing special about them. They were small for my size, delicate even. I spun my ring, which I wore on the fourth finger of my right hand. "Thanks," I said to the Goat. "I've been training hard."

The Goat nodded, looked out the airport windows at the mountains, which, in all the after-storm sunlight, shone bright with snow. "I used to feel that way when I fought. Used to get angry as hell. But then it got old on me after a while. Don't even know why I keep doing it." He shook his head. "Sometimes, the best part of coming over here was flying back to Sitka the next morning."

15. THE WILDFLOWER

All March, Victor had been focused on getting the high school boys ready for their fights in Fairbanks. They sparred endlessly, took extra mitt work, and started dieting. The bouts would last all of three two-minute rounds, six minutes for which they had been training roughly two years, yet when I saw Ethan and Richie and Wyatt in the hallways at school, they looked gaunt and unresponsive, solemn and grave as if preparing for war. The boys seemed more dependent on Victor than ever before. He called them regularly, spoke with their parents, organized their flights, checked in on what they were eating for dinner. I admired that kind of devotion—the way that Victor, without payment, bound himself to the lives of the boys with an unspoken commitment. As if passing down knowledge—even if it was the knowledge of how to hurt someone—existed in its own realm of priority.

Then, one night, Victor didn't show up to practice. At first, I figured he was just busy with Hunter, or caring for Miranda. But the minutes ticked by: six o'clock, six fifteen, and still no sign of Victor. I stood around with the boys, all of us looking at one another for guidance. As the oldest, as a teacher figure, I felt an obligation to step up, but the boys had all been training longer than me, were all Sitka locals, and I didn't feel that it was my place to take Victor's. Finally, Richie went to the front of the room and somewhat awkwardly started us into the workout routine. It got a little bit easier: the boys hit the heavy bag and worked the bob-and-weave rope, and I even tried to give them rounds on the mitts—but we were all lost without Victor there, as if dropping to the floor for push-ups were impossible without the sound of his voice to give the command.

Then, about seven o'clock, Victor burst into the room. His hair was wet—so were his clothes. His eyes were wide open, his face white. "Holy fuck. Holy fuck." He paused. "I almost just fucking died." Victor explained what had happened. He'd been out in his boat after work, just to clear his head, when a wave hit him, tossed him out. His boat kept circling back, almost took his head off. He started to get cold. He hadn't been wearing a life jacket, and his survival suit was in his boat. Just as he was about to go under, another boat saw his boat circling in the distance and plucked Victor out of the water.

"I swear to fucking God, I was just about to go under." Victor looked at us all—Richie, Wyatt, Ethan, me—as we stood still, rapt. "You know what the fucked-up thing is? All I could think about was how pissed I was that I was missing training. I kept thinking, 'Who the fuck's gonna get my guys ready for their fights?'" He shook his head. "Don't tell that to Miranda." Then he dug into the duffel bag, pulled out a pair of gloves and a helmet, and pointed his gloves at the boys. "You ready to spar?"

■

The weekend the boys were out of town, I rode down to Old Thomsen's Harbor to see if I could track Todd down. But when I got to his boat, it was empty, and his dogs weren't in the cabin. I asked around at some other boats—spoke to scruffy, barnacle-faced men—and learned that Todd was living in a trailer park on

Sawmill Creek Road. So I rode out SMC, over Indian River, to the trailer park next to the old movie theater, where Todd's truck was parked in front of a small, tired trailer. I knocked on the door. A small deer carcass hung over the porch.

"Wassup, man!" Todd said, his eyes as happy as they'd been after his first fight.

"You get a deer?" I gestured to the carcass.

Todd nodded. "Hell yeah! A little one, but I can eat off it for a while. People probably wondering if I shot someone's cat." He invited me inside. The trailer belonged to friends who let him live there while they were vacationing in Thailand for the spring. We made small talk. Then I told Todd that I was going to fight in the Showdown soon, and I thought he ought to get back in the gym and consider fighting, or at least help me train.

"No. No. I'm not fighting in the Showdown. I'm done." Todd shook his head. "I'm no winner. I came back from Juneau, thought about it. I been working out with Victor for a while now, but I'm not going to win at Roughhouse. You guys are champions. You're winners. Me, I'm not." Todd paused, his eyes darted around the room anxiously. He cleared his throat. "You want to smoke, Jade?"

I wasn't in the mood for it, but I did—mostly just to clear the awkward air between us. After he was high, Todd's mood softened. He picked up a bass guitar that was sitting in the corner of the trailer. "You like the Chili Peppers? You like Flea?" He started playing the opening line of "Higher Ground." It was dead-on: note for note, nearly virtuosic.

"Man, Todd. You can play."

Todd shook his head. "No. I can mess around. But I'm no good." He put the bass down.

We smoked a little longer, and when Todd had really relaxed, he started showing me his various prized possessions: his harpoon gun and wet suit, and a picture he'd drawn of himself diving for scallops and spearing a big halibut. He'd done it on a piece of notebook paper, with a blue ballpoint pen—but you could feel the emotion in the image: it was lonely down there under the dark sea, but the harpooned fish, the bag of scallops hanging from Todd's belt, told him that life had meaning. "That was right off Eastern Channel. I never have much money, but as long as I can hunt and dive, I'll be all right."

I had not been in Todd's trailer for long when I felt that I needed to leave. I wasn't sure what Todd was up to, but it felt dangerous and sad. On my way out, Todd said, "Good luck at the Showdown, Jade. You're a winner. Victor knows that."

"Thanks." As I rode away, I took another look at Todd's place: the sheet metal and plywood holding the trailer together, the little chimney pumping heat, the inverted deer carcass hanging on the porch, his two dogs in the dirt, heads over their paws—I could see the loneliness of Todd's life glowing from inside the trailer like the lamplight in his windows.

■

When I got back to my apartment, I had a moment of déjà vu. I looked at my couch. I looked at my kitchen, full of plates and cups. My sparse possessions. A stack of books on the shelf. Gray light poured through my windows, colored my carpet a winter shade of blue. The world outside my windows: rainy, cloudy, cold—I had seen it all before.

The apartment was in the town of Winooski, Vermont, a multiunit, which my father shared with a friend. My mother had dropped me off for the afternoon. I was wearing a winter coat with a fur hat. I couldn't have been more than four or five. My father was there, but in my memory he did not appear in the room. I remembered only a card table, with a single pot containing burned rice. And a bed, covered in a blue-and-yellow quilt, which I would later see on the bed he shared with Martha. It was the home of a man who lived alone, who had nothing, who had gone out to sea.

I walked up to the window next to his bed, overlooking a frozen river, a vision of the frigid Vermont skyline fading to dusk. It was a slim moment in my father's life, a period between when he'd left my mother and still hadn't committed to his life at the Birches. The apartment was a sad place. Everything in my memory floated in a pale hue of gray.

I looked at my own apartment, and shuddered. I washed all the dishes in my sink, put them away carefully in the cabinets. I gathered up my laundry, rode my bike to the Laundromat, read a book while the machines spun, then rode back home and carefully folded my clothes and put them in my drawers. I swept my apartment floor, scrubbed my toilet. I opened the windows, like my mother used to do during the Chinese New Year, to let the bad spirits out, the good ones in. I laced up my running shoes, jogged all the way down to the end of HPR, past the mist hanging over Eastern Channel, the dark green mountains crawling along the Pacific horizon, the spruce trees shimmering with rain, silver light dappling the water as it passed through the low clouds. Something about the landscape in Southeast Alaska always called up a tender feeling inside me—less specific than nostalgia, less sentimental. Gazing across the mountains and the ocean, I always got the faraway feeling that no matter how much I remembered about the past, I would always be leaving something behind.

When I got back to my apartment, I did a few sets of push-ups and sit-ups. I showered. Then I sat on my couch, waiting for the next thing to happen. I dug out the bar tab upon which Katrina had written her number. I dialed and waited for her to pick up. When her voice mail came on, I left a message. I tried to keep it short, but my voice grew unsteady, and I ended up over-explaining why I was calling. I said that I hadn't meant to wait so long to call her, I just didn't want her to think I was coming on too strong; and she could call me back when she was ready but it didn't need to be right then . . . and I finally just hung up. I stayed up for a few hours reading, or mostly just pretending to, but the phone never rang.

■

The boys had won two out of three in Fairbanks: Richie by knock-out, in about as violent a brawl as could take place between two 145-pound teenagers. Wyatt won his fight by unanimous decision, scoring a knockdown in the third round. Ethan's opponent was a wiry kid from Seattle with light skin, who came into the ring wearing a red, white, and green helmet and whose nickname was the White Mexican.

On the tape, the two boys matched up evenly, but the White Mexican had a mean streak that Ethan didn't. The rumor was that the kid had knocked out several boys twice his size. At the end of the second round, the boys got into a scrappy exchange in the corner. With just a few seconds left in the round, the White Mexican landed a big looping right hand that dropped Ethan on his ass. Victor tried to wake Ethan up before the bell, but he was too dizzy and the ref had to stop the fight.

"I didn't even know what happened," Ethan said while we watched the footage of him taking the punch in slow motion. Both of his eyes were black now, and his nose was swollen. He'd gotten the shiners after he'd tried to clear his head by blowing his nose, but all the collapsed cartilage wouldn't let the air out, and it popped the blood vessels under his eyes. It was a typical boxing injury that looked a lot worse than it was.

"I told him, 'Don't blow your nose!'" Victor said. "But it was too late."

Now that the boys were done with their fights, Victor had more time to work with me. It had been a few weeks since he'd seen me train, and I was in the best shape I'd been in all season. He was even a bit slow on the mitts and had trouble keeping time with the combinations he'd taught me a month ago. Then, in our last round, he set the beeper and told me to punch for as long as I could without stopping. He called it a three-minute test. The beeper sounded. I started punching: one-two-one-two-one-two. I kept at it. "One minute!" Victor called out. One-two-one-two-one-two. "Two minutes!" Victor said. I had more in me. I kept punching, hissing through the pain in my arms, growling at the growing emptiness inside my chest. I threw a final punch, then dropped my gloves as the beeper sounded. Victor let his mitts fall to the floor. "Damn, Jade. I never seen a guy do that in my gym. You're a fucking horse."

"Thanks."

Before we left, Victor told me that he needed to take a few pictures of me so that Haag could put them on the fight posters that he hung all over Southeast Alaska. Victor mentioned the detail like it was no big thing—but the thought of seeing my face on a boxing poster, hanging outside a bar in Alaska . . . I rarely allowed myself praise, but as I stood against the wall with my fists up, chin down, I was sure that the pose I struck was that of a man.

■

The posters were black, with ROUGHHOUSE FRIDAY written in the *Fight Club* movie font. They were plastered over the front door of the Travelodge. Running up and down the sides of the posters were pictures of all the fighters that Haag wanted to feature for the upcoming Southeast Showdown. It was still a month away, but a lot of fighters who couldn't pull it together to fight during the regular Roughhouse Friday season would sometimes emerge for a weekend of big-money boxing.

There was a photo of Roo in the upper-right corner: shirtless, jacked, wrapped hands under his chin, he looked like an old-time fighter from Hell's Kitchen. The Goat was on there mostly for visibility—even though it was unlikely he'd be flying back to Juneau for another fight. A handful of other local fighters ran along the right side—Sean "the Comeback Kid" Baird, Andrew "the Gun" Swanston—mostly just to bring out fans who wanted to support, as Haag liked to say, "the guy next door!" The Hooligan didn't make the posters—largely, I think, because Haag couldn't track him down for a picture.

My photograph was in the upper-left corner of the poster: hands up, chin down, I was trying to look mean. But my expression was disappointing. I looked unconvincing and unimpressive, more like a teacher dressed up as a boxer than an actual fighter. I had a baby face—round and beardless—and my hair had grown longer; it wasn't my usual shaved head, it was a church-boy haircut.

"Pretty cool," Victor said, admiring the posters. He ripped one off the Travelodge door, handed it to me, then I followed him upstairs to our room.

■

I spent the evening sitting by myself, watching a series of light-weight bouts. Little men thrashing each other, over disputes that Haag announced as he called them into the ring. Over an ex-girlfriend. A wife. A jobsite quarrel. I made the mistake of panning the barroom too carefully, taking in the faces of fans as they whooped and chanted and screamed about nothing. I made the mistake of watching too closely the faces of the winded fighters as they grimaced and squirmed in each other's arms. Marlintini's was a grotesque world of unexamined emotions, unchecked violence, cheap thrills. Everything—the will of the fighters, the blunt slaps of their punches, the shitty music, Haag's voice—felt pointless. These were strange thoughts to be having before a fight. After all, I was the man to beat. I looked across the barroom, contemplating an exit, to where a bouncer was taking tickets. Katrina was at the front of the line, trying to convince the bouncer to let her in.

I crossed the barroom and told the bouncer, "She's with me." Haag's general rule was that fighters' girlfriends got in for free.

The bouncer stepped back and let Katrina pass.

"I was wondering if you were going to come."

Katrina shrugged. "I can't stay." She looked away and then into the barroom, as if searching for someone. "Did you fight yet?"

"In a few minutes."

Katrina nodded. She wasn't paying attention.

"You never called me back."

She shrugged. "I just thought you were a player."

A player. I'd laughed at Miss Mary when she'd asked me if I was a player. I had always thought of a player as someone who played women—who treated them as dispensable, who went from one to the other without looking back. I had thought of the term positively—in an aspirational light. That dating more than one woman at a time was like pulling off some dangerous stunt. But hearing the expression from Katrina made me pause. What had she seen in me that made such a conclusion so obvious? What, from her side of things, did it mean that I was a player? That I was unreliable. That I was someone who didn't have enough sense of who he was to have anything to offer anyone else. That I was too immersed in my own story to think about the needs, the expectations, the emotions, of another person.

Katrina laid her hand on my arm. "I came here because I wanted to tell you that the night you spent in my apartment—it was really nice. It felt really easy." She shrugged. "I liked having you around." She scanned the barroom. "I have to go," she said abruptly. "Good luck in your fight."

Then she disappeared down the stairwell and I went back into the barroom to warm up for my fight.

■

"Here we go, Stone," Victor said. "Four!" Soon we were into a rhythm, working the pads before a small crowd of first-time fighters that had circled around us to watch. *"Whack-whack-whack!"*

Victor hissed during each combination. When I was warm, I stood with him behind the pool table, bouncing on my toes, throwing half punches, watching the crowd move and swell.

The Hooligan came into the barroom wearing a winter hat low over his eyes, a wool coat with the collar up, a satchel over one shoulder. There was no violence in him anymore; I wasn't sure why he was even here. After he'd dressed into his boxing uniform, he stood next to another man, took his beer, and sipped on it for a while, then had a few drags off the man's cigarette. I wasn't sure if it was a performance meant to psych me out or if he just didn't care about the outcome of our fight, but either way, it was working: as I stood in my corner, throwing punches, dressed in my uniform and matching shoes, I felt like a child playing dress-up.

For two minutes, the Hooligan fought with his back to the ropes. He was tired—physically—but also tired of whatever had brought him into Marlintini's in the first place. I kept punching after every clinch, while the Hooligan seemed content to just tie me up. I felt weirdly alone in the ring. The crowd faded away to a muffled chorus. Everything—the ring, the Hooligan, the canvas, the ring girls as they watched us—became a single being moving in the semidarkness of the barroom as if underwater. Time slowed down. I set my feet, feinted right, and threw the lead left to the body that Victor and I had been working on. The punch landed, flush into the Hooligan's right side. He blinked a few times. But his expression was not one of pain; rather, he just looked uninterested in being at the other end of the impact. The final bell rang. I got the win on all three cards, but as the Hooligan and I shook hands, as he left the ring and I remained on the canvas, alone, I didn't feel like I'd finally settled the score. I didn't even feel like I'd beaten him.

■

I sat with Victor at a table in the back corner, watching the final lackluster bouts of the evening. Perhaps it was the imminence of spring, but the Roughhouse season had begun to lose momentum. The lightweight division, without Roo, had little in the way of talent. In one fight, Andrew "the Gun" Swanston asked the ref for a time-out to replace a missing contact lens—then winced heroically through the final round as if fighting with a broken hand. (The Gun, somehow, still got the decision.) The most dangerous of the new fighters was Julio "the Haitian Sensation" Gregoire—who'd come to Juneau from Port-au-Prince while working on a cruise ship and now worked with the Iceman in the Greens Creek Mine. He was young, strong, and unskilled, but his unconventional offense—in which he lifted his right glove high above his head, then brought it down like a club—was difficult for his opponents to avoid. The heavyweight division was even more starved for talent. To find a man over two hundred pounds who was in any kind of fighting shape was like, as Haag sometimes said, finding a Roughhouse fighter who had a working cell phone number. By all accounts, it looked as though the Showstoppah might be the man to beat in the Southeast Showdown.

But that was also the night of the first women's bout of the season. In the March show, in what appeared to be little more than a publicity stunt, the Wildflower had called out a fellow ring girl—an Asian woman named Liesel Weiland—to train for what Haag had determined would be the impromptu ladies' lightweight title. The Wildflower had racked up a half dozen or so fights in her Roughhouse career; Liesel had never so much as tried on a pair of boxing gloves. There was no bad blood between the two women, but by all accounts it appeared that the Wildflower was challenging Liesel to do what so many ring girls had done before her: trade in her bikini for boxing gloves, to experience the other side of the Roughhouse ring. "Bring it on, bitch!" Liesel had said to the Wildflower in front of an eager crowd. But there was no malice in her voice.

The way the two women bounced into the ring in matching

white outfits—white sports bras, white shorts, white socks and shoes—and twin hairdos, two long double braids, gave the event a slapstick flair, like something you'd see at a Hooters restaurant. But as the Wildflower warmed up in her corner, she began to bounce and jump with an energy that was nearly ecstatic. She paced from side to side, swinging her head, pounding her gloves together as if in a trance. I recognized the feelings that boiled inside her. No one entered the Roughhouse ring for something so simple as an adrenaline rush. Meanwhile, across the ring, Liesel threw little punches into space, but her effort was halfhearted; she, compared to the Wildflower, still thought she was just part of a stunt. Then the bell rang.

I knew nothing about the Wildflower then; I had only my vague recognition that every time I fought I had looked to her, standing ringside, hoping that she would recognize me for what I was becoming. Later, I would learn that the Wildflower had grown up in Sitka, spent her youth fighting other girls on the harbor bridge, in the empty lots downtown, while living in and out of temporary housing and the Sitka Hotel. Her father had died when she was young, and she'd been raised by her mother and stepfather—a man who did not treat her well. She'd gone to high school with Victor—whom she remembered as a quiet but serious boy—but had moved to Hoonah on her own when she was eighteen, to live with her aunts and uncles. There, she fell in love with the only blond, blue-eyed boy in town. She'd gotten pregnant, and they'd moved to Juneau to give their daughter a chance at life in the city, but the father was in jail by the time the Wildflower's daughter was born, and the first time she'd introduced him to his little girl was through the window glass at Lemon Creek Correctional Center. After a decade of hard living, the Wildflower had found Roughhouse. For most of her life, she'd earned the attention of men for being pretty. But fighting was different: the sanctioned expression of rage, of anger, made her feel something like dignity.

The night I saw her fight, her sister had died just weeks before, and the Wildflower was living with the grief of losing someone whom she'd always looked up to. Knowing that now, when I remember the way she exploded out of her corner and attacked Liesel with a flurry of punches, I can see the grief beneath her aggression. The Wildflower had little boxing training, but her instincts were good, and she threw straight punches. Liesel, within seconds, shelled up behind her gloves, only fighting back because, I think, she had to. The crowd was drunk now, and for most of the evening they'd seen the Wildflower in a bikini, the way she moved around the canvas strutting and smiling, offering what appeared to be a deep affection for every soul in the barroom. Her turning that affection into violence moved the crowd, and they were all out of their seats, cheering for her. The Wildflower pounded Liesel for two more rounds, and watching the Wildflower battle through the exhaustion of a full bout made me feel good about fighting again. Even the most raw, unskilled bouts, when watched with any empathy at all for the people in them, reveal a tender story about each fighter: what they are made of, who they are, what sadness they carry, what joy. I know it is a bit presumptuous to assume that I can understand what was in the mind of the Wildflower that night, but I believe that the way she fought revealed all that was inside her. Not everyone can fight that way—even in the most vicious battles, one can hold back. I know this because in later fights, I sometimes found myself leaving the ring feeling numb and dull, while on other occasions, I went back to my corner on the verge of confused tears.

As I watched the Wildflower attack Liesel—with volleys of punches, separated by heaving breaths—it became more clear to me that in the ring I was revealing only a small part of myself, in glimpses. I tried too hard to look masculine: tough, violent, uncompromising. I would have been a more interesting fighter, a better fighter, if I had been able to offer, too, the gentleness and quietness that lived inside me. Watching the Wildflower fight was like observing a painting that, over the years, as you remember it, begins to carry new meanings. That I remember that fight so well, so vividly, as clearly as my own, tells me one thing: I was learning that my rage, anger, violence were only temporary tools, meant to take me, always, to some better, more illuminating place. In between rounds, Haag convinced a drunk man from the crowd to enter the ring with his shirt off, to play the part of "ring dude," and his performance was so awful in comparison to the Wildflower's that I could barely watch. If watching her fight made obvious my own reasons for fighting, watching the ring dude perform turned the world outside in again.

When the fight was over, Liesel had a burst eardrum, and her hair was smattered over her face, and the way she hung on the ropes made it clear that she would likely never fight again. The Wildflower could not stop moving. She leaped up and down, danced, waved to her fans, screamed when Haag announced her the winner. When the two women had left the ring and Haag called in the main event—a drab and unmemorable heavyweight bout—the air still crackled with the Wildflower's legacy. After the first round, she came back for an encore: in a bikini and tall leather boots, pumping the cards over her head in tune to the music. The Wildflower offered her face to the crowd—a loving, compassionate face for all the lost souls in Marlintini's. Watching her, I understood something about myself: that all the feelings that had led me into the ring were useless to the world if I could not understand that beneath them—as their cause, their reason and longing—ran a vicious current of love.

PART III

16. SPAWN

Spring had come. The darkness of the winter was replaced by the return of an ever-increasing daylight. I spent my weekends in the mountains, hacking my way up streambeds and scree slopes with a mountaineering ax, ascending above the tree line by midmorning, passing the rest of the day high in the ridges, on nameless crumbling peaks from which you could see straight across Baranof Island. I had gotten to know the mountains well enough that I could enter in one streambed and then exit by another, disappear and wander into one ravine, then climb out along some distant ridge and pop out across town. I knew the names of the peaks—could connect them one by one on a map like a constellation. I began to understand, too, how their contours fit into the others', how a forest became a ridge, which became a peak that descended into a connected valley. What had once appeared to me as a fractured wilderness of forking features was all part of the same map now, the same form, and moving through that territory, in the lengthening days of spring, was like suddenly turning on a light in a room full of shadows.

One clear day, from the summit of Bear Mountain, I spotted what was likely—based on my topographical map—the granite face of Devil's Thumb, the famous route that Jon Krakauer had written about in *Into the Wild*. Standing on that ridge that afternoon, gazing out across the endless peaks and valleys of the Inside Passage, I was struck by how different the experience of mountaineering was from the experience of fighting. There was certainly danger in both pursuits—the likelihood of dying in the mountains far outweighed the likelihood of dying in the ring—but the thrill of climbing, the danger of the wilderness, did not tap into the same vein of feeling that I found throbbing inside me in the Roughhouse ring. I felt alone, and adrift, whenever I wandered into the mountains; I had felt the same way the previous summer, when I'd paddled north. It was a beautiful feeling—a smooth hum of peace, which reminded me that my life was small in comparison to the infinity of the universe. On a bad day, the smooth hum became the droll chant of the void; on a good day, the same hum became the voice of the only kind of God I could believe in. Toward dusk, as I descended from the snowfields along deer trails, I returned to town feeling every bit as alive as I did after a fight. Yet, still, something was missing from that experience: with no crowd, no opponent, no object for my feelings, I remained separate from the world—a spectator of life, wandering through the wilderness.

While admiring a view of the sound from the summit of Bear Mountain, I watched as dozens of seiners—awaiting word from Fish and Game for the opening of the herring fishery—blasted out of the harbor, nets drawn. It was a big quota that year—twenty thousand tons—and for the next forty minutes the water exploded with furious activity. The fishermen had been waiting in town for days to reap their bounty, and now it appeared as though some enormous pressure were being released from deep in the middle of Baranof Island. A few days later, the herring came to shore, to spawn in the shoal waters. I rode my bike down to Mosquito Cove with my fishing pole, hoping to catch some Dolly Varden or maybe snag a few herring for dinner. But when I got there, the cove was already packed with old Tlingit men in skiffs, setting and collecting spruce bow lines—weighed down with rocks, tethered to soda-bottle buoys—which would soon be covered with a coat of golden herring roe. Along the shore, old Filipinas in their husbands' fishing boots tried to kick the silver herring into plastic buckets. As I jigged my line through the milky water of the spawn, the scene appeared before me like one of those vast Buddhist scriptural paintings displayed high along the walls of temples. As the water thrashed with life, as the Tlingit men set their spruce lines, the volcano on Kruzof Island rising up behind them like a portal to another world, the painting told its own story. Never before in my life had I witnessed something in America that so captured the two worlds—of Thailand, of Maine—that fought inside me. Here, far away from both of them, in a passing moment of regeneration, those two channels of blood ran as one.

■

The gym—a place that all winter had become the center of my life—had become, without Victor or Todd or the high school boys to fill it with life, a vacant room that resembled a monastic cell more than a makeshift boxing gym. I tried to stay serious about preparing for the Showdown, even though I knew I'd likely face off with the Hooligan again. But who I fought no longer mattered. Winning didn't matter. All that concerned me was maintaining that sense of completeness that fighting offered me. Maybe it was as simple as being able to call myself a fighter—of having, as my father sometimes said, "a place." My place was the gym, but it could just as well have been the little shop where Paul did his beadwork. But I also knew that the shifting, swirling uncertainty that I had arrived in Sitka with eight months ago had found a home in the gym: not a place to disappear, but to exist. A temple, of sorts, within which that feeling could become what it needed to become, reveal to me its purpose. The ring was that temple, too: a place to fight, but also a corral where I could be contained until my unknown future found its way to the surface.

The high school boys, now that their only fights of the year were behind them, happily stopped showing up to the gym in favor of fishing, hanging out with girls, riding their four-wheelers on Harbor Mountain; Todd was retired from the sport, perhaps content to spend his days high in his houseboat. Victor and I trained on nights when he could break free from work and home, but those nights were rare. He was still making occasional runs back down to Seattle, to be with Miranda, and it seemed unfair to expect him to show up to train me.

One solitary night in the gym, when I'd fallen into a hissing reverie of bag work, Roo showed up, his duffel bag in his hand, dressed in his workout clothes. "I reckon I'll put in a few hours before the Showdown," Roo said as he tied on his boxing shoes. For the next month, Roo and I sparred round after round, sometimes fifteen rounds in a row, chatting about strategy in between rounds, chatting about life after we were done. I still couldn't lay a glove on Roo, but I began to realize that a part of me didn't want to. There was something necessary about knowing that Roo was an unhittable and invincible figure. I'd rarely allowed myself heroes, but Roo—an autonomous, self-reliant man—was one of them. Every time I tried to hit him and missed, I respected him even more.

When we sparred, Roo would sometimes pause in the middle of a round to teach me wily boxing tricks that he'd picked up from better fighters in Australia: holding out a jab stiffly, waiting for me to hit it, then landing a big right once I took the bait; clinching, using my shoulder to open a space between my opponent's elbows, driving uppercuts into the opening, short, quick lethal punches invisible to the crowd.

Roo, too confident in his defense, never bothered to wear any headgear. Ever since I'd first shown up at the gym, I'd been paying careful attention to how he fought, and after five or six rounds we lulled each other into a safe rhythm of punches that found their marks without inflicting any pain. I noticed that Roo kept letting his right hand drop every time he tossed out a jab. It was likely a tic that he'd developed from not having good enough sparring partners to act as correctives. After he let his defense down six or seven times, I started timing my left, without throwing it. I didn't like plotting a trap for someone I admired so much, but I'd taken enough of Roo's punches to know that he'd do the same to me. On the next jab, I punched into the empty pocket over his glove—a chopping southpaw counterpunch that Victor had taught me. I didn't even get to see the punch land. One second, Roo was coming forward; the next second, I felt a clean, sweet-spot sensation in my knuckles, and Roo was on his knees, one glove on the floor in support keeping him upright. When he looked up, a stream of dark blood ran out of his nostril. "Fahk, mate! Ya fahkin' whaled me!" Roo turned to the door, as if someone had been watching. "Sparring, and the guy fahkin' whales me," he said to no one. He took off his gloves, swore, threw the gloves in his duffel bag, dressed, and left the gym.

The next night, Roo invited me over for dinner. When I got to his house, his nose was a bit swollen, but didn't show signs of being broken. I didn't say anything about the punch, and he didn't seem all that angry about it. Instead, we sat on the couch in his living room, watching an old Kostya Tszyu bout.

When Nicole came home from work and saw us sitting on the couch, she laughed. "I don't get it. You guys beat the crap out of each other and now you're best friends?"

Roo shrugged. "Nothing personal, right, mate?"

After dinner he took me out back, to his shop, where he showed me all the things he'd collected during the year of his walkabout before he'd settled down with Nicole: a set of musk-ox horns from the Arctic Circle, several deer he'd stuffed. In a photo album of the walkabout year was a photo of him standing with Tszyu himself, in a gym in Sydney. Another picture was of Roo with a Maasai warrior, who was wearing Roo's ball cap, which Roo had given the man in exchange for a knife that hung on the wall. Then Roo showed me a picture of him and Nicole on top of a mountain range, smiling; another picture of them in Las Vegas, not long after they'd eloped. There was a marked difference in the expression on Roo's face in these photos: he was happy, at peace with the world.

Then he showed his two Southeast Showdown belts, which were lying across a weight bench. I picked them up. They were heavier than I thought they'd be.

"If me and Nicole ever have a son, I'll pass these on to him." Roo laughed to himself. "I reckon not many boys can say their old dad was an Alaskan boxing champion."

■

One afternoon at school, a boy named Bradley came into my classroom. He smelled like weed and cigarettes, his eyes bloodshot. When I asked him what he was doing in Sitka, he explained that he was from a small town in Oregon, but had recently gotten in trouble with a "Mexican skater gang" that had beat him with their skateboards after assuming that Bradley stole their weed. As he told the story, he started crying, so I figured he was telling the truth. He'd been at Sitka High for about two days, and already kids were making fun of him for dressing like a "baby thug." "Fuck them," he said. I pulled out a chair and welcomed Bradley to my classroom.

Over the next week, Bradley and I quickly became friends. He was older than most of my other students, and he treated me with respect and saw me as someone who could help him do well in school. "I don't want no GED," Bradley said. "I want a real diploma." He wanted to go to trade school, to become a mechanic and work on custom cars. The only thing standing between him and graduation was a major research paper in his English class. His teacher was known for holding her students to a high standard and being quite strict with rules, but Bradley accused her of being a "tight-ass bitch."

When I asked him why he was making so little progress on his research paper—he'd chosen surfing as his topic—he told me that he didn't have enough time. He lived in a trailer with his sister and younger brothers and stepmother and father, and it was always noisy, and his parents, he said, drank too much. He also put in long shifts at a grocery store. We tried working on the paper after school, but by the end of the day we were both sick of being stuck in my windowless classroom, and after a few days of consideration, I decided that I—with a whole apartment to myself, and enough money to buy groceries for another person—needed to take matters into my own hands.

A couple of days later, Bradley's dad's truck pulled up in my driveway, and Bradley and his father moved a bunk bed into my apartment. His father was a man of few words and didn't so much as shake my hand before driving away. Then Bradley went about unpacking his things: a samurai sword that he put in a stand over his bureau, a big TV and video game console, a poster of Eminem.

At first, our new arrangement worked out well. Bradley and I would listen to underground rap at night—Jedi Mind Tricks was our favorite—and I'd make us some dinner. Then we'd play video games, or I'd teach him to box, even though he couldn't throw more than a few punches without doubling over and coughing. Then he'd do his schoolwork. Spending so much time with Bradley gave me an idea of what it would be like to have my own child one day—a son, whom I could teach things to, whom I could raise to be like me. I felt an obligation to be home when he was, even if he didn't need anything specific from me. Mostly, I just wanted him to know that no matter what he was up to, he could count on my being around. The long hours I spent staring at my walls, listening to the rain fall outside—they just disappeared from everyday life, and I was glad for it.

A few weeks later, Bradley's paper was in good shape. He was even proud of it. He turned it in on time, but a few days later he came to my class, tears rolling down his cheeks, cursing. "Fuckin' bitch!" Bradley punched the wall. "Fuckin' bitch failed me!" Apparently, he'd forgotten to provide an annotated bibliography of his research materials, and the teacher wouldn't give him a second chance. I went upstairs to talk to the teacher, told her that the mistake was partially my fault, asked her if we might be able to do a rewrite. She agreed to that—even though I could tell she disliked Bradley just as much as he disliked her. But when I brought the news to Bradley, he wouldn't have it. "Fuck her. I'll just get a GED. Anyways, I'm going to mechanics' school."

I came home from the gym the next day to find Bradley's father's truck in my driveway, Bradley's bunk bed disassembled in the back. His dad smelled like beer. He was smiling, glowing with a buzz. Inside, Bradley was packing the last of his things.

"What's going on?"

"I got homesick," he said with a dopey smile. "I just don't think I'm ready to live on my own." He thanked me for helping him out, said it was nothing personal. Then we shook hands. "Just so you know," Bradley said before leaving, "you're the only teacher I ever liked."

From my doorway, I watched him walk toward his father. Next to him, Bradley looked like a little kid.

A few days later, the guidance counselor upstairs told me that Bradley had dropped out of Sitka High, so he could work full-time with his dad.

■

Toward the end of April, Miranda threw Victor a birthday party, at a beach at the end of HPR. As a gift, the high school boys and

I had all chipped in to buy Victor a black hooded sweatshirt that read SITKA BOXING CLUB on the back. We got one for Roo, too, whose birthday fell about the same time as Victor's. Our intention had been to impress the two men with the gifts, to show them how much we appreciated their training. But when they tried on the sweatshirts, they were too big and looked kind of silly. I had bought one for myself, too, which I was planning on wearing into the ring for the Showdown. Standing among Victor's family that night, I was struck by how proud I was to be fighting for a community that had taught me something about who I was. That I was going to represent that community in the ring brought a different gravity to the meaning of fighting.

The grills were full of meat from a moose that Victor had shot the previous fall in Skagway. His mother and father were there, and his brothers, and some cousins and their kids. By now, most people in Victor's family recognized me as the fighter who would carry on Victor's legacy and regarded me with quiet nods of respect. It is hard not to compare that reception to how, later in my life, back in New England, people I had known since I was a boy had received me as a fighter: mostly with confused and judging silence. How that silence would infuriate me, how little it recognized what lived beneath my appearance, how insistently it asked me to remain a child. But in Sitka, among Victor's family, there was something like pride—but more elevated and complex—attached to fighting. It revealed an inner seriousness and discipline, courage and fearlessness—and, perhaps, also a common recognition that fighting was a way of honoring the shared violence that belonged not only to the person fighting but also to the people who believed in him. Some of this, I suppose, had to do with cultural forces, with the deep history that floated around town but was rarely spoken about. Once, Victor showed me a copy of the Tlingit warrior code: to be humble, to be loyal, to fight to your last breath in battle. I'd never come across a warrior code in the circles of middle-class New England; as far as I know, one does not exist.

Toward the end of the party, Victor came over to me with a can of Rainier in his hand. "You feeling good?"

"Yeah," I said. "I'm feeling good." By then I had learned that the question of feeling good was loaded with other questions: about whether your mind was right, your body was prepared, and you had made peace with all the wild anxieties that visited you in the days before a fight. I told him I'd been training, running, keeping myself strong with push-ups and sit-ups.

Victor nodded. "Good. Good. That's good. You know, man, I been bringing the middleweight title back to Sitka for four years in a row." He paused. "I know the season's getting long, but . . . not many guys can say they did that."

"Did what?"

"Showed up in Alaska in a sea kayak and became a boxing champion in one season. You bring that belt back home, and . . . that'd be something."

We shook hands. "Crush skulls, steal souls," I said.

■

When I got back to my apartment, I felt as though I had some specific business to attend to. Without hesitation, I called my father. He was staying on a military base somewhere in the Southwest, after having just met a platoon of soldiers, at 3:00 a.m., on the tarmac, as they came back from Ramadi. In the days ahead, he would debrief each of them, individually, for five minutes at a time, to see whether they were ready to return to civilian life. Few of them ever were, he said.

I asked my father how he was holding up.

"I'm all right. I'm all right. Steady as she goes." The one thing my father could tell the men was that no matter how they felt about the politics of the war, about the politicians who made decisions far from the battlefield, about the country they were fighting in and the causes of the war, the single undisputable thing they could rely on was their love for one another. "I'm not afraid to use that word. I tell them I love them. Some guys think I'm a kook. Other guys, they need to hear it." As my father spoke, I imagined those men standing before my father as he told them he loved them. It was true. He did love them. But I could not see that love in simple terms. I thought of Victor, of my father, and decided that there were just two types of men: the ones who stayed and the ones who didn't.

Then I told my father that I was fighting in the Southeast Showdown in a week.

"No shit." My father mentioned that he was flying back East that same weekend. There was some chance, he said, that he could hop a military flight through Juneau.

I paused—a pang of regret, a desire to take back the implicit invitation. But it was too late. I told my father that if he could come, he should fly right into Juneau, get himself a hotel room at a place called the Travelodge. The bar where I fought was right across the street.

17. THE SHOWDOWN

I knocked on the door of my father's room. He had been living out of his suitcase for the past week. His face looked tired and worn, his clothes were rumpled. As we leaned forward to hug each other, I felt something new and invisible running between us.

"How you feeling, my son?"

"I feel good."

For the next few minutes, my father sat on the bed, asking me questions about my opponents while I stood in front of the mirror with the hood of my Sitka boxing sweatshirt over my head, throwing punches. I was trying to communicate something to him; trying to put into words the mysterious thing that I carried with me into the ring. I threw a few more punches, then told him it was time to go to Marlintini's.

Roo and Nicole met us in the lobby. When I introduced Roo to my father, a strange pride rose up inside me. In Roo, I had a model of the man I wanted to be: autonomous, industrious, single-minded, and tough. My father possessed none of Roo's traits, and I wanted him to know it, and to know that I knew it, too. When my father thanked Roo for "looking after my boy," Roo shrugged and said, "I reckon he does a pretty good job looking after himself." My father nodded. "I reckon he does."

■

It was still unclear who was fighting in each division of the Showdown. To beef up the lightweight division, Haag had flown in a team of men from Anchorage. The most recognized name in the group was Glen "the Backyard Brawler" Laufenberger. He sometimes fought twice in a single night, driving between Eagle River and Anchorage, pocketing a thousand bucks by midnight. The heavyweight title was a wash: all the great fighters from Victor's era had disappeared, and it looked like it was going to be the Showstoppah versus Mike "the Rock" Gravel. As for my division, the Hooligan was still the only middleweight whom Haag could find to fight me, but a single-bout Southeast Showdown wasn't much of a Showdown. Somehow, Haag convinced a Roughhouse veteran named Fernando Pintang to fight me in the semifinals. In his younger years, Pintang had fought as a lightweight, but he'd gained enough weight to move up a division. I wasn't all that worried about facing Pintang: from across the barroom, he looked old and pudgy and uninterested in getting into the kind of battle that I was looking for.

I stood with my father as Haag called all the fighters into the ring.

"Paddled from Seattle, Warshington, to Sitka, Alaska, in a kayak!" Haag said. "Jade the Stone Coffin!"

I climbed through the ropes, saluted the crowd, returned to my father's side.

"You're going by Jade now?" he said.

"Yeah."

"How'd that come about?"

Changing my name had been my way of declaring that I was my own person, that the story of who I was belonged only to a past that I alone had written. But now, insisting on calling myself Jade instead of Jed felt juvenile. "Everyone up here just started saying it that way. I just never got around to telling them they were wrong."

Without Victor to warm me up on the mitts, and with Roo busy preparing for his own fight, I asked my father to step in. First, we tried with a small pair of mitts—the same kind Victor used—that we found lying on the pool table among gloves and wraps, but my father didn't have the coordination or hand speed to hold the targets effectively. Then we found another pair of mitts—two large yellow rectangular pads—that worked better and didn't require the person holding them to do much more than hold them up in front of their face. But even that was difficult for my father. Every time I punched one of the pads, he'd fall off-balance or shift position, so that the next punch I threw missed the target. I tried to show him how to time the mitts with my punches, but he couldn't figure it out, and kept flinching every time my fist hit the mitts. His expressions of surprise made me punch harder.

After a few minutes, I started throwing punches with the same speed and power I used with Victor. But the pads were too big and, behind the yellow wall, my father had difficulty seeing my punches coming. In one instance, he lost his balance, one of the pads fell, and my glove glanced over his guard and clipped him on the side of the head. The impact knocked his glasses off-kilter. I stopped punching. "Keep going," my father said, rearranging the mitts. I was in a full sweat now, all the prefight emotions rising to a crescendo, but the image of his crooked glasses, his earnest, yearning face, took the heat out of me. "I'm warm."

"You sure?"

I waved my father off. "I'm good."

My father pulled the pads off his hands, straightened his glasses. "Jesus, Son. You're a goddamn steam train."

∎

Fighting Fernando was like trying to inflict pain on a soggy blanket. By the second round, he'd lost all interest in winning the fight and calmly fell to his knees after I landed a powerless jab on his forehead. He took the count, got up, but as soon as I jabbed him, he went down again. By the third round, all the aggression I'd built up before the fight had no place to go, and when the final bell rang, I went back to my corner, furious that I hadn't been able to finish him off. When I found my father in the crowd, he patted me on the shoulders. "Looked good in there."

I shook my head. "That guy was nothing. Should have knocked him out."

For the rest of the evening we stood together watching several bouts in the lightweight division. Roo advanced to the finals after beating the Haitian Sensation in an awkwardly matched clash of styles pitting Roo's clean boxing against the Sensation's raw, overhead club-fisted attack. In the second round, the two men butted heads, and Roo's eye swelled up to the size of a grapefruit. He got the decision—the fight was much closer than it should have been—but afterward he wandered around the barroom squinting out of his swollen eye, an expression that made him look like he was scrutinizing the motivations of every fighter in Marlintini's, calling us out for the real reasons we were here.

∎

The next morning my father and I ate breakfast at Donna's. Over biscuits and gravy, we talked about what was next for him. He drummed the table. "You know, there might be an opportunity for me to go over." The work would be entirely administrative, but he'd likely be serving on a base in Afghanistan. I asked him if he wanted to go. He shrugged. The allure of leaving home, of reporting for duty, had already captured him. There was only one thing holding him back. "It'd be hell on my marriage. I'm not sure if Martha would ever forgive me."

He told me a story about being at dinner with Martha and several friends a few months earlier, when Martha had asked him what was more important, his service with the military or their marriage. My father paused. "I was in a dark place. I'm doing work that feels important for the first time in my life. I'm starting to understand what I was put on this earth to do."

"What did you say?"

He took a deep breath, nodded to himself. "Let's just say I made the mistake of telling her the truth."

It was a heroic tale: service over marriage, his loyalty to his brothers-in-arms over his commitment to a woman. But the moral equation of his heroism didn't balance. As my father rambled on about men and sacrifice and truth, I began to calculate the facts of my father's story as I understood it. I saw in his eyes a lack of understanding of what had been left out of the story: her side of it.

And then I started talking, saying everything I had never before said. About betrayal and sacrifice, about lying and cheating and empathy and pain. About my mother. About me. About my father's weaknesses as a man, about my strength and my mother's strength and the strength of her bloodline, about the sacrifices she had made in my name. "You have no fucking idea what that does to a person." Leaving a country behind, raising children, alone, in a culture that is not your own. My voice rose to a pitch I didn't recognize. "You went to live with her best fucking friend. Her best friend. And we had nothing in Maine. Nothing. We were alone." As I spoke, I felt myself come alive: my body filled with power and rage and anger and joy. It coursed through my arms, pumped in my blood, flooded my brain. Not even in the ring had I ever felt such emotions with such clarity. It was like they were all swirling before me, in a cloud of smoke and mist and formless, wordless power. In that power lived all the stories and memories and failures and feelings I had carried with me for twenty years, all the things I had been too young to understand, all the things I had seen but not said, felt but not named, overlooked but never faced squarely. "You'll never know," I told my father. "You have no idea."

By then, several people in Donna's had turned their attention upon us. I paused, leaned back, looked out the window. I was not sure what I had just said. The words did not feel entirely like my own. They were new to this world—expressions of another person still emerging. I knew only what I saw in the moment: that my father, sitting across the table, silent, sullen, the mask of his manliness hanging crookedly from his face, was as separate from me as a stranger, as endemic to my being as my two hands. In that hidden face I could see his own pain—far off and unknowing, tied to the myths of a heritage that lived in my blood, too. I understood only one thing: that my father, as large and powerful and important a man as he appeared to me in my boyhood, had held no power over the pain that possessed him. As I studied his face, examined his skin and eyes and teeth and bald head inscribed with lines of aging, my father became more real to me than he'd ever been, more vivid and human and flawed and complex. And it was only in seeing him this way that a single word rose up inside me, a word so simple and fundamental that for so many years I had not been able to see it hanging before me like a swinging pendulum. I said the word, a single, unanswerable syllable.

"Why?"

The word hung between us. And in it lived all the variations of its meaning. The why was asking my father why he'd left my mother, and me, for another life. But that was the question of my younger self, a question driven by a childish longing to fix what was broken. In time, the meaning of the why would reveal itself as something much bigger: Why do we love? Why do we go to war? Why do we leave our homes? Why do we forget where we come from? Why must we bury the past? Why can we not live without it?

I wanted my father to tell me the answer to every why—as if he alone were my maker, as if I alone were the only person who had ever railed against the most basic facts of existence.

We sat in silence for several minutes.

"You know, my son, I used to tell people that I'd kiss your mother's boots before I ever left her." My father laughed. "I actually believed that."

I remember little of what he said after that. My mind was already floating somewhere above the conversation, lost in the echo of the why. I recall that he tried to defend himself, explained that he'd been out of his mind, that it was a strange time in his life, in the life of the nation, that I shouldn't accuse him until I'd gone through the same situation myself. But I would hear none of it. I was twenty-four years old, hungry for ground to stand on so that I could go forth into a new world on my own terms. Our conversation was just beginning, and we would have it over and over and over, in different ways, in different circumstances, for many years, marveling at the shape of the why in all of its infinite forms. Even now I still find myself believing that out on the horizon, on the other side of the mist that forever hangs between us, is a final redeeming answer.

My father took a long, deep breath. "My only hope is that maybe you'll do a little better than I did. That you don't make this story your own."

I looked out the window, studied the shapes of the mountains beyond town, searched the line of their ridges for some far-off blinking truth. Our server brought our bill to the table, and my father took it to the register to settle up.

The world was a good place to buy in, but the bill always came.

■

The first rounds of my fight with the Hooligan passed in a blur of unmemorable motion. By then, we were in the midst of our fourth fight, and our exchanges became merely the inevitable consequences of the physics of our bodies. I was bigger, stronger; he was faster, leaner. Over the three minutes, my size and wind would wear him down. The other things—my desire to fight, the lack of his—would only shade in the outcome. By the third round, the Hooligan started to tire and, rather than meet me in the ring, retreated to the ropes. I came at him, he tied me up, and while I fought my way out of the clinch, I felt myself detach not only from the Hooligan, but from the action of the fight, from the breathing intensity inside the ring. Then I began to notice things outside the ring: The twisted faces in the crowd. The shimmer of the neon lights. Individual voices floated through my ears, then faded. The clinking of glasses, the distant bark of Haag—"Teacher! Student!"— tumbling across the barroom. As the Hooligan swayed before me, he appeared like a stranger. But around us there rose up a swirling narcotic mist. For a moment, I saw all the faces of the men who had made me. The whalers of Nantucket, as they drifted out to sea. The slouching soldiers, wandering through the jungles of Southeast Asia. The knights of the Round Table, slaughtering their enemies in the name of their king. Lancelot, alone, stricken by sin, exiled by his own betrayals. Kwai Chang Caine, in a Shaolin robe, sparring with the Last Electric Knight, as Muhammad the Asian Buddhist Prince duked it out with the Red Baron. And there was Kostya Tszyu and an angry, seething Jesus, fighting for a welterweight title. Beyond the ropes, in the darkness of the Marlintini's barroom, I could even sense the presence of my father: dressed in his Middlebury College football uniform, kneeling before the broken sword of a Thai warrior in the moments before he brought the man's daughter back to his country. As the faces swirled in the cigarette smoke over the ring, they all became part of the same story, tied to one another in a single mythology. A hero with a thousand faces, squaring off with Iron John. A solemn, tortured Buddha, meeting his son for the first time before deciding, in the middle of the night, to leave him behind.

Ding. Ding. Ding.

The Hooligan and I stood in the middle of the ring. Then Haag came between us and read the cards, then I felt him raising my hand. "The winner! From a little town called Sitka, Alaska!"

The Wildflower wrapped a belt around my waist. There is a picture of this moment: of me, a towel around my neck, staring directly at the camera. For many years I looked at the photo, laughed at it, because in the details surrounding me you could see the small-time-ness of the Roughhouse Friday boxing show: Haag is standing ringside, in a goofy-looking hat and bow tie. The judges sit at a crooked table, in lawn chairs, in front of a drooping American flag. The Hooligan, standing next to me, looks out of shape. My shorts are too big, my frame too bulky for a boxer.

But sometimes when I look at the photo, I see another story: one that, ultimately, is a message to my father. It was, after all, my father who took the picture. And it is me, after all, who is looking back at him from the ring. Do you see? my face asks the camera. Do you see what I've become?

And in that moment, I should have understood the meaning of my name: The quiet vein of violence that ran through me, that made me want to fight, was not my own, did not belong only to me. It was the tail of a much longer story, of friendship and betrayal, race and love, dislocation and war. Of whale hunters and rice farmers, pilgrims and soldiers, sons and lovers. And now it had found its way into my life for a brief moment. And this whole time I had been thinking that I was the weapon, that I was the sword, when, really, I was only its temporary home.

"The Stone!" Haag shouted at the crowd. "Jade 'the Stone' Coffin!"

■

For the main event, the barroom had grown hot and surly with the heat of the crowd. Everyone was drunk and looking for something to yell about. Roo's eye had all but closed, and the wound had turned dark purple. I was working his corner. Nicole stood with my father in the crowd, arms crossed, biting her lip. For two rounds, the Backyard Brawler stumbled around the canvas, stiff legged and lost, lacking all grace. Roo slipped and popped and drove uppercuts and right hands through the Brawler's defense. Between rounds, I told Roo, "You're good. You're way up. Just keep your distance." But Roo wanted more than a mere victory by decision.

The last sixty seconds: Two men, brutally tired, punching blindly, out of their minds with exhaustion. They tumbled and crashed, wrestled and spun, collapsed into each other's arms. Roo couldn't stay away. He fought the only way he knew how: recklessly and without restraint. Every time Roo landed a punch, the crowd roared and rose to their feet, and in the last thirty seconds the whole bar was nearly on top of the ring, starving to be a part of what was happening inside it. The Brawler stumbled forward in a daze, teetered around the canvas, staring at the lights, swatting at Roo occasionally, punching at air. With ten seconds left, Roo dropped his fists, fell forward with a looping right hand. The right hand was meant to stuff the Brawler deep into the cavern that he had come out of, a right hand meant to stuff the winter back into its hole until it was time to come out again.

But the Brawler had one final offering: a short hook, thrown blindly from his waist. As Roo's head dipped forward, the Brawler's fist found his chin. Roo stood upright for a moment, his limp body held erect by the impact. Then, in a smooth, silent, and effortless motion, Roo fell backward in a perfect arc. His head hit the canvas, bounced once, and remained still.

The Brawler blinked several times before realizing that the fight was over. At his feet, Roo lay before him like a dead man. The ref stood over Roo, looked down at him, waved his hands. Nicole tried to enter the ring, but I held her back. Beyond Roo, the Brawler was dancing in his corner. His men were hugging each other. The crowd, Roo loyalists ten seconds earlier, had changed sides entirely. Haag held the mic but said nothing. The Wildflower cried.

It took a full twenty seconds for Roo to come to. When I hoisted him onto his stool, he was barely conscious. His eyes were glossy and loose. He leaned forward and vomited into a bucket. He puked several more times, and I sponged water on him. Nicole came into the ring, held his head in her hands. His first words: "Laysee, mate. Thass just me been laysee." He was still half out when he rose to his feet for the decision. He smiled at the crowd and waved off their cheers. As Roo left the ring, he leaned on Nicole, and they made their way back to the hotel. I looked at my father and he looked at me, then we followed behind them.

■

Katrina waited for me outside the entrance to the Travelodge. We'd made plans over e-mail; her only condition was that she didn't want anything to do with the Roughhouse show. It was a fair request. I gave my father my belt and bag, told him I'd meet him at the airport the next morning. He'd flown five thousand miles to see me fight, but now that I had shown him what I had become, I felt no remorse about leaving him.

"Who's that?" Katrina said.

I looked at the man, worried his appearance would confuse her. "That's my father."

"I feel bad leaving him behind," she said. "He came all the way up here . . ."

"He'll be all right."

We drove into downtown, to a bar called the Viking. We sat at a small table in the back, smoking Katrina's menthol cigarettes and drinking beers and carrying on a light conversation about nothing. I always felt free and calm and at peace after a fight, but now I felt better than I ever had.

Toward last call, a man came up to me, slapped me on the back. "I just saw you fight! You're the champ!"

I thanked the man. We shook hands. He wandered off.

Katrina laughed. "How's that feel?"

"Good," I said.

I looked around the barroom: Marlintini's was less than ten miles down the Glacier Highway, but that night we could have been in another city. After we finished our drinks, we walked outside, into a clear night, into the crowds filing out of the bars, and it was nice to be lost among them, good to be a stranger again.

■

Katrina dropped me off at the airport the next morning. We didn't make plans to see each other again. We barely knew each other, had no precedent for commitment beyond two drunken nights at bars, but the feeling of parting ways was still sad to me. At that point in my life the only good thing I had to give anyone was several hours of company; beyond that I was empty. Perhaps that was cruel, or cheap or disrespectful or even obvious; perhaps if one has nothing good to give, one should refrain from offering. But when I look back at my younger self, I see a young man who still believed that he was getting away with something, that coming and going and giving and taking would have no effect on him, and no effect on the people he was taking from. That life was light, time was cheap, and there would always be an early flight back to Sitka the next morning. As I got out of her truck at the airport, I told Katrina I'd be in touch.

She shrugged. "I'm sure we'll figure something out."

We never saw each other again.

■

I walked with my father down the airport road. He was carrying his suitcase over his shoulder, and as I walked alongside him, I pictured him as a young man, coming back from war with a Thai bride. I pictured him driving away from my apartment building in Maine, headed back to Vermont. I pictured him in full military uniform walking toward me across the tarmac. Even if I knew that he was not the warrior he pretended to be, even if I knew that within him were all the flaws of every man, even if I knew that his intentions with the Thai bride were flawed, that they would not become what they were meant to become . . . Still, even in light of all that, I would be glad to see him there waiting for me.

My father's flight back East left first. What I remember from that moment of our parting is an image of him walking away. I had seen him this way so many times before—over and over, throughout my boyhood, as he left me in Maine—yet, as he disappeared into the sky, I was glad to see him go.

A few minutes later, Kid Roo came into the terminal with Nicole. His eye was swollen shut, black nearly. He sat with his head on Nicole's shoulder. While we waited for our flight, we didn't speak. Then the Anchorage fighters passed us on their way to their gate.

"Good fight," the Brawler said.

Roo shook his hand. "Yeah, mate. Good fight."

I looked at the Brawler. He looked back at me, confused by my stare. As he passed me, I watched him move, calculating the terms of my revenge. In four years, he'd be dead from a drug overdose. In four years, I'd be a father.

18. THE GRAIL

"*Ka-kaw! Ka-kaw!*" The sound was coming from my window. I thought it was a bird, a raven or a crow, but as I searched for my glasses, the bird started speaking English. "*Ka-kaw-ka-kaw*, mother-fucker!" When I saw the silhouette of Victor's baseball-hatted round head in my window, I got out of bed to let him in.

"How's it going, Champ?" He sat down on my couch, next to my new Showdown belt, and picked it up with both hands. "Feel good to be the fucking champ?" Victor seemed happier than I'd seen him for a long time, and for the next several minutes he peppered me with questions about the Showdown. I mentioned that my father had been at the fight, but omitted our argument in Donna's. "I still remember when my dad saw me win the Show-down. Came with all my fishing buddies. He must have spent a thousand bucks at the bar that night celebrating. That was pretty cool." Victor looked at the belt for a moment, this time studying it more carefully. "Haag made 'em a lot nicer this year."

Victor was much less sympathetic than I'd expected him to be about Roo's loss to the Brawler. "That's boxing, man. Roo never respected the Roughhouse show. You saw him. He didn't train. He didn't work out like you did. That other guy, Haag told me he'd been fighting all year up in Anchorage, driving all over the Interior to different towns to fight three, four times a week while working the night shift sweeping floors at a NAPA. That kid worked his ass off for that win. Who knows, maybe the kid deserved it." Victor probably saw a little bit of himself in the Brawler: not the most gifted athlete to ever enter a ring, but more than just another Native kid who was going to slip through the cracks.

When I asked Victor about his trip to Seattle with Miranda, he told me that being in a city for four days had just about driven him mad. "I swear I was losing my fucking mind. I went out walking around a couple times, but there was too much going on, too many fuckin' people, too much pavement everywhere. The only place I could get any peace was in the movie theater. I must have seen the new *Spider-Man* like four times."

Miranda's doctor had advised them that the climate of Sitka—the rain, the cold—was not the best thing for her recovery. She'd be better off someplace Down South—Florida, or maybe Arizona. "You ever been to Arizona?" Victor said. He shook his head. "I don't think we're going anywhere. Miranda was the one who told the doctor that she isn't raising her child anywhere but here." On the flight home, Miranda had even told Victor that as soon as he got up in the morning, she wanted him to go out fishing, to clear his head. Victor looked at me. "You coming?" I told Victor I had to be at school at eight. "Ha! I used to skip school all the time to go fishing!"

We were on the water by six, lines down and gear set and making our first passes along Eastern Channel by six thirty. It was too early in the season for the first run of silvers, but Victor seemed plenty content to fish on luck. It was a gorgeous, clear morning on the water. To the south the horizon shimmered with distant morning light; to the north low shadows spread over the mountains like a massive carpet. A westerly wind curled around the southern tip of Kruzof Island and made the water in the sound choppy, but inside the cabin of Victor's boat the wind was little more than a whisper. When all the lines were straight and the wind was at our back, Victor took a can of dip out of his pocket, put a pinch in his cheek, then sat back in his chair. "So, Jade, what's your plan?"

Plan? The word rang in my ears as if Victor had just cuffed me on the side of the head. All winter, my only plan had been to keep up my training until I brought the Roughhouse Friday title back to Sitka. Now that I'd been back in town for a full twenty-four hours, I hadn't even begun to think about what was next. I told Victor that the only thing on the horizon was the end of my apartment lease.

Victor remembered what it was like being twenty-four. That was the summer he'd bought an old jeep and driven from Skagway all the way up to Fairbanks, for electricians' school. The miles and miles of empty wilderness, all the little outposts along the way—it was one of the coolest experiences he'd ever had, and it showed him what the world was like beyond Sitka. "You know, I bet you could get a job teaching up there in one of those villages in the bush. Up there, you'd pass for Native." After a long pause, Victor said, "You know, Jade, I usually fish with Todd every summer, but this summer, I been thinking: I just don't know." Victor shrugged. "If you want the job, it's all yours. I'd even front the money for your permit to help you get started."

As I sat there watching the rod tips bob and nod, I didn't realize the gravity of Victor's offer: to fish with him for the summer, to run his gear, to care for his boat, to learn about these waters through a medium as intimate as fishing, to work alongside Victor as he performed the necessary rituals of subsistence that his ancestors had performed for thousands of years, in fishing grounds that families like his own had fought to reclaim for over a century—it was more than just an opportunity to work on another boat. That Victor trusted me with all of that—his knowledge, his investment, his heritage—and that I had earned it, perhaps by proving myself in the Roughhouse ring, perhaps by showing him that I was a good friend, was not lost on me.

Then, almost to himself, Victor said, "Or maybe you just don't want to stay in Alaska." I can still remember the tone of that admission: as if the thought had never before occurred to him, ever, that the world beyond Alaska—a world of too many people, too much pavement, where the only place you could get any peace and quiet was in a movie theater—was a place anyone would seek out. "I understand if you want to get out of town. Like I used to tell the Goat: you can only fight Roughhouse for so long before you gotta see what's out there."

We made a few more passes up and down the channel, then, when the hope of an early run of silvers faded, we pulled in our lines, tied off the gear, and steamed back to Mosquito Cove. On his way into town, Victor dropped me off at Sitka High in time for the morning bell. It was not the last time we saw each other, but in my memory this was how we said goodbye.

■

By then, all of my students who were going to pass their classes had no chance of failing, and all of my students who were failing had no chance of passing, so I more or less treated each day as a kind of extended end-of-the-year party. I had pizzas delivered to my classroom, and on days when it wasn't raining, we hung out in a small clearing behind the school where there was a rope swing and several spruce stumps for chairs, just sitting in the sun talking about summer plans. I knew that I had learned a great deal from these young people, had seen in them versions of myself that revealed the forces in my own life—culture, history, the way they never left us—that I had been blind to. In some ways, this seems to be the great flaw of being young: that there is certain knowledge that, even if we are given it, can do nothing to save us from what we are bound to become.

A lot of kids were trying to get jobs in town—usually in the cruise-ship industry, selling fur or trinkets or slinging burgers—but some other kids had signed up for a service program called Young Life, in which they got to travel to Juneau and to other towns across Alaska, volunteering and meeting other Young Lifers from Down South. I'd never heard of Young Life before, and it sounded like a good opportunity for my kids, many of whom had never left Sitka. Then one day a Native kid named Ken came to school wearing a bright orange Young Life T-shirt, and I noticed that the *f* in *Life* was replaced by a small crucifix. I had never heard Ken talk about being a Christian, so I asked him how he'd gotten involved in the program. He told me that one day while he was hanging around downtown, this nice older guy had approached him and invited him to come to the Young Life offices, where some other nice people gave Ken free pizza and let him play video games, then talked to him about Jesus. Several other students had had the same experiences, and when I asked the kids how they planned to pay for their trips, they told me that the Young Life agents said scholarships were available. Also, one of the Young Life missionaries had said that they might take the kids to an amusement park in Canada. None of my kids had been to an amusement park before. I almost started running my mouth about how messed up that sounded—a bunch of evangelical Christians preying on aimless teenagers by luring them to Jesus with pizza and video games—but, since I wasn't sticking around, I felt that I was in no position to talk. The good news was that the school board had voted to continue funding SNEP, and that my position as an academic tutor would continue. On several occasions, Laura had asked me about my plans for the next school year, but I hadn't been able to give her a definite answer.

■

In the days before I left town, I stopped by Roo's house to say goodbye, to tell him I'd be back in the fall, but he didn't fully understand why I was leaving—summer, he said, was the only season worth being up here. We still hadn't spoken a word about his loss to the Brawler—it felt too awkward for me to bring it up—but I did notice that hanging on his refrigerator was a picture of his face taken shortly after the fight: he was smiling, his black eye closed as if winking. Roo said he put the picture up because it made him laugh, but Nicole didn't think it was the least bit funny. What I didn't know at the time: while Roo was plotting his Roughhouse comeback, Nicole was pregnant with his son.

I tracked down Todd at his slip, just as he was leaving to spend the summer at a remote fish hatchery at the end of Baranof Island. He'd be living in a tent and wouldn't see anyone for several weeks at a time, but he was optimistic about the change: the money was right, and he'd be away from the drug scene in Sitka, and all that open wilderness was good for his dogs. He'd loaded up a rickety skiff with gear, and his two dogs were panting in the stern, and as he putted away into the harbor, something about the whole ramshackle assembly of man and boat and dog reminded me of the old pioneer days of the Last Frontier, back when men like Todd didn't have to answer to anybody but themselves.

One day toward the end of May, I was walking down Lincoln Street when I saw a woman riding a bicycle coming toward me. I tried to avoid crossing paths with her, but Miss Mary pulled onto the curb, held out her hand, and congratulated me on my Southeast Showdown title. She'd read about it in the *Sitka Sentinel*. I wanted to tell her that I was grateful for the time we'd spent together, that I had not taken her seriously as a person, that in seeing things in me that I could not see in myself, she had helped me to understand why I fought. But, despite being the toughest guy in Southeast Alaska, I lacked the courage to tell her those things, so I did what I always did: replaced honesty with distant and remote silence passing as masculine cool. When I asked her what she was up to, she said she was living on an island now, and though she didn't say as much, I gathered it was with a man. For a moment, neither of us spoke. Then Miss Mary said, "Jade, I believe that you are a good person," and rode away.

■

As promised, my landlords came back to town in late May, to prep for the fishing season, and shortly afterward the white kid from San Diego showed up in town as well. He started coming around my apartment unannounced, with loads of boxes in his arms, asking if he could store them in the closet. I didn't like the kid: he seemed overly confident about his station in life, but I think my resentment about his arrival mostly had to do with my uneasiness about what I was going to do with myself now that I had to find somewhere else to live. With the Roughhouse season over, I had nothing to train for and no one to report to, no obligation to fill the morass of my future. It was now late May and the sun stayed up until almost midnight, and something about the excess of light drove me mad with anticipation—as if the daylight itself were asking me what was next. I began to have trouble sleeping again—the silence of my apartment felt so thick with uncertainty that I often had to get out of bed and stand in the driveway for a while, taking deep breaths and shadowboxing until my heart stopped thumping and my fists unclenched. In the fall, the darkness had, in its way, protected me from the future. Now, the daylight was forcing me to deal with myself.

One night, sleep just wouldn't come. In a spastic rage, I started drawing all sorts of maps of where I was going next, listing my goals, scribbling down dates of when I wanted to accomplish those goals, until I found myself surrounded by a nest of sticky notes and legal-pad pages. It was useless, circular thinking that solved nothing, but I felt that if I didn't make up my mind about something, anything, my brain was going to explode or I'd poke out my eyes or smash my head through the wall or start punching through the windows. It was a feeling not unlike the experience of getting caught in the middle of the channel on my paddle up here: the size of the world seemed to expand and contract simultaneously, and I felt as though I were being squashed by the vastness of infinity, dangling above the abyss of each second. I began filing through journal entries and dog-eared pages of books and pieces of mail, trying to decode their meanings for an answer. Then, I pulled out the letter my father had written me that fall.

Now, and even more since our conversation in Donna's that morning before the Showdown, I felt a deep resistance to his influence. Bullfights, war, planting flowers, women, heroism, the singular code of the self, the myth of the autonomous hero. The world was a good place to buy in, only if you disregarded all the people in the world who relied on you: wife, son, family. If I had learned anything from Victor, it was that one's devotion to his culture, to his family, to the young men who looked up to him, transcended any devotion to himself. Power was not something to behold, but to give. If I had learned anything from Haag, it was that God was not interested in good and evil, or even aware of good and evil. God as a creator merely placed the ring in the barroom, and it was up to the rest of us to step through the ropes and face the things we feared, give physical language to what violence lived inside us. For now, Haag was the kind of God I could believe in: an indifferent and often drunk huckster who put one man against another, then cleared town on the first flight north. But as I read my father's words again, his voice amplified by the silence of my apartment, their meaning exploded off the page like a holy directive. Hemingway's *beautiful girls, gorgeous, bright shawls over their shoulders, dark, dark-eyed, black lace mantillas over their hair* called out to me like distant sirens. I could feel the heat of the Spanish afternoon baking my skin. I had four thousand dollars in the bank. I had an entire summer—at least—to burn. Something would come next.

Then I felt the same sudden impulse to hear my father's

voice—the same urgency I had experienced after many long hours on the water, or the morning after a fight when the surge of aggression still burned in my forearms, when the question Why?—unasked, unspeakable, still promising an answer—throbbed in my brain as a single syllable.

After about eight rings, my father's answering machine came on. I got about halfway through a garbled, bumbling message when my stepmother picked up. I was impatient with her—that was the beginning of a period when even the sound of her voice made me sick with resentment—and quickly asked to speak with my dad.

"My son," he said, in a tired, distant voice. It had been three weeks since he'd come to watch me fight, but I still felt like I had not seen him in a long time. He listened carefully, sleepily, as I laid out the high stakes of the moment: I had to move out of my apartment. I wanted to keep fighting. But Victor himself had told me that if I didn't leave town, I'd never take my fighting to the next level . . . but then there was that letter about Spain that my father had sent me . . . and as I continued rambling, my chest tightened, my voice became high and tight and grandiose, and the silence of the night screamed in my ears as if any minute the entire universe might explode through my windows. I said, "I'm moving to Spain."

My father was quiet for a moment. "Spain?"

"Spain." I reminded him of the article he'd sent me. I reminded him of the dark girls in shawls and the bullfights and all the other fantasies I held about a place that did not exist. Fantasies that were projections of our own losses, of our own longings to imagine ourselves into realized men. They were limited dreams—but the only ones we had in common.

"Hmm," my father said calmly. He didn't tell me I was crazy. He didn't ask me to reconsider. All he said was "Well, my son, if that's what you want to do . . . you ought to do it."

"Do what?"

"Move to Spain."

■

I packed up the contents of my apartment into two piles. In the first pile was everything that I had acquired over the past year that I was giving to the White Elephant. In the second pile were all the things I was bringing back with me: my boxing and camping gear, and my Southeast Showdown belt. I'd sold my sea kayak to a friend—and then gave him my banjo, on the condition that I'd come back for it one day.

The night before I left, I didn't sleep much. But it wasn't the anxious insomnia of the fall and winter. Instead, I lay in a quiet, almost meditative silence, an emptiness so vast that when the early light of summer began to paint my windows around 4:00 a.m., I was almost sad to see the darkness go. I shouldered my backpack and took one last look at my basement apartment: after a single Roughhouse season, it looked exactly as it had when I'd first moved in.

I rode downtown through a sunny morning, the light bright over the mountains, the sky clear and featureless. As I pedaled over the harbor bridge, no mist hung over the channel. The water shimmered, and time seemed to move backward and then forward and then it just stopped. I ditched my bike in the woods, just deep enough into the tree line so that someone might find it and put it to good use.

As the plane left the tarmac, I felt the familiar anticipation of flying to Juneau for a fight. But as I looked off the wing, I saw in the mountains below, in the waters of the Inside Passage running between them, a different world: the hills and pine forests of northern New England, the dark waters of Lake Champlain, the tidal rivers of Maine. As that world faded beneath me, I took the Showdown belt out of my backpack, recognized myself for what I had become: a certain version of a young man, rising through the clouds with something golden in his hands.

EPILOGUE: RETURN

Over the next few years I fought a handful of times, in several different states, against opponents whose names I half remember. I lived in Portland, worked out with a club of high-level amateurs and pros, and trained with even more fervor and devotion than I had in Sitka. But before long I realized that, at twenty-six years old, I'd never be more than a valuable sparring partner to up-and-coming boxers who'd never questioned their instincts to fight. I remember those years less as a series of fights than as a chain of memories—lights, punches landed and taken—always shadowed with a restless desire to find something at the other end of them, some place in the world to call my own.

The only bout I recall with total clarity took place during the Northern New England regional finals, in the city of my birth, Burlington, Vermont, just after the New Year a few years later. When I told my father that I was coming to fight in his stomping grounds—at the hallowed Memorial Auditorium, right down the street from his office—he went overboard and invited just about every man he knew: friends from the military, friends from his mental health firm, all his old buddies from the Champlain Islands, my stepbrothers. The annual tournament was a big deal in

Vermont: local kids from the rural parts of the state trained all year for a shot at glory, for a chance to advance into the next stage of Golden Gloves competition. I had no idea whom I was fighting—didn't even pause to look at his name before stepping into the ring before one thousand people.

I could feel that my father was in the audience. He'd mentioned the names of the men who had come to watch me fight. They were the husbands of my mother's old friends, the fathers of boys who I'd known for much of my life. They were the same men who had likely been standing along the road some twenty years earlier, when I, in that yellow GALAHAD T-shirt, running next to my father, had fallen to the ground at the finish line of the Fourth of July race. They had all known about the terms of my parents' separation. In the years since, on the occasions when I had run into these men, a part of me still believed that they still saw me as that broken little child who'd flopped at the finish line on purpose.

The bell rang. I shuffled toward my opponent. Our bodies came together. In a tangle of elbows and arms, fists and shoulders, I began to work through his defense, to find holes in his guard for the tight hooks, for the short uppercuts—*appakats!* The punches landed. One after another. The kid was strong—like many of the Vermont fighters, he was a working-class, country-raised farm boy. When I dug into his body, I could feel his strength—working strength—in all the muscles that fought to protect him. By the second round, he had begun to tire. In our clinches, he began to hang on me a bit more. When he broke apart, he paused to take a deep breath.

By the third round, when we'd taken each other into the deep water of the fight, I backed him up onto the ropes, waited for him to throw his desperate right hand, which he did, then I slid beneath it and drilled his lower back with a series of left hooks. The kid was too blind with exhaustion to recognize that I was going to keep throwing the punch as often as he would let me. Every time the punch landed, I slid out with my back foot and tapped jabs off his forehead, to keep him pinned. Then I slid back in, pivoting to my right, to put new pain in a new opening in my opponent's guard. It was lethal, brutal work, but my hands moved effortlessly, as if being commanded by invisible levers in the sky.

For what felt like a full minute, I kept on like this—three years of bag work, thousands of hours in front of the mirror, hundreds of miles of running, enough uppercuts to flatten my nose and give me chronic sinus infections—all of it coming together in a single moment. As a fighter, I knew already that I had no future: I was too old, the wrong size, probably not fast enough to ever be more than a bottom-rung pro. But once or twice in a lifetime, it can feel as though the world is bending toward your purpose, as though the arc of all things has specific regard for the story you are trying to beat into meaning. That night, in the city where my mother had brought me into the world, in the little patch of this country that she had intended to make her home, in front of the community that my father came from and the community that I had always felt rejected my mother, I found myself moving in that unspoken realm of a power greater than me. It did not last long. From that night, I have a single picture: my opponent, backed up against the ropes, shelled up behind his gloves, me, diving forward, leaning left, my left hand cocked as I prepare to throw a hook to his body. But it is not the damage of landing the punch that continues to haunt me; rather, it is the expression on my face: one of beautiful, uninhibited and unrepentant anger. "You got good wind," my opponent said after the final bell. "You hit hard." We shook hands and went our separate ways. I never did get his name.

I left the ring, walked through the crowd, holding a tall golden trophy in one hand, and found my father. He hugged me, slapped me hard on the cheek, then turned with me under his arm, so that the men he'd invited could bear witness to the young warrior that his son had become. Even now as I write this, I can feel myself resisting this final moment, because I know that it was merely one of many false professions of finality in my relationship with my father, a relationship that, now that I am a father myself, is forever unfolding. But that night, I, fully grown and semirealized, walked forward to meet those men with no secret shame inside me, no questions about the past, no inclination to pretend that I was injured. The confused anger that had possessed me as a boy had been made visible in the ring. It had taken two decades to reclaim what I believed I had lost, but in that passing moment I had all of it back.

"Holy shit," one of my stepbrothers said, stepping forward, holding out his hand. "You're a fucking badass."

Behind him, in the stunned and fearful eyes of the men who had come to watch me fight, and in the proud eyes of my father as he paraded me in front of those men, and even in the omniscient invisible eyes of that original city of my birth, I saw the figure of who the confused little boy of my youth had been waiting all these years to see: the angry young man who, one day—in some other kingdom, in some other time—would come back to name him.

ACKNOWLEDGMENTS

Thank you first to Betsy Lerner: for your radical loyalty, confidence, belief, and support. I am so grateful to have you in my corner.

Thank you to my editor, Colin Dickerman, for giving this story a home. I appreciate greatly the time and care that you and the people at Farrar, Straus and Giroux have devoted to my book. It means so much to me to finally see it in print.

In the writing world, I have been helped by so many friends and mentors that to name one demands that I name you all. So I will say only that your presence has been essential to my emotional and spiritual life as well as to my creative process. A number of institutions and fellowships have supported me and my family during these last years: the University of New Hampshire, Stonecoast MFA in Creative Writing, the Telling Room, the Salt Institute for Documentary Studies, Bowdoin College, Deerfield Academy, the Island Institute in Sitka, Alaska, and the Bread Loaf Writers' Conference.

There is a long and very complicated history of non-Native people writing about Native people in order to understand themselves, and I am very aware that this book is part of that often delinquent canon. During the five or so years in which I traveled back and forth to Southeast Alaska, many people offered me enormous kindness and generosity, including the families of George Bennett, Victor and Miranda Littlefield, Scott and Niecole Robinson, Jessika Beam, and my former coworkers at the Sitka Native Education Program: Laura Castillo, Judy Brady, and Sam Payenna. I also wish to thank Eric for being such a good friend and climbing partner during the first year I lived in town. I'd like to thank Ethan, Wyatt, Richie, Roman, Jay, Jack, and Scott for being such good friends and sparring partners. And Cliff, Amber, Tasha, Matt, Angelika, and many others for being such good friends during those strange, molten years when none of us knew where we'd end up.

Thank you to Bob Haag for giving me a place to fight. Thank you to Anthony Lindoff, Mike Edenshaw, Ben Reed, Chuck McCracken, and Fernando Pintang for being good opponents. Thank you to the writers at the *Juneau Empire* for your coverage of the Roughhouse show, which I relied on heavily: Charles Bingham, Ron Wilmot, Courtney Nelson, and Klas Stolpe. Thank you to Ethan Billings and the people at Marlintini's Lounge who hosted the fights. Thank you to Edna Abbott and the many other Roughhouse fighters who spoke with me over the years about their experiences. I wish I could have written about you all instead, but that, I suppose, is not the point of a memoir.

Thank you to Bobby Russo and the many fighters at the Portland Boxing Club, who gave me a boxing home. I know that the image of the boxing writer is a well-used cliché, but without the opportunity to spend much of my twenties fighting and training, I would not have been able to engage with myself—or this story—in any functional way.

Lastly, to my father and mother: I know it is probably not your preference to have your son tell the story of our family. My aim in writing in this book was only to understand our past so that, in understanding, I might be a better father and husband.

Finally, to my wife and two daughters: you fill my life with meaning and purpose and love.

A NOTE ABOUT THE AUTHOR

Jaed Coffin is the author of the memoir *A Chant to Soothe Wild Elephants*. He teaches creative writing at the University of New Hampshire and lives with his family in Maine.